"In every corner of the world, millions commem~~orated the five hundredth anniver~~ of the Protestant Reformation (1517–2017). But ~~central was the Reformers' own em~~phasis on Scripture as the very Word of God, the norm to norm all others in the teaching of the church, given such clear expression as in the lectures published here. This is a treasure trove for students, Christian laity, and clergy. It will take you to the engine of the evangelical movement and remind you that its founders still have much to teach us all about the power of the Bible to convict, save, sanctify, and put us in touch with God, showing us how to live and love in ways that truly make a difference."

Douglas A. Sweeney, distinguished professor of church history and the history of Christian thought, Trinity Evangelical Divinity School

"Scott Manetsch and his contributors provide fresh and lively essays on Scripture and Reformation history, indispensable for the church today. Protestant reformers studied Scripture not simply as 'a collection of devotional insights,' and today, we should not view Scripture as a cudgel of first-century values over twenty-first-century ideas on issues such as the role of women's leadership in the church but rather as 'the very essence of the Christian gospel.' For example, Manetsch's essay on Jean Crespin's book of martyrs conveys the excitement that sixteenth-century Christians found in the Word and their tenacity until death. Likewise, Michael Haykin brings to life in a minibiography the great English preacher and martyr Bishop Hugh Latimer. And Timothy George uses nonevangelicals such as Dietrich Bonhoeffer to exhort evangelicals to hold on to their Reformation roots and the charisma of the Bible rather than that of individual preachers. As a Lutheran, I find this book attractive to evangelicals within denominations founded in the sixteenth century as well as to evangelical churches today."

Jeannine Olson, professor of history, Rhode Island College

"This book brings us back to the heart of the matter: the centrality of the gospel and Scripture for the Protestant reformers. By demonstrating the guiding role the Bible played in the sixteenth century for pastoral care, preaching, the devotional life of lay and clergy alike, understandings of justification and sanctification, and practices of the priesthood of all believers, the various authors not only illuminate the key commitments of the Protestant reformers: they also deftly connect these matters to crucial questions facing evangelical Christians today."

G. Sujin Pak, Duke Divinity School, vice dean of academic affairs, associate professor of the history of Christianity

"These eight essays and the afterword both stimulate and edify. Everywhere we see the evidence of a strong team with an expert coach. The result is a scholarly but accessible book that advances Reformation studies and offers a clear win for a magisterial doctrine of Scripture. I heartily recommend it to students and experts alike."

Chad Van Dixhoorn, professor of church history, Westminster Theological Seminary

"Martin Luther and the Reformation were inextricably connected. But perhaps surprisingly, it is often forgotten how intimately bound Luther saw the Reformation to Scripture. His mission insisted on it being recovered by the church so it could be assiduously studied and carefully read by clergy and laity alike. In these excellent essays, leading scholars explore the heart of the Reformation revealing Luther's passion for the reformation of the church according to the Word of God. The contributions consider Luther's insights on biblical interpretation, preaching, pastoral care, justification by faith, and the Christian life. These biblical themes, once so precious to the Reformer, are again recommended to all as Luther's vision to have a church true to the Scriptures remains essential for the proclamation of the gospel of Christ. Don't miss the opportunity to add an outstanding study to your books on the Reformation. Luther's trust in the Word of God will encourage you in your ministry for Christ and his people."

Peter A. Lillback, president, Westminster Theological Seminary, Philadelphia

THE REFORMATION
and the IRREPRESSIBLE
WORD OF GOD

INTERPRETATION, THEOLOGY, *and* PRACTICE

EDITED BY SCOTT M. MANETSCH

IVP Academic

An imprint of InterVarsity Press
Downers Grove, Illinois

InterVarsity Press
P.O. Box 1400, Downers Grove, IL 60515-1426
ivpress.com
email@ivpress.com

InterVarsity Press® is the book-publishing division of InterVarsity Christian Fellowship/USA®, a movement of
students and faculty active on campus at hundreds of universities, colleges, and schools of nursing
in the United States of America, and a member movement of the International Fellowship of Evangelical Students.
For information about local and regional activities, visit intervarsity.org.

Cover design: Cindy Kiple
Interior design: Daniel van Loon
Images: © Reformation Monument in Geneva / Godong / UIG / Bridgeman Images

ISBN 978-0-8308- 5235-2 (print)
ISBN 978-0-8308- 7285-5 (digital)

Printed in the United States of America ⊗

Library of Congress Cataloging-in-Publication Data
Names: Manetsch, Scott M, editor.
Title: The Reformation and the irrepressible word of God : interpretation,
  theology, and practice / edited by Scott M. Manetsch.
Description: Downers Grove : InterVarsity Press, 2019. | Includes
  bibliographical references and index.
Identifiers: LCCN 2019002869 (print) | LCCN 2019009713 (ebook) | ISBN
  9780830872855 (eBook) | ISBN 9780830852352 (pbk. : alk. paper)
Subjects: LCSH: Bible—History—16th century. | Bible—History—17th century.
  | Reformation.
Classification: LCC BS447 (ebook) | LCC BS447 .R44 2019 (print) | DDC
  220.09/031—dc23
LC record available at https://lccn.loc.gov/2019002869

P 25 24 23 22 21 20 19 18 17 16 15 14 13 12 11 10 9 8 7 6 5 4 3 2 1

Y 38 37 36 35 34 33 32 31 30 29 28 27 26 25 24 23 22 21 20 19

CONTENTS

PART FOUR: THE CHRISTIAN LIFE
in the REFORMATION

Abbreviations

ANF	The Ante-Nicene Fathers. 10 vols. Edited by Alexander Roberts and James Donaldson. Buffalo, NY: Christian Literature, 1885–1896. Several reprints; also available online.
CTS	Calvin Translation Society edition of Calvin's commentaries. 46 vols. Edinburgh, 1843–1855. Several reprints but variously bound; volume numbers (when cited) are relative to specific commentaries and not to the entire set.
DBWE	Dietrich Bonhoeffer Works. Vol. 15. Theological Education Underground, 1937–1940. Edited by Victoria Barnett. Minneapolis: Fortress, 2011.
EEBO	Early English Books Online. Subscription database: http://eebo.chadwyck.com.
HAB	Herzog August Bibliothek
Institutes	John Calvin. *Institutes of the Christian Religion*. 2 vols. Edited by J. T. McNeill. Translated by F. L. Battles. Philadelphia: Westminster, 1960.
LCC	Library of Christian Classics
LW	Luther's Works [American Edition]. 55 vols. St. Louis: Concordia; Philadelphia: Fortress, 1955–1986.
NPNF	A Select Library of the Nicene and Post-Nicene Fathers of the Christian Church. 28 vols. Edited by Philip Schaff et al. Buffalo, NY: Christian Literature, 1887–1894. Several reprints; also available online.

OER   *Oxford Encyclopedia of the Reformation.* 4 vols. Edited by Hans J. Hillerbrand. New York: Oxford University Press, 1996.

PL   Patrologia cursus completus. Series Latina. 221 vols. Edited by J.-P. Migne. Paris, 1857–1866.

WA   D. Martin Luthers Werke: Kritische Gesamtausgabe. 66 vols. Weimar: Hermann Böhlaus Nachfolger, 1912–1921.

INTRODUCTION

SCOTT M. MANETSCH

THE PROTESTANT REFORMATION OF THE SIXTEENTH century had many different faces and many surprising features. It was a constellation of social events that changed how people related to their families and communities, ushering in wide-ranging reforms in education, poverty relief, marriage and divorce, the clerical office, and social discipline. The Reformation was also a collection of political events that empowered rulers to extend authority over their subjects while at the same time fragmenting the German-speaking world into rival confessional groups that delayed the unification of Germany for more than three hundred years. In addition, the Reformation was a cluster of revolutionary events that crystalized and intensified widespread discontent against the received feudal agrarian system, a social protest that exploded in the German Peasants' War of 1525. And, certainly, the Reformation was a mass media event as Martin Luther and other Protestant leaders harnessed new print technologies to articulate their evangelical message and dismantle traditional religious institutions and customs.

While each of these features is important, they fail to capture what the Protestant reformers themselves understood to be the substance and essential core of the sixteenth-century Reformation. For early Protestant leaders such as Martin Luther, Huldrych Zwingli, Nicholas Ridley, John

Knox, and John Calvin, the Reformation was a religious renewal movement that called the church back to the Scriptures and the centrality of the Christian gospel. The Reformation was not first and foremost about changing the social or political order but rather about recovering from Scripture the central message of Christianity—that God extends grace to sinners who trust in Jesus Christ alone—and applying that theological insight to the spiritual needs of men and women as well as the practical concerns of church and community. In their view, the Protestant Reformation was a divinely orchestrated *religious* or *spiritual* event that found its origin in the recovery, reading, and faithful application of the Bible.

Both the literature and lived experience of early Protestants provide ample testimony to these primary religious concerns. One striking example is seen in Martin Luther's "Exhortation to the Clergy Assembled at the Diet at Augsburg," written by the Reformer in May of 1530 from the safety of Coburg Castle as he anxiously awaited updates from the imperial diet.[1] In this largely forgotten treatise—which has been called Luther's own Augsburg Confession—the Saxon Reformer offered a general assessment of the progress of evangelical teaching, showing "what great and glorious fruit the word of God has produced" and "what the world would be like if our gospel had not come."[2] Luther described in graphic detail the state of medieval Catholic religion without the Reformation: the "unspeakable thievery" of indulgences, the "hellish" sacrament of penance, the travesty of clerical celibacy, the "scandalous huckstering" of endowed masses, the "false and shameful" devotion shown Mary and the saints, the patent failure of episcopal leadership, and the shocking ignorance of the parish clergy.[3] Through these abuses the medieval church had detracted from Christ's unique sacrifice for sins, tortured the consciences of God's people, encouraged blatant idolatry,

---

[1]The "Exhortation" is found in WA 30/2:268-356. An English translation is available at bookofconcord .org/exhortation.php. Accessed November 21, 2017. I am thankful to my colleague John Woodbridge for calling my attention to this fascinating document.
[2]WA 30/2:281.
[3]WA 30/2:284-85, 288, 293.

championed works righteousness, and condemned faithful Christians to death as heretics. All these errors and abuses, Luther believed, had resulted from the fact that the traditional church had elevated its theologians and traditions above God's holy Word. Luther commented:

> Their best work, however, was in despising the Holy Scriptures, and letting them lie under the bench! "Bible, Bible?" said they. "The Bible is a heretics' book! You must read the doctors! There you find what is what!" I know that I am not lying about this, for I grew up among them and have heard and seen all this from them.[4]

From Luther's perspective, then, the central contribution of the Protestant Reformation was to restore to their rightful place in Christ's church the Scriptures and the "free and pure gospel" (what later Protestants called the formal and material principles of the Reformation).[5] This was what set the Lutherans apart from their Catholic opponents, the Reformer believed: "You and we know that you live without God's word, but we have God's word. . . . We ask nothing more, and never have asked anything more, than that the gospel shall be free."[6] Armed with God's Word and God's gospel, Lutheran preachers now served as agents for spiritual renewal as they dismantled the numerous Catholic errors and superstitions and provided true Christian consolation to the souls of those in despair. Previously, Luther noted,

> No one knew how to preach the gospel otherwise than to teach out of it examples of good works, and no one of us ever heard a gospel that aimed to give comfort to the conscience and to lead to faith and trust in Christ. That is how it ought to be preached, and, praise God! it is now preached that way again.[7]

In the final paragraphs of his "Exhortation," Luther identified 114 additional unbiblical customs and doctrines taught by the Roman Church—ranging from Lenten fasts to kissing and adoring the cross—and he

---

[4]WA 30/2:300.
[5]WA 30/2:355.
[6]WA 30/2:339, 341.
[7]WA 30/2:291.

urged the clergy at the Diet of Augsburg to reform the church in light of the message of Scripture. "The true Church," he insisted, "must be the one that holds to God's Word and suffers for it, as, praise God! we do, and murders no one and leads no one away from God's Word. . . . God help you to a reformation on this point!"[8]

While Martin Luther anxiously awaited reports from the Diet of Augsburg during the late spring and summer of 1530, he entertained a steady stream of friends and curious visitors to Coburg Castle who sought his audience and advice. One of these visitors was a remarkable woman named Argula (von Stauff) von Grumbach, whose life experience reflected the deep religious convictions that motivated many early Protestants. Born around 1492 into a distinguished German noble family near Beratzhausen in Bavaria, Argula was raised by pious parents who taught her to pray and to read the German Bible, a copy of which her father gave her as a gift on her tenth birthday. As a young woman of fifteen or sixteen, she was sent to the imperial court in Munich, where she served as a lady-in-waiting to Queen Kunigunde (daughter of Emperor Frederick III).[9] Around 1516, she married Friedrich von Grumbach, and the couple soon settled in the town of Dietfort, near Ingolstadt. Though it is uncertain when or how Argula von Grumbach first came into contact with Luther's ideas, it is clear that by the early 1520s she had become a supporter of the Wittenberg theology and was avidly studying Luther's writings in light of Scripture—much to her husband Friedrich's displeasure. What began as private religious conviction erupted into public controversy in 1523 when Argula defied cultural norms and her husband's wishes by writing a blistering letter to the University of Ingolstadt, protesting the harsh treatment shown to a young student named Arsacius Seehofer, who had been forced by the theological faculty to recant his evangelical beliefs.[10] Among the doctrines that Seehofer had

---

[8]WA 30/2:321-22.
[9]Peter Matheson, ed., *Argula von Grumbach: A Woman's Voice in the Reformation* (Edinburgh: T&T Clark, 1995), 7-8.
[10]Matheson, *Argula von Grumbach*, 14-16.

disavowed under duress were Luther's teachings on justification by grace alone through faith alone and Scripture's supreme authority over the church.[11]

Argula von Grumbach's letter to the University of Ingolstadt, which subsequently appeared in sixteen printed editions, was courageous, passionate, and brutally frank, reflecting her confident command of Scripture and deep spiritual conviction. In this long letter, Argula quoted no fewer than seventy biblical texts, many, it seems, from memory. In the opening lines of her letter, Argula addressed the obvious question that would have troubled most of her readers: What gave her license, as a woman with no university training, to confront and correct learned theologians of the church? She argued that it was Scripture itself that gave her this right, for Christ's statement in Matthew 10:32 ("So everyone who acknowledges me before men, I also will acknowledge before my Father who is in heaven") and the prophetic command in Ezekiel 33 ("If you see your brother sin, reprove him") applied to all Christians regardless of gender or educational background.[12] Hence, in obedience to these divine commands, Argula felt compelled to set forth her confession of faith and, at the same time, reprove the Catholic theologians at Ingolstadt for their gross neglect of God's Word. Argula presented herself as well-studied in the religious controversies of her day. Several years earlier, she had disregarded the warnings of Franciscan monks and begun reading the German Bible for herself, a practice that provided rich spiritual illumination and soon reshaped her theological convictions. "Ah, but what joy it is when the Spirit of God teaches and gives us understanding, flitting from one text to the next—God be praised—so that I came to see the true, genuine light shining out."[13]

At the same time, as she read Luther's writings and compared them with his German New Testament, she became convinced that the

---

[11]For the seventeen articles that were deemed heretical by Ingolstadt's faculty, see Matheson, *Argula von Grumbach*, 91-93.

[12]Matheson, *Argula von Grumbach*, 75. Argula here is paraphrasing Ezek 33:6-8.

[13]Matheson, *Argula von Grumbach*, 86-87.

Wittenberg theology accorded with the teachings of the Bible. "For my part," she wrote, "I have to confess, in the name of God and by my soul's salvation, that if I were to deny Luther and Melanchthon's writing I would be denying God and his word, which may God forfend forever."[14] The theologians of Ingolstadt, by contrast, had condemned Luther's teaching and declared him a heretic without even consulting Scripture. Indeed, these reputed doctors of the church were completely ignorant of the teachings of the Bible and thus had to resort to threats and coercion rather than godly persuasion.[15] "I beseech you for the sake of God," Argula demanded, "tell me in writing which of the articles written by Martin or Melanchthon you consider heretical. In German not a single one seems heretical to me."[16] Argula's belief that Scripture should have supreme authority for defining Christian doctrine and practice echoed the conviction of Luther and other evangelical Reformers. As she put it, "No one has a right to exercise sovereignty over the word of God. . . . For the word of God alone—without which nothing was made—should and must rule."[17] At the conclusion of her letter, Argula von Grumbach struck the pose of a modern-day prophet as she confidently announced God's Word to the Catholic theologians at Ingolstadt. "What I have written to you is no woman's chit-chat, but the word of God; and (I write) as a member of the Christian Church, against which the gates of Hell cannot prevail. . . . God give us his grace that we all may be saved."[18]

Both Martin Luther's "Exhortation" to the clergy at the Diet of Augsburg and Argula von Grumbach's letter to the faculty at the University of Ingolstadt illustrate particularly well the significant impact that Scripture had in shaping the theological convictions and spiritual experiences of

---

[14]Matheson, *Argula von Grumbach*, 76-77.

[15]Elsewhere, Argula states that the Ingolstadt theologians were "as well informed about the Bible as a cow is about chess." See Argula von Grumbach to Adam von Thering, in Matheson, *Argula von Grumbach*, 146.

[16]Matheson, *Argula von Grumbach*, 86.

[17]Matheson, *Argula von Grumbach*, 82.

[18]Matheson, *Argula von Grumbach*, 90.

men and women in the sixteenth century. The eminent Reformation scholar G. R. Elton in the early 1960s lent support to this view, noting that "if there is a single thread running through the whole story of the Reformation, it is the explosive and renovating and often disintegrating effect of the Bible."[19] In the past half-century, however, this perspective has fallen out of favor with many social and cultural historians, who, being suspicious of traditional confessional narratives of the Reformation, have focused instead on (what they see as) the primary political, economic, and social factors underlying and effecting religious change. Though these lines of scholarship have proven fruitful in many ways—not least in that they have given voice to previously marginalized groups, prioritized institutional histories, and recognized the social and political impact of religious ideas—they have too often understated or completely ignored the Bible's central role in the "story" of the Reformation.[20] Fortunately, recent developments in the field of Reformation studies indicate that attention to the Bible and its impact in the sixteenth century might be making a comeback. Among the most fruitful of these research trajectories are studies of the Bible that focus on its production and reception,[21] studies of early modern preaching,[22] studies of the doctrine

---

[19]G. R. Elton, *Reformation Europe, 1517–1559* (New York: Harper & Row, 1963), 52. Cited in Timothy George, *Reading Scripture with the Reformers* (Downers Grove, IL: IVP Academic, 2011), 11.

[20]To give one example, *The Oxford Illustrated History of the Reformation*, ed. Peter Marshall (Oxford: Oxford University Press, 2015), whose stated goal is to help orient readers to the most important approaches, discoveries, and compelling questions of contemporary Reformation research, devotes one sentence to Luther's work as a translator of the German Bible, says little about Protestant ministries of preaching and commentary writing, and completely ignores recent scholarship on the history of Reformation exegesis. For an evaluation of this volume, see Scott Manetsch, "Reassessing the Reformation: Contemporary Themes and Approaches," *Fides et Historia* 48 (2016): 131-40.

[21]See, for example, Jaroslav Pelikan, *The Reformation of the Bible: The Bible of the Reformation* (New Haven, CT: Yale University Press, 1996); Bettye Thomas Chambers, *Bibliography of French Bibles: Fifteenth- and Sixteenth-Century French Language Editions* (Geneva: Librairie Droz, 1983); and Jennifer Powell McNutt and David Lauber, eds., *The People's Book: The Reformation and the Bible* (Downers Grove, IL: IVP Academic, 2017).

[22]See, for example, Larissa Taylor, ed., *Preachers and People in the Reformations and Early Modern Period* (Leiden: Brill, 2001); T. H. L. Parker, *Calvin's Preaching* (Louisville: Westminster John Knox, 1992); and John Frymire, *The Primacy of the Postils: Catholics, Protestants, and the Dissemination of Ideas in Early Modern Germany* (Leiden: Brill, 2010).

of Scripture espoused by individual Reformers,[23] and studies in the history of biblical interpretation in the Reformation era.[24]

The present volume seeks to contribute to this growing scholarly literature devoted to the Bible and its reception, interpretation, and impact during the sixteenth-century Reformation. The nine chapters that follow originated as papers delivered at a conference titled "The Reformation and the Ministry of the Word," held at Trinity Evangelical Divinity School (Deerfield, Illinois) in the fall of 2017 to commemorate the five hundredth anniversary of Martin Luther's posting of the Ninety-Five Theses to the door of the Castle Church in Wittenberg. Because all the contributors to this volume are both active scholars and church leaders, their chapters explore the Bible's decisive role in shaping early Protestant doctrine and practice in such a way as to encourage contemporary Protestants to celebrate their theological heritage and appropriate its riches.

The Reformation and the Irrepressible Word of God is divided into four sections plus a concluding afterword. Section one explores the interpretation of the Bible in the Reformation. In chapter one, Scott M. Manetsch describes the important contribution of early Protestant biblical scholarship and interpretation, and then shows the pervasive—and skillful—use of Scripture among ordinary Protestants whose histories are reported in Jean Crespin's famous *History of the Martyrs* (1570). In chapter two, David S. Dockery describes the development and substance of Luther's distinctive christological interpretation of Scripture and then

---

[23]See, for example, Robert Kolb, *Martin Luther and the Enduring Word of God* (Grand Rapids: Baker Academic, 2016); Matthew Barrett, *God's Word Alone—The Authority of Scripture: What the Reformers Taught . . . and Why It Still Matters* (Grand Rapids: Zondervan, 2016); and Mark Thompson, *A Sure Ground on Which to Stand: The Relation of Authority and Interpretative Method in Luther's Approach to Scripture* (Eugene, OR: Wipf & Stock, 2007).

[24]See, for example, Richard Muller and John Thompson, eds., *Biblical Interpretation in the Era of the Reformation* (Grand Rapids: Eerdmans, 1996); Timothy George, *Reading Scripture with the Reformers* (Downers Grove, IL: IVP Academic, 2011); Donald McKim, ed., *Dictionary of Major Biblical Interpreters* (Downers Grove, IL: IVP Academic, 2007); David Steinmetz, *Luther in Context*, 2nd ed. (Grand Rapids: Baker Academic, 2002); and G. Sujin Pak, *The Judaizing Calvin: Sixteenth-Century Debates over the Messianic Psalms* (New York: Oxford University Press, 2010). See also individual volumes published in the Reformation Commentary on Scripture series of InterVarsity Press.

recommends its use to modern exegetes as a valuable canonical/theological principle in conjunction with the grammatical-historical method of interpretation.

In section two, attention is devoted to preaching and pastoral care in the Reformation. Michael A. G. Haykin's chapter on Hugh Latimer demonstrates the strategic importance that preaching played in Latimer's ministry as bishop of Worcester and chaplain to Edward VI as well as in the religious renewal of the English church. Next, in chapter four, Ronald K. Rittgers offers a fascinating study of how early Protestants in their pastoral and devotional writings treated Scripture as a kind of sacrament or conduit of God's grace that conveyed divine comfort, help, and wisdom to those who were afflicted of conscience or body. What this shows, Rittgers believes, is that early modern Protestants did not altogether "disenchant" the world, as some scholars have argued, but adopted forms of sacrality that were different from those popular in the medieval church. Hence, while the topic of the Protestant sacraments will not be addressed in detail in this volume, the sacramental nature of the Word is not entirely absent from the essays that follow.

Section three explores the doctrine of justification in the Reformation. In chapter five, Michael S. Horton demonstrates conclusively that Protestant reformers such as Luther, Calvin, and Peter Martyr Vermigli were not innovators in their interpretation of "justification passages" in Romans but instead followed an exegetical tradition derived from John Chrysostom (and other early Greek fathers), who recognized Paul's antithesis between works of the law and faith, distinguished between justification and sanctification, and understood justification as a "great exchange" of the sinner's guilt for Christ's righteousness. If the Protestant doctrine of justification has deep historical roots, it also has continued relevance for people living in the contemporary world. Thus, in chapter six, Kevin DeYoung shows how the Pauline doctrine that sinners are both pardoned and accepted as righteous through faith in Christ is truly "good news" for modern men and women weighed down by the burden of guilt imposed by the Western secular world, with all its legalistic demands, intense suffering, and psychological angst.

The two chapters that make up section four address the Christian life in the Reformation. Thomas H. McCall's chapter on Christian sanctification provides a timely reminder that, even as Luther and his Protestant colleagues affirmed that Christ, through his death, achieved the gracious justification of sinners, they also emphasized that Christ bestowed on believers the gift of the Holy Spirit, whose indwelling presence empowers them to grow in righteousness and holiness. Justification does not obviate the need for Christian holiness but rather makes it possible. Finally, in chapter eight, David J. Luy argues persuasively that Luther's doctrine of the universal priesthood was not intended to displace ecclesial institutions or church hierarchies but was rather a constructive vision whereby Christians, as beneficiaries of God's grace, become conduits of Christ and his life-giving benefits to the church. Thus, the universal ministry of God's people is never divorced from Word and sacrament.

The Reformation and the Irrepressible Word of God concludes with an afterword, written by Timothy George, that addresses the timely question "What can evangelicals learn from the Reformation?" Dr. George argues that the distinctive qualities of modern evangelicalism—conversion, the Bible, the cross, Christian activism—all find articulation and significant expression in the sixteenth-century Reformation. Evangelicalism will not endure as a religious movement if it does not remain firmly rooted in the Protestant heritage of the Reformation, with its commitment to God's authoritative Word, its celebration of God's gracious salvation through Jesus Christ, and its vision of the Christian church, renewed by the power of the Holy Spirit.

I would like to express my heartfelt gratitude to a number of different people who have made this book possible. First, I would like to thank the administration of Trinity Evangelical Divinity School, especially President David S. Dockery and Dean Graham Cole, for their consistent encouragement and financial support of the Reformation and the

Ministry of the Word Conference that was held on our campus in September 2017. I am also deeply grateful to my dear colleagues who so capably organized and implemented the Reformation conference, including Doug Sweeney, David Luy, Martin Klauber, Felix Theonugraha, Mark Kahler, Mary Guthrie, Chuck King, and Taylor Worley. Thank you to each one of you. A special word of appreciation is also in order to my research assistants, Taylor Sexton, Viktor Palenyy, and Caleb Jenkins, who improved the quality of this book by their careful editing work and by compiling the bibliography and index. In a similar fashion, I am also grateful to my friends at InterVarsity Press, especially associate editor David McNutt, for their support of this project and their meticulous labors bringing it to publication. Finally, I wish to thank the outstanding group of scholars who participated in the conference and contributed their essays to this volume. I am most grateful for your warm collegiality and friendship. May this book, in some small way, expand readers' love for God and his Word, intensify their longing for renewal of Christ's church, and permit them to exclaim (with Luther), "What great and glorious fruit the Word of God has produced!"[25]

Soli Deo gloria

---

[25]WA 30/2:281.

PART ONE

BIBLICAL
INTERPRETATION
in the REFORMATION

Chapter One

"I HAVE *the* WORD *of* GOD"

SCRIPTURE, INTERPRETATION, *and* CRESPIN'S *HISTORY of the* MARTYRS

SCOTT M. MANETSCH

ONE OF THE MOST MEMORABLE EXAMPLES of Protestant iconography in the sixteenth century was a map printed in 1566 by Jean-Baptiste Trento and François Pierre Eskrich bearing the title *Mappe Monde Nouvelle Papistique* (*New Papal World Map*). This enormously creative piece of Protestant cartography depicts the monstrous world of Catholic Rome—located within the yawning jaws of the devil. Here the Protestant reformers are depicted as Christian commandos or freedom fighters, wielding the Word of God to destroy false religion and rescue the Christian church.

In the Province of Pilgrimages, the Reformers Jan Hus, Martin Luther, and Philipp Melanchthon—all armed with Holy Scripture as arrows and spears—battle wily Jesuits and depraved Catholic bishops. In the Province of the Catholic Saints, the French Reformers Pierre Viret and Guillaume Farel—with Bibles raised above their heads—attack the idolatry and seduction of Lady Superstition. At the same time, the Swiss Reformers Huldrych Zwingli and Heinrich Bullinger mount an assault against the seemingly impregnable Province of Scholasticism, with the Word of God flaming like

torches in their hands. And finally, it is left to John Calvin and Theodore
Beza to battle the papal curia in the province nearest to hell. The pope is
seated between his two nefarious captains, identified as Beelzebub and
Lucifer. As with the other Protestant commandos, Calvin and Beza wield
the sacred weapon of Holy Scripture as they storm the very gates of hell.[1]

As a choice sample of Protestant propaganda, the *New Papal World
Map* illustrates well the fierce confessional conflict that divided Christian
churches during the age of the Reformation. At the same time, the map
suggests the central place that the Bible, the written Word of God, had
in Protestant theology and practice. For Protestants, the Bible constituted the supreme source of religious authority for doctrine and daily life.
It was an infallible guide for Christian living, a source of hope and comfort for the afflicted, a call to arms for those committed to religious reformation. For Protestant reformers such as Luther, Zwingli, Calvin, or
Bucer, the study of Holy Scripture offered readers not simply a collection
of devotional insights but the very essence of the Christian gospel.[2] It was
through the Bible that God himself spoke to his people. As Luther once
commented, "This book, the holy Scripture, is the Holy Spirit's book."[3]

This chapter will highlight the central role that the Bible played in
Protestant church life during the sixteenth century. The first part of this
essay surveys terrain that is well known to most students of the Reformation as it describes the strategic contribution of Protestant humanist
scholarship in the recovery of the biblical languages, the translation of
the Scriptures, the generation of Bible study resources, and the advent of
new approaches to Scripture interpretation. The second part of this
chapter covers territory that is largely unchartered as I examine Jean

---

[1]See [Jean-Baptiste Trento and Pierre Eskrich,] *Mappe-Monde Nouvelle Papistique: histoire de la
Mappe-Monde papistique, en laquelle est déclairé tout ce qui est contenu et pourtraict en la grande
Table, ou Carte de la Mappe-Monde (Genève, 1566)*, ed. Frank Lestringant and Alessandra Preda
(Geneva: Droz, 2009).

[2]Jaroslav Pelikan, *The Reformation of the Bible: The Bible of the Reformation* (New Haven, CT: Yale
University Press, 1996), 23.

[3]"Das ist des heiligen Geists buch, nemlich die heilige Schrifft, darin mus man Christum suchen
und finden." WA 48:43.

Crespin's classic book *History of the Martyrs,* unveiling ways that the Bible shaped the convictions and spirituality of ordinary Protestant clergy and laity during the age of the Reformation.

THE BIBLE IN THE REFORMATION

Protestant biblical scholarship in the sixteenth century owed a significant debt to the cultural and educational program known as northern humanism, which was committed to the pursuit of the humane letters (*studia humanitatis*), the cultivation of eloquence, the retrieval and mastery of classical texts, and the sustained study of the Christian Scriptures in their original languages of Hebrew and Greek. During the fifteenth and sixteenth centuries, Catholic humanists such as Lorenzo Valla, John Colet, Johannes Reuchlin, Jacques Lefèvre d'Étaples, and Desiderius Erasmus made major advances in biblical philology and exegesis by producing grammars and lexicons, commentaries on Scripture, and superior Latin translations of the Greek and Hebrew texts.[4] Of all these contributions, none was of greater importance than Desiderius Erasmus's famous *Novum Instrumentum,* first published in 1516, which provided scholars a complete Greek text of the New Testament, an elegant Latin translation from the Greek, along with extensive exegetical notes or annotations.[5] In the years that followed, Erasmus expanded these textual notes and published them in four separate editions under the title *Annotationes*—a theological and exegetical commentary that served as a baseline for Protestant biblical interpretation thereafter.

The impact of northern humanism on Protestant pedagogy and biblical scholarship was both profound and extensive. Magisterial Reformers such as Martin Luther, Huldrych Zwingli, Philipp Melanchthon, Martin Bucer, and John Calvin were shaped significantly by the values and commitments of the humanist educational program and became enthusiastic

---

[4]See my more extensive treatment in Scott W. Manetsch, ed., *Reformation Commentary on Scripture: 1 Corinthians* (Downers Grove, IL: InterVarsity Press, 2017), xliii-lxii.

[5]Erasmus's Greek New Testament drew from four Greek texts, the earliest of which was dated from the twelfth century.

proponents of its vision for cultural and religious renewal. Here we will highlight four important ways that the humanist program of biblical scholarship shaped the ministry of the Reformers and changed the face of early modern Protestantism.

The languages of the Bible. The Protestant reformers recognized that the careful study of the Christian Scriptures in the original Greek and Hebrew languages was necessary for recovering the Christian gospel and achieving the reformation of the church. Martin Luther and his colleagues believed that recovering the knowledge of the biblical languages was not merely an isolated cultural achievement but God's providential design for the renewal of biblical Christianity. The health of the church—indeed, the integrity of the gospel—depended on the knowledge of the Christian Scriptures in the language of their original composition. As Luther stated,

> In proportion then as we value the gospel, let us zealously hold to the languages. For it was not without purpose that God caused his Scriptures to be set down in these two languages alone—the Old Testament in Hebrew, the New [Testament] in Greek. Now if God did not despise them but chose them above all others for his Word, then we too ought to honor them above all others. . . . And let us be sure of this: we will not long preserve the gospel without the languages.[6]

Accordingly, nearly all the major Protestant reformers were *homines trilinguarum* (men of three languages): conversant in classical Latin, Greek, and Hebrew. Moreover, their commitment to the biblical languages found expression in the academic programs of their universities and academies. At the University of Wittenberg, for example, Luther and his colleagues pushed for curricular reforms that led to the creation of professorships in Greek and Hebrew in 1518.[7] The first professor to occupy the Greek chair was a brilliant young humanist named Philipp Melanchthon, who would soon become Luther's disciple and chief

---

[6]LW 45:359-60.
[7]For the impressive growth of Hebrew instruction at Lutheran, Reformed, and Catholic universities before 1660, see Stephen Burnett, *Christian Hebraism in the Reformation Era (1500–1660)* (Leiden: Brill, 2012), 27-42.

confidant.[8] Similarly, when Calvin established his academy in Geneva in 1559, a liberal arts curriculum, including instruction in Greek and Hebrew, took pride of place.[9] The first rector of Calvin's academy was an accomplished French humanist, expert Hellenist, and poet named Theodore Beza. The city of Zurich, by contrast, could boast neither a university nor an academy. To fill this lacuna, in 1525 the Reformed minister Huldrych Zwingli established a pastoral assembly called the *Prophetzei* (The Prophecy), where the city's ministers and theological students met five days a week to study the Bible in the original languages of Hebrew and Greek.[10] For the Reformers, the recovery of the biblical languages was an essential step closely tied to guarding right doctrine in the church.

Translations of the Bible. Equipped with a knowledge of Greek and Hebrew, Protestant scholars began to question the authority of the Latin Vulgate Bible and soon produced new and improved translations of the sacred text. Even before Luther posted his Ninety-Five Theses, northern humanists such as Valla, Lefèvre d'Étaples, and Erasmus were already raising serious doubts about the reliability of the traditional Latin Vulgate. These concerns grew exponentially as early Protestant leaders compared the old Latin translation to recently published versions of the Hebrew Bible[11] and the Greek New Testament.[12] The acuteness of the problem was impressed on

---

[8]See Martin Brecht, *Martin Luther: His Road to Reformation, 1483–1521*, trans. James L. Schaaf (Minneapolis: Fortress, 1993), 276-77. In his treatise "To the Councilmen of All Cities in Germany" (1524) Luther also urged that secondary schools be established that taught children the liberal arts and the biblical languages. See LW 45:356-64.

[9]Karin Maag, *Seminary or University? The Genevan Academy and Reformed Higher Education, 1560–1620* (Aldershot, England: Scolar Press, 1995), 14-15.

[10]W. P. Stephens, *The Theology of Huldrych Zwingli* (Oxford: Clarendon, 1986), 39. For a firsthand description of Zurich's Prophecy, see Heinrich Bullinger's comments on 1 Cor 14:27, found in Manetsch, *1 Corinthians*, 335-36.

[11]A number of different versions of the Hebrew Bible were available to the Protestant reformers. Martin Luther appears to have used the Hebrew Bible of Gershom Soncino (1494) in his translation of the Bible into German. Later generations of Protestants usually consulted Bomberg's *Biblia Rabbinica* (1517–1518, 1525–1526) or the Hebrew Bibles of Sebastian Münster (1534–1535) and Robert Estienne (1539–1544). See Hans Hillerbrand, ed., *Oxford Encyclopedia of the Reformation* (New York: Oxford University Press, 1996), 1:158-59. Hereafter abbreviated as OER.

[12]Erasmus's *Novum Instrumentum* (eds. 1516, 1519, 1522, 1527, and 1537) was surpassed by successive editions of the Stephanus Bibles (1546, 1549, 1550, 1551), which employed a number of superior Greek codices.

Luther as early as 1517 when he discovered that the Vulgate's translation of the Greek word *metanoia* as "do penance" badly missed the biblical authors' call for heartfelt repentance.[13] The obvious deficiencies of the Latin Vulgate invited Protestant scholars such as Konrad Pellikan, Robert Estienne, and Theodore Beza to generate new Latin versions of the Bible. In so doing, they decisively broke the monopoly of the Latin Vulgate in the Christian West.

During these decades, Protestant scholars also engaged in a massive program of Bible translation and publication that made available the sacred Scriptures in most of Europe's vernacular tongues. The Protestants, of course, were not the first Christians in the West to produce vernacular Bibles. John Wyclif's English translation of the Bible, which first appeared between 1380 and 1384, predated William Tyndale's "Protestant" Bible by almost one hundred and fifty years.[14] Similarly, the first printed German Bible was published in 1466, nearly sixty years (and at least eighteen versions) before Luther completed his famous September New Testament in 1522.[15] Nevertheless, the Protestant program of Bible translation broke new ground in several important ways. For one, the vast majority of Protestant vernacular Bibles were translated directly from the Hebrew and Greek, assuring that they would avoid the most egregious textual errors found in the Latin Vulgate.[16] Equally important, Protestant translators like Luther and Tyndale employed all their skill and artistry to render the language and message of the Bible in an idiom familiar to ordinary lay people. The Bible was to be the people's book.[17]

---

[13]Thus, Luther's first thesis in his Ninety-Five Theses stated, "When our Lord and Master, Jesus Christ, said 'Repent,' he called for the entire life of believers to be one of penitence." See also Luther's letter to Johann von Staupitz, May 30, 1518, in LW 48:63.

[14]See F. F. Bruce, *The English Bible: A History of Translations* (Oxford: Oxford University Press, 1961), 14-15. See also Pelikan, *Reformation of the Bible*, 52-54.

[15]The first printed German Bible was the *Biblia Germanica*, published in Strasbourg by Johann Mentelin in 1466. See Pelikan, *Reformation of the Bible*, 49-51.

[16]Thus, for example, Luther's German New Testament (1522) was the first German edition translated directly from the Greek. See Karl Krueger, "Bible Translation," in *Dictionary of Luther and the Lutheran Tradition*, ed. Timothy J. Wengert (Grand Rapids: Baker Academic, 2017), 90-91.

[17]For more on the popular reception of the Bible, see Jennifer Powell McNutt and David Lauber, eds., *The People's Book: The Reformation and the Bible* (Downers Grove, IL: IVP Academic, 2017).

As Luther once commented, "I endeavored to make Moses so German that no one would suspect he was a Jew."[18]

Finally, Protestant church leaders recognized the breathtaking opportunities offered by the printing press and harnessed this technological revolution to produce an unprecedented number of vernacular Bibles for Europe's reading public. The figures are staggering: Luther's September New Testament of 1522 was followed by more than 443 complete or partial editions of the German Bible during the next quarter century.[19] Similarly, between 1550 and 1600, Genevan printers produced more than eighty editions of the French New Testament and another eighty editions of the entire French Bible.[20] By the end of the century, humanist scholars had completed new versions of the Bible in Arabic, Czech, Danish, Dutch, English, French, German, Italian, Portuguese, and Spanish.[21] The fact that many of these Bibles were printed in a relatively inexpensive, pocket-sized format is further testimony to the Protestants' commitment to make the written Word of God available to all people, no matter their social status or economic station.

The study of the Bible. The Protestant reformers believed that the fruitful reading and faithful proclamation of the Bible was essential for the spiritual health of God's people and the true reformation of the Christian church. As Melanchthon stated in his *Loci Communes* (1543):

> Thus, we should understand that it is a great blessing of God that He has given to His church a certain Book, and He preserves it for us and gathers His church around it. . . . [T]he church is the people who embrace this Book, hear, learn, and retain as their own its teachings in their worship life and in the

---

[18]Martin Luther, *Tischreden* [Table Talk]. 6 vols. 2771a, cited in Roland Bainton, *Here I Stand: A Life of Martin Luther* (New York: Abingdon, 1950), 327.

[19]Andrew Pettegree, *Brand Luther* (New York: Penguin, 2015), 188. Moreover, Wittenberg printers alone sold around 200,000 copies of Luther's German Bible before 1620. See M. H. Black, "The Printed Bible," in *Cambridge History of the Bible* (Cambridge: Cambridge University Press, 1970), 3:432.

[20]Bettye Thomas Chambers, *Bibliography of French Bibles: Fifteenth- and Sixteenth-Century French Language Editions* (Geneva: Librairie Droz, 1983).

[21]Pelikan, *Reformation of the Bible*, 49-62.

governing of their morals. . . . Therefore we should love and cultivate the study of this divinely given book.[22]

The problem, of course, was that the majority of men and women during this period were unable to read the Scriptures for themselves. Recent scholarship estimates that only around 12 percent of Western Europeans were literate in 1500, a figure that increased to around 18 percent a century later.[23] As a general rule, literacy rates were significantly higher in the cities than in the countryside, and men were far more likely to be literate than women. Given this stark reality, how could one meaningfully describe the Bible as the people's book?

Early Protestant leaders were aware of this problem, and they created a variety of ministry programs and resources to promote biblical literacy. Nearly all of the magisterial Reformers wrote catechisms to instruct boys and girls, as well as ignorant adults, in the central tenets of the Christian religion, including the Apostles' Creed, the Ten Commandments, and the Lord's Prayer. The Reformers established multiple dozens of Latin schools and academies in which children (mostly boys) learned to read and write, memorized the catechism, and studied Bible doctrine. In Protestant cities such as Wittenberg and Geneva, worship services were conducted seven days a week in which the congregation recited liturgies, pregnant with the language of Scripture, and sang psalms and Christian hymns. Most important of all was the Protestant sermon. In Wittenberg, Luther and his colleagues preached nine vernacular sermons each week; in Geneva, the Reformed ministers preached as many as thirty-three sermons each week in the city's three parish churches. The sermon was the primary way in which Protestants imparted evangelical doctrine,

---

[22]Philipp Melanchthon, *Loci Communes* (1543), trans. J. A. O. Preus (St. Louis: Concordia, 1992), 117. See Mark Thompson's discussion of this passage in his chapter "Sola Scriptura," in *Reformation Theology: A Systematic Summary*, ed. Matthew Barrett, (Wheaton, IL: Crossway, 2017), 163-64.

[23]See, for example, Eltjo Buringh and Jan Luiten Van Zanden, "Charting the 'Rise of the West': Manuscripts and Printed Books in Europe, a Long-Term Perspective from the Sixth Through Eighteenth Centuries," *The Journal of Economic History* 69, no. 2 (2009): 432-35. See also David Cressy, "Literacy in Context: Meaning and Measurement in Early Modern England," in *Consumption and the World of Goods*, ed. John Brewer and Ray Porter (London: Routledge, 1993), 305-19.

promoted Christian sanctification, and cultivated biblical literacy. As Calvin stated, "For God there is nothing higher than preaching the gospel, because it is the means to lead people to salvation."[24]

In addition to ministries that promoted biblical literacy, the Protestant reformers also published an almost countless number of books and pamphlets to help clergy and educated laypeople study and interpret the Bible. This vast literature included printed sermons, hermeneutical guides, paraphrases of Scripture, Hebrew and Greek grammars, Bible concordances and dictionaries, Gospel harmonies, and biblical commentaries. It is with good reason, then, that scholars have sometimes called the sixteenth century the golden age of biblical interpretation.[25] Something more needs to be said regarding Protestant commentaries. During the Reformation, Lutheran, Anglican, and Reformed church leaders applied their knowledge of sacred philology and the biblical languages to compose a vast library of exegetical and theological commentaries on every book of the Bible. Scholars have identified, for example, seventy different commentaries on the book of Romans and nearly one hundred commentaries on the Psalms written during the sixteenth century alone.[26] The roll call of Protestant commentators included Luther, Zwingli, and Calvin, to be sure, but also a battalion of lesser-known humanist biblical scholars such as Melanchthon, Johannes Brenz, Heinrich Bullinger, Martin Bucer, Wolfgang Musculus, Theodore Beza, and Peter Martyr Vermigli, whose erudition and mature exegetical judgments were on display in their penetrating (and often massive) commentaries. Although Reformation commentaries appeared in a variety

---

[24]John Calvin, *Supplementa Calviniana Sermon inédit*, ed. Erwin Mülhaupt et al. (Neukirchen: Neukirchener, 1936), 8:210.

[25]See Timothy George's general introduction to the Reformed Commentary on Scripture series in Manetsch, *1 Corinthians*, xxvii.

[26]See OER 1:167-71. Most, though not all, of these commentaries were written by Protestant scholars. Today, the most complete collection of sixteenth-century Protestant commentaries can be found in the Post-Reformation Digital Library, which lists around 950 discrete biblical commentaries published during the period. See the rubric "Biblical Commentary" at www .prdl.org.

of literary genres and adopted different interpretive strategies, all were intended to make clear the Bible's message for the benefit of the church. Protestant commentators would thus have agreed with the early church scholar Jerome, who stated that the task of exegesis is "to explain what has been said by others and make clear in plain language what has been written obscurely."[27]

It is important to recognize, finally, that Reformation commentaries had a number of different intended audiences. Undoubtedly, many pastors and lay people read these commentaries for their personal instruction and edification. But biblical commentaries also had a public life, serving as indispensable resources for preachers as they proclaimed God's Word in sermons or for professors as they lectured on the sacred text at universities. Through the media of pulpit and lectern, therefore, humanist biblical scholarship reached a broader lay audience and shaped Protestant belief and moral behavior during the age of the Reformation.

The interpretation of the Bible. Finally, we need to make a few brief comments about the way in which early Protestants interpreted their Bibles. Yale historian Jaroslav Pelikan once credited Luther and the Protestant reformers with achieving a Copernican revolution in hermeneutics.[28] And that is partially true. As noted earlier, Protestant leaders championed the humanist program of biblical scholarship that accented philology, challenged the monopoly of the Vulgate Bible, and stimulated a veritable flood of exegetical tools and vernacular Bible translations. Equally important, the magisterial Reformers defended the literal interpretation of Scripture while at the same time launching blistering attacks on the medieval exegetical tradition, which they believed had too often disregarded or distorted the literal meaning of Scripture in search of "deeper" spiritual meanings found in the allegorical, tropological, and anagogical senses of the text. Calvin compared such figurative exegesis to children "playing

---

[27]Quoted in Kenneth Hagen, "What Did the Term *Commentarius* Mean to Sixteenth-Century Theologians?," in *Théorie et pratique de l'exégèse. Actes du troisième colloque international sur l'histoire de l'exégèse biblique du XVIe siècle*, ed. Irena Backus and Francis Higman (Geneva: Droz, 1990), 19.
[28]Pelikan, *Reformation of the Bible*, 29.

games with the sacred Word of God, like tossing a ball back and forth."[29] Bucer repudiated allegorical interpretation as a "blatant insult to the Holy Spirit" contrived by Satan.[30] Luther routinely denounced the fanciful allegories of patristic and medieval interpreters, calling them "silly," "senseless," "foolish," "absurd," "disastrous," "nonsensical"—they were "empty dreams" and "amazing twaddle" that desecrated the sacred writings.[31] Instead, the Protestant reformers insisted that Christian exegetes should interpret the Bible according to its natural or literal sense, governed by the grammar, genre, history, and literary context of a passage. Luther summarized the Protestant approach this way: "We must everywhere stick to the simple, pure, and natural sense of the words that accords with the rules of grammar and the normal use of language as God has created it in man."[32] Although this literal hermeneutic of Scripture was not entirely new with the Reformers (medieval exegetes such as Thomas Aquinas and Nicholas of Lyra had also given priority to the letter of the text), nevertheless, the Protestants popularized this approach and defended it as the only faithful manner of handling the Word of God.

But with that said, early Protestant interpreters were to a significant degree traditional in their approach to Scripture.[33] Along with their patristic and medieval forebears, they believed that Holy Scripture was the divinely inspired Word of God—infallible in its content and message, authoritative in its commands, relevant for their present day. Likewise,

---

[29]John Calvin, *Commentary on 2 Corinthians 3:6-7*, CTS 40:175. See also Ioannis Calvini Opera quae supersunt omnia. 59 vols. Corpus Reformatorum 29-88, ed., G. Baum, E. Cunitz, and E. Reuss (Brunswick, 1863–1900), 50:40-41.

[30]Cited in David Wright, "Martin Bucer," in *Dictionary of Major Biblical Interpreters*, ed. Donald McKim (Downers Grove, IL: IVP Academic, 2009), 249. Similarly, Luther commented: "I urge students of theology to shun this kind of interpretation in the Holy Scriptures. For allegory is pernicious when it does not agree with history, but especially when it takes the place of the history, from which the church is more correctly instructed about the wonderful administration of God." (LW 5:345). For more on Luther's attitude toward figurative exegesis, see Robert Kolb, *Martin Luther and the Enduring Word of God* (Grand Rapids: Baker Academic, 2016), 92-93.

[31]See Luther's *Lectures on Genesis*, LW 1:90, 93, 98, 99, 122, 184, 185, 188, 231, 232, 233.

[32]LW 36:30.

[33]See Richard Muller and John Thompson, eds., "The Significance of Precritical Exegesis: Retrospect and Prospect," in *Biblical Interpretation in the Era of the Reformation* (Grand Rapids: Eerdmans, 1996), 335-45.

in agreement with the Christian tradition, the Reformers recognized the unity of the biblical canon and believed that passages of Scripture must be interpreted within this larger canonical frame. At the same time, the majority of Protestant exegetes recognized that faithful interpretation of Scripture must occur in conversation with biblical scholars throughout the ages. Hence, while the Reformers believed in the authority and clarity of the Bible and affirmed that Scripture should interpret Scripture (the so-called *analogia scripturae*), they also "recognized the value of consulting the scholarship of patristic and medieval exegetes—not only as apologetic foils, but also as faithful guides to interpreting God's Word."[34]

Finally, although Protestant leaders regularly excoriated the allegorical excesses of the medieval church, they did not endorse a bare literalism that ignored the spiritual message of Scripture. Reformation commentators like Luther, Zwingli, Bucer, and Calvin recognized that the literal or natural sense of Scripture frequently contained various layers of spiritual meaning or typological significance that spoke of Christ, Christian morality, and Christian hope to believers in their own day. The task of the faithful interpreter, then, was to excavate these rich spiritual deposits while remaining true to the plain, historical meaning of the biblical author. Spiritual exegesis must always be subject to the letter of the text. Some magisterial Reformers (like Luther and Zwingli) displayed a fair degree of freedom in drawing spiritual and mystical meaning from Scripture; others (like Calvin and Bucer) were more restrained in their uses of spiritual or typological exegesis.[35] All agreed, however, that allegories were never to be used to establish points of doctrine; they functioned only to elucidate or illustrate Christian truth.

They also agreed that all interpretations—literal as well as spiritual readings—must accord with the analogy of faith (*analogia fidei*)—that is,

---

[34]Scott M. Manetsch, "The Gravity of the Divine Word," *Concordia Theological Quarterly* 81 (2017): 63.

[35]For an excellent description of Calvin's restrained use of typological exegesis, see G. Sujin Pak, *The Judaizing Calvin: Sixteenth-Century Debates over the Messianic Psalms* (New York: Oxford University Press, 2010).

the broader message of scriptural teaching. Luther explained this hermeneutical approach to his students in this fashion: "I do not try to find [allegories] unless they in some way enhance the historical meaning that is comprehended from the simple story itself. There they are like flowers strewn about, but they prove nothing."[36]

For these reasons, therefore, most scholars today rightly reject the idea that Luther, Calvin, and other early Protestant exegetes were progenitors of modern historical critical approaches to Scripture interpretation. To be sure, they did break new ground in their use of humanistic biblical scholarship and in the priority they gave to the simple or literal meaning of the text. However, their general attitude regarding the divine nature and authority of Scripture as God's written word was in overall continuity with the Christian tradition that preceded them.

THE BIBLE IN JEAN CRESPIN'S *HISTORY OF THE MARTYRS*

As we have seen, the Bible occupied a central place in Protestant scholarship, pedagogy, and public worship in the sixteenth century. But what role did the Bible play in the everyday lives of *ordinary people* during the Reformation? How did village pastors, common laborers, university students, tailors, and dressmakers view the Bible? How did they interpret it? What importance did it play in their daily lives? Jean Crespin's monumental work *History of the Martyrs* is one of only a handful of written sources from the Reformation period that sheds light on this largely forgotten world of popular perception and belief. In the second part of this chapter, I will briefly introduce Crespin and his martyrology and then examine this important source for clues as to how the Bible shaped the convictions and spirituality of ordinary Protestants during the age of the Reformation.[37]

---

[36]LW 5:88. For an insightful treatment of Luther's attitude toward allegories and his development as an exegete, see Kolb, *Martin Luther and the Enduring Word of God*, 158-67.

[37]The term *ordinary Protestant* is not intended to assume illiteracy. Though Crespin's martyrs included men and women from a variety of social and economic backgrounds, most of those who interacted with Scripture appear to have had some level of literacy. Other martyrs probably gained knowledge of the Bible's message through oral conversations, memorized catechesis, and sermons.

First, a few words about Crespin himself. Jean Crespin was one of the most prolific printers of French Protestant literature in the sixteenth century.[38] Born around 1520, Crespin received a humanist education at the University of Louvain before returning to his hometown of Arras in the Spanish Netherlands to pursue a career in law. In November of 1541, he witnessed the public execution of a goldsmith named Claude le Painctre, who was burned at the stake for his evangelical convictions. Four years later, Crespin himself was accused of being a secret Lutheran and was thereafter stripped of his family's inheritance and banished from the city, leading to his eventual relocation to Reformed Geneva in 1548. With Calvin's support, Crespin soon established a successful print shop in Geneva that employed four presses and around sixteen employees, a business that produced a vast quantity of religious books, including Bibles, commentaries, catechisms, liturgical manuals, and polemical writings.[39]

One of the most popular books that issued from Crespin's press was the martyrology that he penned and first published in 1554 under the title *Le Livre des Martyrs* (*The Book of Martyrs*). This work, which consisted of 687 pages (in octavo), recorded the bold confessions and described the courageous deaths of around ninety named evangelical martyrs, beginning with Jan Hus's execution in 1415 and concluding with the death of Pierre de la Vau, who was burned at the stake in Nîmes in 1554.[40] Crespin continued to supplement and revise his martyrology until a thirteenth and final edition appeared in 1570 under the title *The*

---

[38]For basic information on Jean Crespin (ca. 1520–1572) and his martyrology, see Jean-François Gilmont, *Jean Crespin: Un éditeur réformé du XVIe siècle* (Geneva: Librarie Droz, 1981); Jeannine Olson, "Jean Crespin, Humanist Printer Among the Reformation Martyrologists," in *The Harvest of Humanism in Central Europe*, ed. Mandred Fleischer (St. Louis: Concordia, 1992), 317-40; David Watson, "Jean Crespin and the Writing of History in the French Reformation," in *Protestant History and Identity in Sixteenth-Century Europe*, ed. Bruce Gordon (Aldershot, England: Scolar, 1996), 2:39-58; David Watson, "Jean Crespin and the First English Martyrology of the Reformation," in *John Foxe and the English Reformation*, ed. David Loades (Aldershot, England: Scolar, 1997), 192-209. For an excellent treatment of martyrdom in the sixteenth century, see Brad Gregory, *Salvation at Stake, Christian Martyrdom in Early Modern Europe* (Cambridge, MA: Harvard University Press, 1999).
[39]Olson, "Jean Crespin," 322-24.
[40]See Crespin, *Le Livre des Martyrs* (n.p., 1554), accessed at books.google.com on August 23, 2017.

History of True Witnesses to the Truth of the Gospel (which thereafter became known as *History of the Martyrs*). By that time the work had grown into a hefty volume of 1,450 pages (in folio) that memorialized the deaths of nearly six hundred Protestant martyrs.[41] It would be difficult to overstate the impact that *History of the Martyrs* had among French Protestants in the centuries that followed. The martyrology became an essential part of Huguenot memory and spirituality, read alongside the French Bible and the Genevan Psalter. The Catholic poet and propagandist Agrippa d'Aubigné once commented, "After the Bible, I have found no book more dangerous than this one, and none more powerful to make one a heretic."[42]

Jean Crespin's stated purpose in writing the *History of the Martyrs* was to present his readers with a faithful narrative of historical events cast within the frame of God's broader providential plan for his church.[43] The martyrology was to serve as a kind of mirror through which Reformed Protestants might observe "the power, wisdom, justice and goodness of God."[44] Crespin constructed his narrative around a patchwork of historical sources, including published documents, private letters, eyewitness accounts, oral testimonies, trial records, and personal confessions, stitched together with his own historical and theological commentary. Crespin's reliability as a historian has sometimes been questioned due to his confessional bias, his uncritical use of sources, his providential view of history, and occasional embellishments that he introduces to the

---

[41]Jean Crespin, *Histoire de vrai Tesmoins de la verité de l'Evangile, Qui de leur sang l'on signée depuis Jean Hus jusques autemps present* (Geneva: Ancre de J. Crespin, 1570). After Crespin's death in 1572, his son-in-law Eustache Vignon and the Genevan minister Simon Goulart continued to update the martyrology until it reached its final form in 1619, a massive edition of 1760 pages (in folio) that described the deaths of around eight hundred Protestant martyrs. See Crespin, *Histoire des Martyrs*, Édition Nouvelle Précédée de Notes, ed. Daniel Benoit and Matthieu Lelièvre, 3 vols. (Toulouse: Société des livres religieux, 1885–1889). My analysis is based on the 1570 edition of Crespin's martyrology.

[42]Cited by Benoit and Lelièvre in the introduction to their edition of the *Histoire des Martyrs*, xix.

[43]See especially David Watson, "Jean Crespin and the Writing of History," 39-58.

[44]Crespin states in the 1561 edition of the work that he will "proposer aux lecteurs, comme en un miroir, la puissance, la sagesse, la justice et la bonté de Dieu." Cited in Gilmont, *Jean Crespin*, 188.

historical record.[45] But even if Crespin's method does not meet the critical standards of modern historical scholarship, his martyrology transcends mere Protestant hagiography as it provides the reader with a vast collection of primary source materials that shed precious light on Protestant religious belief and behavior in the sixteenth century. In particular, these historical traces give a rich and detailed description of how early Protestants viewed Scripture and how the Bible shaped the spirituality and religious identity of ordinary men and women in the age of the Reformation. Crespin's martyrology makes clear that, for sixteenth-century Protestants, the Bible was the people's book.

References to the Christian Scriptures saturate Crespin's work. His narrative employs a variety of words and phrases to refer to Holy Writ, including the Bible (*la Bible*), the Holy Scripture (*la saincte Escriture*), the Old and New Testament (*le vieil & nouveau Testament*), and the Word of God (*la parole de Dieu*). This latter term has a wide semantic range for Crespin; he uses it variously to describe the message of the gospel, Christian preaching, and Christian doctrine in general; he also uses the term more narrowly to describe God's written revelation. Thus, for example, a member of the parlement of Paris and Protestant martyr Anne du Bourg identifies Christian Scripture as "the true Word of God, dictated by the Holy Spirit, written by the Prophets and Apostles" who were "true secretaries of our good God."[46]

Because they understood Scripture to be God's written word, Crespin's martyrs revered it and ascribed divine qualities to it. They recognized the Bible as "celestial teaching" and "infallible truth." Its message therefore was "firm and eternal," "completely true," and "certain and perfect."[47] Charles Favre, a student from Lausanne who was executed in Lyons in

---

[45]For a largely critical assessment of Crespin's reliability as a historian, see William Monter, *Judging the French Reformation: Heresy Trials by Sixteenth-Century Parlements* (Cambridge, MA: Harvard University Press, 1999); and Watson, "Jean Crespin and the Writing of History," 39-58. For Brad Gregory's more positive assessment, see *Salvation at Stake*, 18-22.

[46]Crespin, *Histoire de vrai Tesmoins* (1570), 531.

[47]Crespin, *Histoire de vrai Tesmoins* (1570), 148, 240v, 348, 690.

1554, captured these convictions in his written confession: "I believe and confess that the Scripture alone is the rule of religion and the Christian faith, which is contained in the Old and New Testament, and that it is firm, certain and true, infallible and perfect."[48] As they faced opponents who challenged their religious beliefs and threatened them with physical harm, Protestant martyrs found particular confidence and comfort from the fact that the Bible's message of salvation was true, did not change, and remained eternal. The martyr Pierre Brully, for example, informed his accusers that "I have no fear of error when I speak according to the Word of God."[49] Similarly, Richard Le Fevre confidently asserted that the Christian's faith should be founded "on the word of Jesus Christ alone, which cannot fail and does not lie."[50] Several decades later, a Flemish martyr named Christophe Smith wrote from prison, "Let them burn; let them strangle; let them kill and murder, by fire, nooses, the sword, and water as much as they want, the Word of God still remains and will remain eternally."[51]

In their judicial hearings and confessions, many of Crespin's martyrs articulated the Protestant doctrine of *sola Scriptura*, that Scripture alone is the Christian's highest authority in matters of faith and practice. For Englishman John Philpot, God had established and ordained Scripture "as the judge of all human wisdom and all the words and works of all the people in the world." Thus, he continued, "I hold no doctrine which is contrary to the indubitable authority of holy Scripture."[52] In a similar fashion, when interrogated by Catholic authorities in 1552, Denis Peloquin stated that Scripture was "infallible truth, certain and perfect . . . the only rule of the Christian religion."[53] Seven years later, Anne du Bourg concluded his defense by affirming that "all the laws made by the

---

[48]Crespin, *Histoire de vrai Tesmoins* (1570), 226.

[49]Crespin, *Histoire de vrai Tesmoins* (1570), 135v.

[50]Crespin, *Histoire de vrai Tesmoins* (1570), 278v.

[51]Crespin, *Histoire de vrai Tesmoins* (1570), 642.

[52]Crespin, *Histoire de vrai Tesmoins* (1570), 401.

[53]Crespin, *Histoire de vrai Tesmoins* (1570), 240v.

popes or others concerning the Christian religion cannot force Christians to follow any other rule or doctrine than what is contained in the book of the Bible."[54] Several of Crespin's martyrs acknowledged the theological contribution made by early church fathers, such as Ambrose, Augustine, and Chrysostom, but insisted that their judgments must always be tested by Scripture. One French martyr put the matter this way: "I in no way reject the writings of the doctors that are conformed to the holy Scripture, inasmuch as they are drawn from it as the true source and fountain of all pure doctrine; but those that are not conformed to the holy Scripture, I hold them as a fable and lie."[55] Evidently, the question of authority stood at the center of the confessional divide that separated the evangelical churches from Rome. Thus, when a Catholic judge ordered Richard Le Fevre to explain the difference between the Roman Church and the Reformed churches in Geneva, Lausanne, and Bern, the defendant responded: "The difference is that the Church of Rome is governed by human traditions and the other, by contrast, is governed by the Word alone and the ordinance of God."[56]

The trial of Jean Rabec provides a good example of how Protestant martyrs appealed to Scripture's authority against their Catholic opponents. Rabec had once been a Franciscan monk who, having tasted evangelical teaching, renounced his monastic vows and relocated to Lausanne to study theology at the city's Reformed academy. After completing his studies, he returned to the city of Angers as a missionary to share with his fellow countrymen "the inestimable treasure of the Lord's grace" and, if possible, to "rescue from the abyss of hell those who were perishing."[57] In August of 1555, Rabec was arrested and imprisoned when he was caught reading aloud the first edition of Crespin's martyrology to a group of onlookers. During the long trial that followed, Rabec was rigorously questioned by episcopal judges as to his views regarding the intercession

---

[54]Crespin, *Histoire de vrai Tesmoins* (1570), 531.
[55]Crespin, *Histoire de vrai Tesmoins* (1570), 604.
[56]Crespin, *Histoire de vrai Tesmoins* (1570), 279v.
[57]Crespin, *Histoire de vrai Tesmoins* (1570), 408v.

of the saints, the Virgin Mary, purgatory, the pope, auricular confession, the Mass, transubstantiation, baptism, Catholic traditions, and monastic vows. From his prison cell, Rabec wrote a precious letter describing his responses to his interrogation. When asked about praying to the saints, he responded that the practice "was not acceptable, inasmuch as it cannot be proven from Scripture."[58] When asked about papal authority, he answered: "I do not believe that there is any other head of the Church than Jesus Christ, inasmuch as Scripture proposes no other."[59] Regarding the doctrine of Mary's immaculate conception, Rabec was even more direct: "You have as the foundation of your [belief] an explanation based in the human brain; as for me, I have the Word of God. Judge who is the most wise, God or you; and what is most certain, his judgment or yours!"[60] At one point in the trial, Rabec paraphrased the famous statement by Luther: "I would place more value in the words of a child who has the Word of God than the rest of the whole world who does not have it."[61] After months of intense interrogations and cruel treatment, Rabec was finally excommunicated as a heretic, defrocked, and sentenced to death by burning. On April 24, 1556, the executioner came to Rabec's prison cell, cut out his tongue, and then led him to the place of execution, where he was suspended above the ground by his wrists for half an hour before being burned alive at the stake. Remarkably, according to Crespin's account, the courageous martyr Jean Rabec—without a tongue and with blood streaming out of his mouth—was heard praying and reciting Psalm 79 minutes before his body was burned to ashes.[62]

Of course, bold assertions like that of Jean Rabec—"I have the Word of God"—were contested by Catholic opponents at every turn. In Crespin's account, Catholic judges and inquisitors regularly rejected the

---

[58]Crespin, *Histoire de vrai Tesmoins* (1570), 408v.

[59]Crespin, *Histoire de vrai Tesmoins* (1570), 409v.

[60]Crespin, *Histoire de vrai Tesmoins* (1570), 409.

[61]Crespin, *Histoire de vrai Tesmoins* (1570), 409. At the Leipzig Disputation, Luther famously stated: "A simple layman armed with Scripture is to be believed above a pope or a council without it." Cited in Bainton, *Here I Stand*, 117.

[62]Crespin, *Histoire de vrai Tesmoins* (1570), 413v-14.

martyrs' private interpretations of the Bible, asserting that the Catholic Church alone defined canonical Scripture and thus had the sole right to interpret it. In a letter to friends back in Geneva, the martyr Jean Vernon from Poitiers offered a typical Protestant response to these epistemological concerns. The monk interrogating him had asked how he knew that the Old and New Testaments were the Word of God except for the fact that the church defined them as such. Vernon answered that "he believed that Scripture was the Word of God because the style and language of Scripture is the language of God dictated by the Holy Spirit." Moreover, those who have experienced the new birth "are taught by God and have the Holy Spirit in them, who gives testimony to their spirit that they are from God." Vernon proceeded to quote from Isaiah 54, Jeremiah 31, John 18, and Romans 8 in support of his viewpoint.[63] In a similar fashion, the martyr Jean Trigalet also appealed to the Holy Spirit's role as witness to Scripture's divine origin and authority. "We have a sure witness of this fact in our conscience by the Spirit of Adoption, who works in our hearts, and gives us complete confidence in the promises of God, causing us to cry Abba Father, as Saint Paul says in Romans 8."[64]

But what of the hermeneutical problem? How could Protestants have confidence that they rightly interpreted Scripture without appealing to the teaching authority of church and tradition? Crespin's martyrs addressed this hermeneutical concern in various ways, although the overall message was that ordinary Christians could understand the central teachings of God's Word if they studied the Bible carefully, allowed Scripture to interpret Scripture, and depended on the Holy Spirit for illumination. Thus, for example, two English martyrs, Thomas Hygby and Thomas Causson, challenged the Catholic interpretation of Jesus' words, "This is my body broken for you," in this fashion: "We do not at all deny these words, but we determine the true sense of these words by comparing other passages of Scripture to this passage, which easily

---

[63]Crespin, *Histoire de vrai Tesmoins* (1570), 341v.
[64]Crespin, *Histoire de vrai Tesmoins* (1570), 345.

provides the true interpretation of this particular passage."[65] Similarly, when a theological professor from the Sorbonne in Paris rebuked a poor teenager named Jean Morel for interpreting the Scripture for himself, Morel responded: "My faith is founded on the doctrine of the prophets and apostles. And, although I may not be well trained in sacred letters . . . I can learn from [the Scriptures] what is necessary for my salvation; and the passages that I find difficult, I pass over them until such a time when it pleases God to give me the ability to understand them. And thus I drink the milk that I find in the Word of God." Morel supported his statement by quoting from St. Chrysostom, who once wrote, "The Holy Spirit wished that the sacred Scripture should be written in such a way that all might read it, both great and small, even servants and chambermaids."[66]

The role of the Holy Spirit in biblical interpretation was an especially important theme in Crespin's martyrology. When Geoffroy Guerin was asked in 1558 how one could adjudicate between rival interpretations of Catholics and Protestants, he answered simply, "This will be the Holy Spirit."[67] In the same year, a Catholic judge demanded of a sixty-year-old vinedresser named Pierre Chevet how it was that he knew so much Scripture and how he could be so confident of its meaning. Chevet quoted from Isaiah 54:13 ("All your children shall be taught by the LORD") and then replied, "Why should I not know what pertains to my salvation, when I have such a good teacher [*docteur*], the Spirit of God?"[68] When asked how he dared to assert that he possessed the Holy Spirit, Chevet answered confidently: "I am a child of God, and the Spirit of God was given to me as a deposit of my adoption" (alluding to Rom 8:15).[69] François Varlut, a poor drapemaker and lay preacher from Tournay, also described the Holy Spirit as the chief doctor of Scripture. Arrested in

---

[65]Crespin, *Histoire de vrai Tesmoins* (1570), 316.
[66]Crespin, *Histoire de vrai Tesmoins* (1570), 508.
[67]Crespin, *Histoire de vrai Tesmoins* (1570), 498.
[68]Crespin, *Histoire de vrai Tesmoins* (1570), 517.
[69]Crespin, *Histoire de vrai Tesmoins* (1570), 517.

1562, Varlut was brought before the city's magistrates, who asked how he, an ignorant tradesman, could claim to be wiser than the learned doctors of the church who had studied theology most of their lives. Varlut answered:

> Monsieur, as for me, I know and confess that by nature I am so ignorant that I am not able even to think a good thought, as Saint Paul says, and that before God had changed my perverse and hard heart into a submissive heart, I knew nothing of the good nor of God. But when it pleased God by his grace to touch my heart, and when he had made me aware of my ignorance, then . . . I asked him for wisdom [and] to be instructed by his Holy Spirit in the knowledge of the truth. He granted my request and instructed me in the true knowledge of his Word, so that I am certain that what I believe is the true word of God and not an opinion.[70]

The magistrates ridiculed Varlut's response, pointing out that the hated Anabaptists also boasted of the Spirit's inspiration. Varlut remained unmoved, however: he would continue to trust Jesus and the apostles, who promised that Christians who asked for the Spirit's wisdom would certainly receive it.

The Protestant martyrs in Crespin's martyrology were people of the Bible. They not only defended its authority and debated its message, they also bought and sold it; they read it; they memorized it; they sang it; they talked about it; they found comfort from it; some even died for it. For many of these martyrs, the message of sacred Scripture profoundly shaped the way they viewed God, his nature and purposes, and the way they conducted their daily lives. An English noblewoman named Anne Askew stated before her accusers that she would "prefer to read five verses in the holy Bible of God than to hear the same number of Masses," for she "felt great edification in reading the Bible but none when listening to the Mass."[71] Estienne Brun, a peasant farmer from Dauphiné, devoted the majority of his time to ploughing his fields and reading his French

---

[70]Crespin, *Histoire de vrai Tesmoins* (1570), 603.
[71]Crespin, *Histoire de vrai Tesmoins* (1570), 164v.

New Testament—the first activity was "for the nourishment of his family," and the second was "for the instruction of himself in all fear of God."[72] The two sons of Robert Ouguier of Lille warned their father against handling a wooden crucifix, pointing instead to the spiritual illumination that came from the Word of God: "We do not at all want a Jesus Christ made of wood, because we bear Jesus Christ, the living Son of God, in our hearts and we feel his holy Word written in letters of gold in the deep recesses of our hearts."[73] Likewise, shortly before his execution in 1546, the Spanish martyr Jean Diaze urged fellow believers to embrace the message of God's Word, which "illumines the eyes of our understanding with all celestial light so that it burns in all of our hearts as a divine fire, inciting us to good works, worthy of a Christian man."[74]

In addition to spiritual illumination and moral guidance, many of Crespin's martyrs experienced comfort from Scripture in the darkest moments of their lives. When the French martyr Pierre Gabart found himself in a filthy prison cell, teeming with rats, he "did not stop singing the Psalms and crying out in a loud voice the consolations of the Word of God so that others might hear."[75] Many other Protestant martyrs, including the German pastor Wolfgang Schuch, sang psalms and recited Scripture as they were led to the scaffold or bound to the stake.[76] A couple of martyrs even died with Bibles in hand. Thus, for example, an unnamed bookseller was burned at the stake in Avignon in 1543 with copies of the Scripture strapped to his chest and back as punishment for selling illegal vernacular Bibles in the city. According to Crespin, the poor book merchant "had the Word of God in his heart and mouth, and did not cease along the road to his execution exhorting and admonishing the people to read the holy Scripture."[77] The central role that the Scripture

---

[72]Crespin, *Histoire de vrai Tesmoins* (1570), 95.

[73]Crespin, *Histoire de vrai Tesmoins* (1570), 426v.

[74]Crespin, *Histoire de vrai Tesmoins* (1570), 160v.

[75]Crespin, *Histoire de vrai Tesmoins* (1570), 484v.

[76]Crespin, *Histoire de vrai Tesmoins* (1570), 67.

[77]Crespin, *Histoire de vrai Tesmoins* (1570), 118v.

played in shaping Protestant spirituality and practice is also illustrated in the final letter that the martyr Jean Le Grain wrote to his wife shortly before his death by sword in June of 1568: "I urge you to remain in peace and harmony among yourselves, meditate constantly on the holy Scripture of the Lord. Do not forget to give to each of my children a Bible, which I leave them for a last will and testament. My very dear wife, I ask you to continue to teach our children in the fear of God, being always content with what he gives to you. To conclude, I bid you *adieu*, my very dear wife, if it happens that I should not see you again."[78]

CONCLUSION

This chapter has explored the important place that the Bible occupied among Protestants in the sixteenth century. As we have seen, early Reformers such as Luther, Melanchthon, Zwingli, and Calvin believed that the recovery of the Christian gospel and the reformation of the church was in large part dependent on a renewed commitment to the careful study, right interpretation, and faithful proclamation of the Christian Scripture. Accordingly, the Reformers worked tirelessly not only in teaching and preaching the Scriptures but also in producing study resources such as improved vernacular translations of the Bible, catechisms, and commentaries to help God's people mature in Christian understanding and sanctification. The Bible was never intended to be the preoccupation or property of scholars alone; it must be the people's book. The martyr accounts that we have consulted in Crespin's *History of the Martyrs* illustrate this conviction particularly well. As we have seen, Protestant martyrs from various social backgrounds and occupations professed their commitment to God's written Word and cherished its message. In the face of extraordinary difficulties, Crespin's martyrs turned to Scripture again and again. They studied it; they defended it; they recited it; they memorized it; they sang it; they found comfort from it.

---

[78]Crespin, *Histoire de vrai Tesmoins* (1570), 702r-v.

The trial and execution of a twenty-three-year-old widow named Philippe de Luns from Périgueux provides one final example of the formative role that Scripture played in shaping Protestant identity and spirituality in the Reformation. Philippe was arrested in 1557 for hosting a Protestant conventicle in her home, at which the believers were frequently heard by neighbors singing the Psalms. Moreover, her husband had recently died without receiving last rites from the Roman Catholic Church. From her prison cell, Philippe wrote the lieutenant, "Monsieur . . . I see clearly that my death approaches and yet, if I have ever needed consolation, it is now. Please allow me to have a Bible or a New Testament to comfort me."[79] Throughout her trial, Philippe remained resolute in her commitment to the Scripture and the Protestant faith. When asked from whom she had learned her doctrine, she replied that "she had no other instructor than the text of the New Testament."[80] When asked whether or not she wanted to believe in the Catholic Mass, she replied that "she only wanted to believe that which was in the Old and New Testament."[81] As the time of her execution approached, Crespin reports, Philippe laid aside the griefclothes of her widowhood and clothed herself instead with a velvet cape and other bright accessories in joyful preparation for her triumphal martyrdom and union with her spouse, Jesus Christ. On September 27, 1558, Philippe de Luns was brought to the Place Maubert in Paris and tortured; she then mounted the gallows and died with a radiant courage befitting a true martyr.[82]

---

[79]Crespin, *Histoire de vrai Tesmoins* (1570), 482.
[80]Crespin, *Histoire de vrai Tesmoins* (1570), 482v.
[81]Crespin, *Histoire de vrai Tesmoins* (1570), 482v.
[82]Crespin, *Histoire de vrai Tesmoins* (1570), 484.

Chapter Two

MARTIN LUTHER'S CHRISTOLOGICAL PRINCIPLE

IMPLICATIONS *for* BIBLICAL AUTHORITY
and BIBLICAL INTERPRETATION

DAVID S. DOCKERY

MARTIN LUTHER (1483–1546) BEGAN TO FASHION a distinctive method for interpreting the Bible while he prepared his preface for the book of Romans in 1522. Throughout his life he looked to this significant Pauline book in the New Testament as the entry and key for interpreting all of Holy Scripture. In and through this epistle, Luther came to understand the meaning of human sin and the atoning sacrifice of Christ.[1] For the Wittenberg Reformer, this Pauline book summed up Christian doctrine and provided an introduction to the Old Testament, both of which were shaping factors in Luther's approach to biblical interpretation. Luther exhorted others to be familiar with Paul's teaching in Romans and to return to it often. Here could be found the things one ought to know, the body of doctrine—namely, what is law, gospel, sin, punishment, grace, faith, righteousness, Christ, God, good works, love, hope, and the cross.

---

[1]See Robert Kolb, *Martin Luther and the Enduring Word of God* (Grand Rapids: Baker Academic, 2016), 113-14.

THE FORMATION OF LUTHER'S THEOLOGY
AND APPROACH TO BIBLICAL INTERPRETATION

We will begin this chapter by exploring how Luther's approach to biblical interpretation developed. We often think of the themes of gospel, faith, and righteousness found in Romans 1:16-17, quoting the prophet Habakkuk, as the key verses for Luther's understanding of Romans. That Habakkuk's words were of special importance in Jewish circles can be seen in the famous remark of Rabbi Simlai (ca. AD 250) recorded in the Talmud in Makkot 23b: "Moses gave Israel 613 commandments, David reduced them to 10, Isaiah to 2, but Habakkuk to 1: 'the righteous shall live by his faith.'" No doubt this text, also quoted in Galatians 3:11 and Hebrews 10:38, had a catalytic effect in leading to the Reformation. It has sometimes been observed that these words of Habakkuk, on which his "son" the apostle Paul brilliantly elaborated, became the great clarion call of the Protestant Reformation in the theology of Habakkuk's "grandson," Martin Luther.[2]

Others would likely point to Romans 3:21-26 as the entry way into Luther's thought. Here we find Paul's theocentric gospel, which shaped his theological "children," that courageous and godly generation that led the Protestant Reformation in the sixteenth century. The central gospel message of justification by faith alone shines so gloriously here that the Reformers considered these verses to be Scripture's clearest explication of this precious doctrine. According to Luther, if the epistle to the Romans is a "little" New Testament, then Romans 3:21-26 deserves to be called the "little" Romans.[3] These two key Pauline passages were pivotal for Luther in the formation of his thought.

---

[2]For an expanded discussion, see David S. Dockery, "Romans 1:16-17," *Review and Expositor* 86 (1989): 87-91; David S. Dockery, "The Use of Hab. 2:4 in Rom. 1:17: Some Hermeneutical and Theological Considerations," *Wesleyan Theological Journal* 22, no. 2 (1987): 24-36; also C. E. B. Cranfield, *A Critical and Exegetical Commentary on the Epistle to the Romans* (Edinburgh: T&T Clark, 1975), 1:86-102.

[3]See David S. Dockery, "A Reformation Day Sermon (Romans 3:21-26)," *Preaching Magazine* (September-October 1989): 33-34; also Richard N. Longenecker, *The Epistle to the Romans* (Grand Rapids: Eerdmans, 2016), 378-87.

Yet, as Steven Paulson indicates in his outstanding introduction to *Lutheran Theology*, it may well have been Romans 1:1-4 that opened the door for Luther to his hermeneutical method, which shaped his understanding of the gospel, of preaching, and of theology. Moreover, according to Luther, Paul's letter, introduced by these verses, served as "the best introduction to the Old Testament that a person could have."[4] The apostle began this grand epistle with these words:

> Paul, a servant of Jesus Christ, called to be an apostle and set apart for the gospel of God—the gospel he promised beforehand through his prophets in the Holy Scriptures regarding his Son, who as to his earthly life was a descendant of David, and who through the Spirit of holiness was appointed the Son of God in power by his resurrection from the dead: Jesus Christ our Lord. (Rom 1:1-4 NIV)

The young Luther began the serious study of theology while in the monastery at Erfurt. He was initially sent to lecture at the newly founded University of Wittenberg in 1508 and returned in 1511, where he completed his studies for the doctor of theology degree in 1512. His permanent appointment to the chair of Bible took place that same year, prior to his thirtieth birthday. His serious study of the Scriptures and his extensive reading of Augustine as he prepared for his lectures paved the way for Luther's understanding of biblical authority and his approach to biblical hermeneutics.

His preparation for these important and formative lectures at Wittenberg provided a laboratory for developing his hermeneutical principles in general and his interpretive approaches in particular as he worked through key portions of Scripture, beginning with his lectures on the Psalms from 1513 to 1515. Other important lectures and sermons during those years

---

[4]See Steven D. Paulson, *Lutheran Theology* (London: T&T Clark, 2011), 13-26. One can begin to understand why Philipp Melanchthon began with the book of Romans when he started to construct the theological curriculum for the young ministers at Wittenberg. See David S. Dockery, "Theological Education: An Introduction," in *Theology, Church, and Ministry: A Handbook for Theological Education* (Nashville: B & H, 2017), 8-12; see also further comments on Romans 1:1-4 in Douglas J. Moo, *The Epistle to the Romans* (Grand Rapids: Eerdmans, 1996), 39-51.

included Romans (1515–1516); Hebrews (1517–1518); Luke (1521); 1 Peter, 2 Peter, and Jude (1522–1523); 1 Corinthians 7 (1523); Deuteronomy (1523–1525); minor prophets (1524–1526); Ecclesiastes (1526); John (1527); 1 Timothy and Titus (1527–1528); Isaiah (1528); Song of Songs (1530–1531); Galatians (1531); Psalms (1531–1545); 1 Corinthians 15 (1532); and Genesis (1535–1545).

In the early years of the sixteenth century, Luther initiated and fostered a hermeneutical revolution, what some have called a Copernican revolution in biblical interpretation that changed the course of history. The Protestant Reformation would have been impossible apart from this shift of emphasis in Luther's approach to the interpretation of both the Old Testament and the New.[5] In a very real sense, Luther was the father of Protestant biblical interpretation, and his influence has been incalculable.[6] Before turning our attention to Luther's approach to biblical interpretation, a brief look at Luther's understanding of the Bible and its authority will be in order.

LUTHER'S UNDERSTANDING OF BIBLICAL AUTHORITY

Luther adopted the commitments representative of Augustine as well as the late medieval church's understanding that the inspired Scriptures of the Old and New Testaments serve as the foundation of all belief and practice. Luther's teachers had taught the young monk that the inspired Scriptures were the authority on which his teaching was to be based. As Hermann Sasse has observed, "It has to be stated that he (Luther) took over the traditional doctrine of Scripture as having been given by

---

[5]See Gerald Bray, *Biblical Interpretation: Past and Present* (Downers Grove, IL: InterVarsity Press, 1996), 171-73; see also Kolb, *Martin Luther and the Enduring Word of God*, 75-131; R. F. Surburg, "The Presuppositions of the Historical-Grammatical Method as Employed by Historic Lutheranism," *The Springfielder* 38 (1975): 279; also, Oswald Bayer, "Martin Luther," in *The Reformation Theologians*, ed. Carter Lindberg (Oxford: Blackwell, 2002), 51-66; and Heiko A. Oberman, *Luther: Man Between God and the Devil* (New Haven, CT: Yale University Press, 1989), 151-74.

[6]A. Stevington Wood, "Luther as an Interpreter of Scripture," *Christianity Today* 3 (November 24, 1958), 7; see also David C. Steinmetz, *Luther in Context*, 2nd ed. (Grand Rapids: Baker Academic, 2002), 12-22.

inspiration of the Holy Spirit."[7] Luther never questioned this doctrine, nor did he try to create a different understanding of biblical inspiration and authority while he developed a new approach to interpretation. He had no hesitation in declaring the entirety of the Bible to be God's word. As Kenneth Hagen has noted, Luther was a medieval, Augustinian monk who inherited the tradition of Scripture as the *sacra pagina*.[8] Luther maintained this deep commitment throughout his life. Shortly before his death, Luther stated, "Thus, we attribute to the Holy Spirit all of Holy Scripture."[9]

It must be observed that Luther did not reject Christian tradition, the church fathers, nor the confessional statements from the important church councils of the fourth and fifth centuries. He did, however, contend that the authority of Scripture took priority over these matters; in fact, they were normed by Scripture (*norma normata*) so that Scripture was the norming norm (*norma normans*) rather than the other way around. Luther's words at the Diet of Worms in 1521 epitomize the Reformation's prioritizing of Scripture over church tradition in all matters, but especially in resolving theological disputes. These well-known words are worth repeating:

> Unless I am convinced by the testimony of the Scriptures or by clear reason, for I do not trust in the pope or councils alone, since it is well known that they have often erred and contradicted themselves, I am bound by the Scriptures I have quoted, and my conscience is captive to the Word of God. I cannot and will not retract anything, since it is neither safe nor right to go against conscience.[10]

---

[7]Hermann Sasse, "Luther and the Word of God," in *Accents in Luther's Theology: Essays in Commemoration of the 450th Anniversary of the Reformation*, ed. Heino O. Kadal (St. Louis: Concordia, 1967), 84.

[8]See Kenneth Hagen, "The History of Scripture in the Church," in *The Bible in the Churches: How Various Christians Interpret the Scriptures*," ed. Kenneth Hagen (Milwaukee: Marquette University Press, 1994), 1; Timothy George, *Theology of the Reformers* (Nashville: B & H, 2013), 79-86; and Mark D. Thompson, *A Sure Ground on Which to Stand: The Relation of Authority and Interpretive Method in Luther's Approach to Scripture* (Eugene, OR: Wipf & Stock, 2007), 47-53; and Hans J. Hillerbrand, ed., *The Reformation* (repr., Grand Rapids: Baker, 1978), 32-103.

[9]See *On the Last Words of David* (1543) in LW 15:275.

[10]LW 32:112; see Erik M. Heen, "Scripture," in *Dictionary of Luther and the Lutheran Tradition*, ed. Timothy J. Wengert (Grand Rapids: Baker, 2017), 673-76.

With this framework for understanding Luther's commitments to biblical inspiration and authority, we can now turn our attention to Luther's approach to biblical interpretation. The burning desire in the heart of Luther to get the Word of God into the hands of the people was so great that he not only translated the Bible into the language of the people but also provided guidelines concerning its interpretation.

Luther's Approach to Biblical Interpretation

Observations regarding the "early" Luther's approach to biblical interpretation cover many aspects of his developing approach to hermeneutics as it slowly distanced itself from the medieval practices. During these early years, Luther gradually moved away from the fourfold system of exegesis, known as the medieval Quadriga, which included the literal, allegorical (or mystical), tropological (or moral), and anagogical (or heavenly) senses of Scripture. This time period also saw Luther bring together an understanding of a literal approach to Scripture and his developing and distinctive christological interpretation of Scripture.[11]

The first priority for Luther, as we have seen, was built on a commitment to Scripture as the supreme and final authority for theology and life, for faith and practice, free from all ecclesiastical authority or interference. He recognized that the Christian tradition had gone seriously off course when it viewed the church as the way to Christ rather than Christ as the way to the one true church. Similarly, the Reformer asserted not only the supreme authority of God's Word but also its sufficiency and clarity. Realizing that diverse perspectives could be found among the church fathers on most doctrines, with the exception of those cardinal teachings affirmed by the first ecumenical councils, Luther emphasized the priority of the Scriptures in contrast to the writings of the patristic fathers.

While adopting the Augustinian and medieval consensus regarding biblical inspiration, Luther set aside the fourfold exegesis of the medieval

---

[11]See William M. Marsh, *Martin Luther on Reading the Bible as Christian Scripture: The Messiah in Luther's Biblical Hermeneutic and Theology* (Eugene, OR: Pickwick, 2017), 28-99.

period. He maintained that the historical/literal sense was essential for Christian faith and theology. Luther was likely more dependent on the thought of Erasmus on this point than some realize.[12] Luther differed from Erasmus, as Robert Kolb has noted, by emphasizing the clarity or perspicuity of the Bible's teaching, whereas Erasmus tended to note the obscurity, diversity, and complexity of Scripture.[13] Luther stressed the clarity of Scripture, but that was not intended to mean that the right interpretation came without hard work or struggle. He also observed that a proper rendering of the literal sense as the grammatical-historical sense does not necessitate a wooden literalistic understanding on the one hand, nor does it allow for an ahistorical spiritual sense on the other.[14]

As we will see, Luther advanced the approach of Erasmus, not only by focusing on the perspicuity of the text's message but also in his development regarding the referencing of all Scripture to Christ. Erasmus proposed a christological reading of the biblical text through the window of the teaching of Christ in the Gospels, whereas Luther placed the emphasis on the redeeming Christ of the epistles.[15] Luther can indeed be identified as the father of Protestant biblical interpretation, but it should also be remembered that Luther's way was paved by Erasmus.

In various places, Luther identified specific guidelines to help people read and understand the Holy Scripture in their vernacular tongue. In particular, he insisted on

1. the necessity of grammatical knowledge;

2. the importance of taking into consideration the times, circumstances, and conditions;

---

[12]See David S. Dockery, "The Foundation of Reformation Hermeneutics: A Fresh Look at Erasmus," in *Evangelical Hermeneutics*, ed. Michael Bauman and David Hall (Camp Hill, PA: Christian Publications, 1995), 53-75; J. W. Aldridge, *The Hermeneutics of Erasmus* (Richmond: John Knox, 1966); and Alister E. McGrath, *Reformation Thought: An Introduction* (Oxford: Blackwell, 1999), 50-63, 87-90.

[13]Kolb, *Martin Luther and the Enduring Word of God*, 35-97.

[14]See Marsh, *Martin Luther on Reading the Bible as Christian Scripture*, 4-10.

[15]See I. D. K. Siggins, *Martin Luther's Doctrine of Christ* (New Haven, CT: Yale University Press, 1970); and J. B. Payne, *Erasmus: His Theology of the Sacraments* (Richmond, VA: Bratcher, 1970), 54-70.

3. the importance of identifying the context;

4. the need of faith and spiritual illumination;

5. the importance of keeping what he called the "proportion of faith" for maintaining the clarity of Scripture, often called the analogy of faith principle, which at times he labeled the "body of doctrine" or the "rule of faith"; and

6. the necessity of referring all Scripture to Christ.[16]

Luther's commitment to the necessity of grammatical knowledge, the consideration of circumstances and conditions, the observance of the context, and the reference of all Scripture to Christ certainly echoes principles offered by Erasmus. The "body of doctrine," according to the Wittenberg theologian, provided a proper theological framework for interpreting the narrative construction of the Bible as a whole. Like others before him, Luther observed that some biblical books addressed the central message of faith more clearly than others. He regarded John's Gospel, 1 John, the letters of Paul (especially Romans, Galatians, and Ephesians), and 1 Peter as books that emphasize Christ and teach believers all that is necessary to know.[17] The last of these principles, the reference of all Scripture to Christ (often referred to as the "christological principle"), will be the focus of the remainder of this essay. We should not miss Luther's emphasis at this point. For him, the function of all good interpretation for both the Old Testament and the New pointed to Christ.

THE DEVELOPMENT OF LUTHER'S CHRISTOLOGICAL PRINCIPLE

Luther's interpretation of Scripture centered on the christological principle. For the Reformer, Christ stood at the heart of the Bible.[18] Even

---

[16]See Kolb, *Martin Luther and the Enduring Word of God*, 98-100.

[17]See Kolb, *Martin Luther and the Enduring Word of God*, 94-119; Christopher Ocker, *Biblical Poetics Before Humanism and Reformation* (Cambridge: Cambridge University Press, 2002), 21-22; and Steinmetz, *Luther in Context*, 126-41.

[18]See David S. Dockery, "Martin Luther's Christological Hermeneutics," *Grace Theological Journal* 4, no. 2 (1983): 189-203; and A. Skevington Wood, *The Principles of Biblical Interpretation as Enunciated by Irenaeus, Origen, Augustine, Luther, and Calvin* (Grand Rapids: Zondervan, 1967).

before the key events of October 31, 1517, while a professor at Wittenberg, Luther's interpretation began to move toward this principle. He came to believe that Christ must be understood as both the content and meaning of the Psalms.[19] This was more than a hermeneutical principle. As J. S. Preus has shown, the Reformer also believed it necessary to make personal and moral application of this christological reading of the text to one's life.[20] Though reminiscent of the moral sense of the Quadriga, Luther's hermeneutic increasingly adopted a more consistent christological interpretation.[21]

Luther insisted that the correct use of Scripture is at once the plain sense and the sense that expounds Christ, believing not that there were two senses of interpretation but only one. He thus connected the christological principle with the grammatical-historical principle. As I. D. K. Siggins has made clear, the christological principle for Luther was plainly stated by Scripture itself and was not an extrabiblical norm of interpretation.[22]

In principle, every portion of the Old Testament proclaimed Jesus Christ and anticipated its fulfillment in him. At the same time, everything in the New Testament was understood to look back to and shed light on the Old. Siggins comments, "The New Testament is not more than a revelation of the Old, while the Old Testament is a letter of Christ."[23] For Luther, the entirety of Scripture, if viewed properly, must lead to Christ, a principle developed from the teachings of Christ himself in the Gospel of John: "You search the Scriptures because you think that in them you have eternal life; and it is they that bear witness about me" (John 5:39).

William Marsh identified the maturing of Luther's approach by 1522, noting Luther's explication of the christological principle in the preface

---

[19]See R. F. Surburg, "The Significance of Luther's Hermeneutics for the Protestant Reformation," *Concordia Theological Monthly* 24 (1953): 241-61.

[20]J. S. Preus, "Luther on Christ and the Old Testament," *Concordia Theological Monthly* 43 (1972): 490.

[21]See Gerhard Ebeling, "The New Hermeneutics and the Early Luther," *Theology Today* 21 (1964): 34-46.

[22]See Siggins, *Martin Luther's Doctrine of Christ*, 17-18.

[23]Siggins, *Martin Luther's Doctrine of Christ*, 17-18.

for the New Testament in that year, pointing not only to John 5:39-46 but also to Genesis 3:15; Deuteronomy 18:15-18; 2 Samuel 7:12-14; Luke 24; Acts 17:11; Romans 1:1-4; and 1 Peter 1:10-12.[24] These are not only the most frequently cited passages but also the ones around which Luther shaped his hermeneutical approach. The primary text Luther offered in this regard was Romans 1:1-4, as noted at the beginning of this chapter. In Luther's "Preface to the New Testament" (1522) he contended, "God has promised this gospel and testament in many ways, by the prophets in the Old Testament, as St. Paul says in Romans 1, 'I am set apart to preach the gospel of God which he promised beforehand through his prophets in the holy scriptures, concerning his Son who was descended from David.'"[25] Once again, Marsh's insights are helpful:

> Between *A Treatise on the New Testament* (1521) and the *Preface to the New Testament* (1522), Luther's portrayal of "how all Scripture tends toward him [Christ]" comes in the form of a "gospel" declaration that incorporates essential characteristics that God has long-promised through the prophets in the OT Scriptures about the coming person and work of the Messiah. Because Luther is a theologian of the whole Christian Bible, he trusts the apostolic testimony of passages such as Romans 1:1-4, Luke 24, John 5:39-46 (Christ's own instruction), and 1 Peter 1:10-12 as authoritative pronouncements about the literal sense of the OT's textual referentiality.[26]

These observations lead us to the second way of stating this principle, which is theological rather than exegetical. For Luther, the great weakness of allegorical exegesis was that it imposed an interpretive approach that tended to discount or ignore the importance of the historical setting of the text. Luther recognized that at times the christological principle could lead him into the same hermeneutical difficulties. Aware of this potential danger, Luther devoted himself to painstaking exegesis, though he always thought of himself as one who had never arrived as an

---

[24]Marsh, *Martin Luther on Reading the Bible as Christian Scripture*, 102-10.
[25]LW 35:358.
[26]Marsh, *Martin Luther on Reading the Bible as Christian Scripture*, 109-10.

interpreter of Scripture.[27] The ways in which he related the literal sense to Christ were, however, quite flexible.[28] Luther could exercise great freedom and adaptability in his interpretation since for him the tension was primarily between law and gospel and not between letter and spirit.[29] Sometimes Luther's hermeneutical principles were better than the outworking of them, something true for most biblical scholars throughout the history of biblical interpretation.[30]

When Luther discerned reflections of the Holy Trinity and the work of Christ in Old Testament texts, he ran the risk of adopting an approach rejected in the fourth and fifth centuries by the Antioch School of interpretation.[31] Luther criticized the Antioch School for its rigid stance just as he criticized the allegorists for their opposite position. While Luther appreciated typology, he did not distinguish typology from the literal sense in the manner that the Antiochenes did.[32] In their treatment of Old Testament texts, the Antiochenes saw the shadows of Christ, an adumbration of what was to come. For Luther, however, the Old Testament was not a figure or shadow of what would be but a testimony of God's special and unchanging relationship with humankind.[33]

---

[27]See Kenneth Hagen, *Luther's Approach to Scripture as Seen in His "Commentaries" on Galatians, 1519–1538* (Tübingen: Mohr Siebeck, 1993). See also the chapter by Scott Manetsch in this volume.

[28]Siggins, *Martin Luther's Doctrine of Christ*, 18; see also Kolb, *Martin Luther and the Enduring Word of God*, 24-26, 90-93, 158-61.

[29]See Marvin Anderson, "Reformation Interpretation," in *Hermeneutics*, ed. Bernard Ramm (Grand Rapids: Baker, 1971), 81-93.

[30]See L. Berkhof, *Principles of Biblical Interpretation* (Grand Rapids: Baker, 1950), 26; Bray, *Biblical Interpretation: Past and Present*, 165-220; David S. Dockery, "New Testament Interpretation: A Historical Survey," in *New Testament Criticism and Interpretation*, ed. David Alan Black and David S. Dockery (Grand Rapids: Zondervan, 1991), 41-69; and Kevin J. Vanhoozer, ed., *Dictionary for Theological Interpretation of the Bible* (Grand Rapids: Baker, 2005).

[31]See David S. Dockery, *Biblical Interpretation Then and Now* (Grand Rapids: Baker, 1992), 103-78; Rowan A. Greer, *Theodore of Mopsuestia: Exegete and Theologian* (London: Faith, 1961); Maurice F. Wiles, *The Divine Apostle: The Interpretation of St. Paul's Epistles in the Early Church* (Cambridge: Cambridge University Press, 1967).

[32]See David S. Dockery, "The Value of Typological Exegesis," in *Restoring the Prophetic Mantle: Preaching the Old Testament*, ed. G. Klein (Nashville: Broadman, 1992), 161-78.

[33]See B. Moeller, "Scripture, Tradition and Sacrament in the Middle Ages and in Luther," in *Holy Book and Holy Tradition*, ed. F. F. Bruce and E. G. Rupp (Manchester, England: Manchester University Press, 1968), 120-22; Jaroslav Pelikan, *Luther the Expositor* (St. Louis: Concordia,

Luther maintained that the Old Testament is Christian Scripture and the New Testament is proclamation because what the former promised is now heralded by the apostles as realized. The Old Testament served as the ground of the New Testament's proclamation of Jesus Christ, while the New Testament enables the interpreters to see how the Old Testament witnessed to Christ as the Messiah in the literal sense.[34]

For the Wittenberg Reformer, allegory eradicated the historicity of the Old Testament, while typology too often disregarded Christ's presence in the Old Testament. The weakness of Luther's christological interpretation, however, was that it could easily diminish the historicity of the Old Testament.[35] Because Luther looked for Christ everywhere in the Scripture, he opened the door to the possibility of a forced interpretation—though it is important to note that Luther worked hard to avoid distorting the biblical text.

As Siggins has noted, Luther allowed for two kinds of historical applications. The first of these pertained to texts that Luther often quoted when preaching. In these the Reformer confidently applied the christological principle where the details of the grammar or subject matter could refer to Christ. The second kind of historical application pertained to those texts whose message was general enough to permit a valid application in various contexts.[36] While these concerns must not be overlooked, we must, on the other hand, not fail to see the many strengths of the christological principle.

Luther's christological interpretation helped to provide the framework for him to become one of the most influential leaders of the

---

1959); and Raymond Barry Shelton, "Martin Luther's Concept of Biblical Interpretation in Historical Perspective" (PhD diss., Fuller Theological Seminary, 1974).

[34]See David W. Lotz, "Sola Scriptura: Luther on Biblical Authority," *Interpretation* 35 (1981): 258-73. As Marsh notes, Lotz provides a perspective that grounds Luther's "christocentric" view of Scripture in the Reformer's christological understanding of the doctrine of the Word of God. See Marsh, *Martin Luther on Reading the Bible as Christian Scripture*, 194-95.

[35]See Heinrich Bornkamm, *Luther and the Old Testament*, ed. V. I. Gruhn (Philadelphia: Fortress, 1966), 250.

[36]Siggins, *Martin Luther's Doctrine of Christ*, 20-21.

Reformation.[37] From a historical vantage point, we see that the gospel of salvation in Jesus Christ was illuminated and advanced through this principle. Luther underscored in his biblical interpretation, his theology, and his preaching that it was Christ and his words which brought life for sinful men and women, the message that became the backbone of the Reformation.

The christological interpretation as articulated by Luther became the breakthrough for many to read Scripture afresh during the time of the Reformation. Luther's approach pointed to precedents in the apostolic tradition and practices found among many of the church fathers.[38] More importantly, Luther's hermeneutical approach challenged the fourfold sense of medieval exegesis. In its place appeared the centrality of Christ and the proclamation of faith in him for eternal life.[39]

Although the results do not necessarily justify the means, it was chiefly the christological principle that set Luther apart from medieval exegetes.[40] Moreover, Luther's christological hermeneutic has profoundly shaped the subsequent history of biblical interpretation in the West, from the sixteenth century to the present day. Luther's most enduring achievement in the field of biblical interpretation was his distrust of and direct assault on allegorical interpretation and the fourfold method of exegesis popular in the medieval period—and this accomplishment was possible in large part as he worked out his christological interpretive principle. Thus, it is important to recognize that Luther's christological approach was determinative for his whole hermeneutical program.

---

[37]Bornkamm, *Luther and the Old Testament*, 249.

[38]See Dockery, *Biblical Interpretation Then and Now*, 158-60; and Timothy George, *Reading Scripture with the Reformers* (Downers Grove, IL: IVP Academic, 2011).

[39]See Anderson, "Reformation Interpretation," 85.

[40]See Gerhard Müller, "Luther's Transformation of Medieval Thought: Discontinuity and Continuity," in *The Oxford Handbook of Martin Luther's Theology*, ed. Robert Kolb, Irene Dengel, and L'Ubomir Batka (Oxford: Oxford University Press, 2014), 105-14.

THE CHRISTOLOGICAL PRINCIPLE BRIEFLY
ILLUSTRATED: PSALM 117

At this point, we want to take a brief look at how Luther applied the christological principle in his reading of the Old Testament's hymnbook. Psalm 117 is a short and simple psalm, which reads:

> Praise the LORD, all nations!
>> Extol him, all peoples!
> For great is his steadfast love toward us,
>> and the faithfulness of the LORD endures forever.
> Praise the LORD!

Luther broke this psalm into four parts: a prophecy, a revelation, a doctrine, and an admonition. The *prophecy* is the promise of the gospel and the kingdom of Christ, for if the nations are called to offer praise to God, he must initially have become their God. In the first place, he must be proclaimed to them, and all idolatry must be overcome by the power of the Word of God for them to place their trust in him.[41] The *revelation* points to the kingdom of Christ. It will be a spiritual and heavenly kingdom—not a temporal and earthly kingdom—for the psalmist permits the unbelievers from the nations to remain in their respective countries and does not call them to gather together in Jerusalem. The command is to praise God in all the nations. For this to happen, God's message of salvation must have been proclaimed throughout the world "as the gospel of Christ."[42] The *doctrine* that Luther identifies in this psalm is the doctrine of justification by faith, that people can stand before a holy and righteous God by faith alone (*sola fide*), for with his free grace God reigns over his people, thereby nullifying all human righteousness sought in the Jewish law, the Catholic Mass, monasticism, or any other good work. Finally, the *admonition* provides instruction concerning service to the Lord, stimulating praise and thanksgiving. Only those things based

---

[41]See Bornkamm, *Luther and the Old Testament,* 99.
[42]LW 14:10-18.

exclusively on Christ, the font and cornerstone of all righteousness, will endure.[43]

Luther has taken this brief psalm and brought out of it the brilliance of the gospel. He offered additional comments on this psalm that included attacks on the papacy, the monastic system, and various practices related to the cult of the saints. Even though the interpretation may encourage one toward Christ, it must be maintained that this interpretation extends beyond the literal, grammatical-historical sense of the biblical text. Luther's flexibility led him beyond the historical interpretation to find Christ and the gospel in the passage.

According to Luther, all the promises of the Old Testament look toward Jesus Christ for their ultimate fulfillment. For Luther, the christological principle took precedence and priority; everything pointed to Christ.[44] Luther's interpretations often called for a direct response to the Old Testament world, providing valuable examples for his exhortations and admonitions. Now, we will turn our thoughts in a different direction. Building on the insights from how Luther applied his principles of biblical interpretation, we will attempt to understand how succeeding generations applied, adopted, and adapted Luther's approach.

THE CHRISTOLOGICAL PRINCIPLE AS ADAPTED BY SUCCEEDING GENERATIONS

Steven Paulson's careful look at the developments in Lutheran thought over the past five hundred years indicates that succeeding generations who claimed to follow Luther often chose the practical over the theoretical and the spirit over the letter, emphasizing the experiential aspects of Luther's interpretations, including the freedom and flexibility with which he applied his own principles. Beginning with the Pietists in the seventeenth century (e.g., Jakob Spener's *Pia Desideria* [1675]) and

---

[43]LW 14:22-37.
[44]See E. F. Klug, *From Luther to Chemnitz* (Grand Rapids: Eerdmans, 1971), 49.

continuing with nineteenth-century liberals such as Albrecht Ritschl
(1822–1889) and Ernst Troeltsch (1865–1923), such freedom and flexibility extended into the twentieth century with existentialist theologians
like Rudolf Bultmann (1884–1976), Gerhard Ebeling (1912–2001), and
Ernst Fuchs (1903–1983).[45] Though the influences of liberalism and existentialism no longer have the same widespread presence they once enjoyed, these movements, nevertheless, continue to influence biblical
interpretation and the shape of theology in the twenty-first century.[46]
Because of this ongoing influence and because followers of these influential nineteenth- and twentieth-century thinkers continue to point to
Luther as a forerunner of their proposals, it is important for us briefly to
take note of both comparisons and contrasts with Luther.

Representatives of these various movements have pointed to Luther
as their spiritual father. The basis for the claim that Luther is the father
or forerunner of their efforts has come from Luther's statement, "The
Word of God, experienced in the heart, is the foundation of the doctrine
of biblical inspiration."[47] It may be granted that Luther's focus and interest regarding certain passages of Holy Scripture seemingly created a
"canon within the canon," and this, combined with his own experiential-
ist approach, influenced his interpretive practices. The question, however, is did his experience stand over his view of Scripture, which then
became God's Word through his own experience, or did he believe that
Scripture stood over his experience as revelation proclaiming the truth
of God?[48]

---

[45]See Paulson, *Lutheran Theology*, 6-12.

[46]See Gregory Walter, "Existentialism," in Wengert, *Dictionary of Luther and the Lutheran Traditions*, 240-43; and Walter "Liberalism," in Wengert, *Dictionary of Luther and the Lutheran Traditions*, 421-23.

[47]J. T. Mueller, "Luther and the Bible," in *Inspiration and Interpretation*, ed. John F. Walvoord (Grand Rapids: Eerdmans, 1957), 94; see also Anthony Thiselton, "The New Hermeneutic," in *New Testament Interpretation: Essays on Principles and Methods*, ed. I. Howard Marshall (Grand Rapids: Eerdmans, 1977), 308-33.

[48]See the discussion in John Warwick Montgomery, *In Defense of Luther* (Milwaukee: Northwestern, 1970), 63-64; and W. J. Kooiman, *Luther and the Bible* (Philadelphia: Muhlenberg, 1961).

The twentieth-century existentialists claimed that medieval exegesis is to Luther's exegesis as the grammatical-historical principle of evangelical hermeneutics is to an existential hermeneutic. Thomas Parker confirmed this assessment:

> In contrast to Calvin, Luther's interpretations tend to be subjective, directed toward the individual believer; accordingly Luther's hermeneutical principles can lead to an extreme—to a subjectivism which stresses the religious feeling or the existential dimensions of subjective faith over against the object of faith, thus losing realism.[49]

Luther's well-known statement at the Diet of Worms, along with his thoughts and writings when he faced opposition, however, point us back to the primacy of Scripture.[50] This statement has been heard so often that its significance is often overlooked. Luther more than once affirmed that his conscience or existential life was taken captive by the Word. Not only at the Diet of Worms, but at all critical times in his career, his experience was placed in subjection to the Scriptures, which can be seen in Luther's debates with Erasmus, Zwingli, and others. In these situations, time after time, Luther appealed to the authority of the Scripture.

Rather than the claim of the existentialists, which we noted earlier, the reality is that medieval exegesis is to existential hermeneutics what Luther's approach has been to evangelical or orthodox hermeneutics.[51] The existential hermeneutic is a restoration of the very approach to the Bible that Luther opposed, for Luther's primary concern as a biblical interpreter was to overthrow the dominant fourfold method of exegesis that was dominant in the medieval West.

It must be remembered that Luther thought of his role first and foremost as a preacher. This practical orientation had a large influence on his interpretation of Scripture in which he primarily saw Christ, whom he

---

[49]T. D. Parker, "The Interpretation of Scripture: A Comparison of Calvin and Luther on Galatians," *Interpretation* 17 (1963): 68.

[50]See G. Rupp, *Luther's Progress to the Diet of Worms* (New York: Harper, 1964), 96.

[51]See Montgomery, *In Defense of Martin Luther*, 67; and Mueller, "Luther and the Bible," 89.

adored, as the Savior of the world.[52] In addition to the assertion that Luther's christological principle led to an unbalanced existentialist hermeneutic, some have argued that his christological approach to the Bible liberated him from a traditional, orthodox view of biblical inspiration. The Existentialist School has often appealed to Luther's christological principle to support their claim that the Bible only *bears witness* to Christ.

Luther, however, recognized both the divine and human aspects of Holy Scripture.[53] He insisted that just as the accepted doctrine of Christ's person requires us to believe in the two natures of our Lord without confusion, without mutation, without division, and without separation, so the twofold nature regarding the concursive inspiration of Scripture should be recognized in both its full humanity and its divinity.[54] While advocates of an existential hermeneutic might agree that the Bible shares in the glory of Christ and the lowliness of his humanity, it is here that the comparison ends.

Other scholars have claimed that modern existential and liberal interpreters of Scripture follow and fulfill the trajectory initiated by Luther. For just as Luther saw the complete inadequacy of humanity's moral efforts toward salvation, so the liberals and existentialists recognize the inadequacy of humanity's intellectual efforts to justify itself by way of a verbally inspired Scripture. Thus, they posit that since the Scripture is a historical document written by humans, the Bible, then, also participates in the frailty of all that is human. Therefore, it has been suggested that the pages of Scripture contain the relativity of all that is historical.

Although Luther and the Existentialist School start at similar places, their conclusions are quite different. Luther, by contrast, pressed the analogy between the incarnation and the nature of Scripture, stressing

---

[52]See Kolb, *Martin Luther and the Enduring Word of God*, 125-28, 174-208; Mueller, "Luther and the Bible," 88-90.

[53]See Wood, "Luther as Interpreter of Scripture," 8-9.

[54]See David S. Dockery, *Christian Scripture: An Evangelical Perspective on Inspiration, Authority, and Interpretation* (Nashville: B & H, 1995), 44-56, 129-33.

that the human element of Scripture is no more impervious to error than was the human nature of Christ.[55] The christological principle, rather than leading Luther to a view advocating the fallibility of Scripture, was actually shaped by and grounded on his commitment to a verbally inspired Bible.[56]

It was Luther's conviction that wherever Scripture speaks, it speaks with absolute authority and clarity.[57] While understanding that Luther's christological principle cracked the door for some to challenge his orthodox view of biblical inspiration, it cannot be concluded that Luther's hermeneutic led him to a limited view of inspiration.[58] Scripture was Luther's primary authority. His christological principle is best understood as a hermeneutical guide that reinforced and exemplified his orthodox view of the Bible's inspiration and authority.

IMPLICATIONS FOR CONTEMPORARY INTERPRETERS

As we move toward the conclusion of this chapter, we must briefly explore the implications of Luther's approach for contemporary interpreters and pastoral ministry. Luther maintained that the correct interpretation of Holy Scripture begins with the literal, historical-grammatical sense, contending that a text of Scripture has to be taken as it stands unless there are compelling reasons for doing otherwise.[59] He saw no inconsistency between the *sensus literalis* and the christological principle. The grammatical-historical principle has traditionally attempted to take Scripture at its plain sense, understood in its primary, ordinary, literal meaning within the

---

[55]See John D. Woodbridge, *Biblical Authority: Infallibility and Inerrancy in the Christian Tradition* (Grand Rapids: Zondervan, 2015), 49-68; also Bray, *Biblical Interpretation: Past and Present*, 191-200.

[56]See Kolb, *Martin Luther and the Enduring Word of God*, 35-173.

[57]See Robert Kolb, "The Bible in the Reformation and Protestant Orthodoxy," in *The Enduring Authority of the Christian Scriptures*, ed., D. A. Carson (Grand Rapids: Eerdmans, 2016), 89-114.

[58]L. W. Spitz Sr., "Luther's Sola Scriptura," *Concordia Theological Monthly* 31 (1960): 740-45.

[59]See Marsh, *Martin Luther on Reading the Bible as Christian Scripture*, 8; Katherine E. Green-McCreight, "Literal Sense," in Vanhoozer, *Dictionary for Theological Interpretation of the Bible*, 455-56; and Kevin J. Vanhoozer, *Is There Meaning in This Text? The Bible, the Reader, and the Morality of Literary Knowledge* (Grand Rapids: Zondervan, 1998), 303.

immediate context.[60] The question for contemporary biblical interpreters is whether the *sensus literalis* and the christological principle can be tied together as closely as Luther connected them in the sixteenth century.

With little or no disagreement, it is generally affirmed that Luther's overall approach is consistent with his preaching and his Reformation teachings. It remains difficult, however, to see how his interpretations, at least at times, could be derived from and be consistent with the plain sense of Scripture, with a primary, literal, grammatical interpretation of the historical and literary context. The premier Lutheran scholar Robert Kolb, however, cautions us at this point, saying, "By no means did Luther see Christ in every passage."[61] Still, Luther's chief concern in the interpretation, teaching, and preaching of Holy Scripture was to convey the message of salvation and to cultivate faith in Jesus Christ as Lord and Savior.[62]

Although it may be difficult to fault Luther, he was guilty at times of weighting the biblical text's meaning and significance toward his own context in such a way as to obscure the historical reality underlying the text. Other interpreters, by contrast, have so focused on the historical meaning of the text that they have ignored the christological meaning or contemporary significance of Scripture. It is important to observe that Luther did in fact recognize "the two horizons of Scripture."[63] Interpreters in our day must go to the historical context and back again without

---

[60]See David S. Dockery, "The Study and Interpretation of the Bible," in *Foundations for Biblical Interpretation* (Nashville: B & H, 1994), 36-54; David S. Dockery and George H. Guthrie, *The Holman Guide to Interpreting the Bible* (Nashville: B & H, 2004), 25-70; and David S. Dockery, "A Historical Model," in *Hermeneutics for Preaching: Approaches to Contemporary Interpretations of Scripture*, ed., Raymond Bailey (Nashville: Broadman, 1992), 27-52.

[61]Kolb, *Martin Luther and the Enduring Word of God,* 127.

[62]Kolb, *Martin Luther and the Enduring Word of God,* 128; see also Scott H. Hendrix, "Luther Against the Background of the History of Biblical Interpretation," *Interpretation* 37 (1983): 229-39; and Scott H. Hendrix, "The Authority of Scripture at Work: Luther's Exegesis of the Psalms," in *Encounters with Luther*, ed., Eric W. Gritsch (Gettysburg, PA: Institute for Luther Studies, 1982), 144-59.

[63]See Anthony Thiselton, *Two Horizons* (Grand Rapids: Eerdmans, 1980); also, Rhyne R. Putnam, *In Defense of Doctrine: Evangelicalism, Theology, and Scripture* (Minneapolis: Fortress, 2015), 123-72.

de-emphasizing either the historical context or the text's present-day significance.[64] Luther's goal in the interpretation of God's Word was built around his understanding of the christological principle whereby everything must serve the central truth of God's gospel witnessed in the atoning work of Jesus Christ.[65] Such a goal is worthy of imitation.

In response to the objection that Luther's christological interpretation imported into the biblical text something not originally intended by the author, Luther would likely reply that the New Testament's fulfillment of the Old Testament promise should be understood as part of the larger historical and literary context of Old Testament passages. God, the author of the whole of Scripture, Luther would contend, is able to set forth the true, intended meaning of the Old Testament passage through and by means of the New.[66] I would propose that Luther's approach points us not in the direction of the Existentialist School of theology but toward a canonical and theological approach to hermeneutics.[67]

The basis for this response comes from Christ's own words on the way to Emmaus after his resurrection:

> "How foolish you are, and how slow to believe all that the prophets have spoken! Did not the Messiah have to suffer these things and then enter his glory?" And beginning with Moses and all the Prophets, he explained to them what was said in all the Scriptures concerning himself. (Luke 24:25-27 NIV).

Surburg offers these thoughts: "When Luther finds Christ in the Old Testament he is not allegorizing as some might contend, but merely

---

[64]See C. H. Dodd, *There and Back Again* (London: Hodder, 1932).

[65]See Klug, *From Luther to Chemitz*, 49; and Surburg, "Presuppositions of the Historical-Grammatical Method," 285.

[66]See Bornkamm, *Luther and the Old Testament*, 11-45; and Marsh, *Martin Luther on Reading the Bible as Christian Scripture*, 193-99.

[67]See important discussions of canonical and theological interpretation in Robert B. Sloan, "Canonical Theology of the New Testament," in *Foundations for Biblical Interpretation*, 565-94; Daniel J. Treier, "Contemporary Theological Hermeneutics," in Vanhoozer, *Dictionary for Theological Interpretation of the Bible*, 787-93; Kevin J. Vanhoozer, *First Theology: God, Scripture, Hermeneutics* (Downers Grove, IL: InterVarsity Press, 2002); Kevin J. Vanhoozer, "What Is Theological Interpretation of the Bible?," in Vanhoozer, *Dictionary for Theological Interpretation of the Bible*, 19-25; Charles Wood, *The Formation of Christian Understanding* (Philadelphia: Westminster, 1982); and Putnam, *In Defense of Doctrine*, 173-208, 375-400.

reading the Old Testament in the light of the New. In doing this he finds a deeper meaning than an exegete who ignores the New Testament."[68]

Even though Luther's practice was not always consistent with his hermeneutical principles, his goals were admirable. In Luther's interpretation (as in other areas of life), he consistently sought to magnify the Lord Jesus Christ. It must be concluded, however, that the christological principle should best be understood and implemented today as a theological principle that accompanies the *sensus literalis.* Therefore, the two are complementary and not inconsistent.

The christological principle is valid for twenty-first-century interpreters as a canonical/theological principle, a second step beyond the grammatical-historical method. Christological interpretations, when consistent with the literary and historical context as well as with the teaching of the New Testament, should be encouraged regarding the experiences, promises, and prophecies of the Old Testament, pointing us to the gospel promised beforehand through the prophets in the Holy Scriptures (see Rom 1:1-4).

There is great insight and spiritual wisdom to be gained from this approach to theological interpretation and application. In doing so, one must remember not to divorce a passage from its historical background. A canonical/theological interpretation will not stop at the grammatical-historical level but will seek the canonical and christological sense of the passage for the enrichment of the teaching and preaching of Holy Scripture and for the building up and strengthening of the church.

CONCLUDING THOUGHTS

In conclusion, with Luther, we confess that the Bible is the ultimate standard of authority for God's people. We further believe the Bible is our only and all-sufficient rule of faith and practice. We trust the Spirit's work

---

[68]Surburg, "Presuppositions of the Historical-Grammatical Method," 285; see also Daniel I. Block, "Old Testament Theology," in *Theology, Church, and Ministry,* 192-216, who proposes that we should think of Christ as the goal of Old Testament study rather than thinking of Christ as the center of Old Testament interpretation and theology.

of illumination that enables believers to interpret the biblical text in its original context in such a way as to understand both the *sensus literalis* as well as its canonical/theological significance for our contemporary world.

Ultimately, the Bible is to be interpreted in light of the centrality of Jesus Christ, who himself affirmed the complete veracity of the Bible and lived his life in fulfillment of Holy Scripture. The message of the Bible for our day, as in the sixteenth century with Martin Luther, remains the foundation on which the people of God can work together in the proclamation of the gospel while moving forward in faithful witness, ministry, and mission to a watching, hurting, and fallen world.[69]

Following Luther, it is now our privilege to tell people that what unites us with God is faith, not faith in faith but in the crucified, resurrected, and exalted Christ, the content and substance of the christological principle that not only helped to bring about a major hermeneutical development but provided a foundation for the sixteenth-century Reformation that has continued to shape the church and influence the world for the past five hundred years.[70] For the best aspects of Luther's legacy, we join together to say, "Thanks be to God."

---

[69]See Henry Allen, "The Historical Legacy of Luther," in *Reformation 500: How the Greatest Revival Since Pentecost Continues to Shape the World Today*, ed. Ray Van Neste and J. Michael Garrett (Nashville: B & H, 2016), 173-87.

[70]See Robert W. Jenson, *A Theology in Outline* (Oxford: Oxford University Press, 2016), 85-87.

PART TWO

Preaching *and* Pastoral Care *in the* Reformation

Chapter Three

"MEAT, NOT STRAWBERRIES"

HUGH LATIMER *and* BIBLICAL PREACHING
in the ENGLISH REFORMATION

MICHAEL A. G. HAYKIN

MODERN HISTORIES OF THE REFORMATION RIGHTLY cite a number of different factors—political, religious, economic, technological, and psychological—for the advent of the Reformation. To the Reformers themselves, though, one factor above all needed to be stressed. As Martin Luther (1483–1546) once put it in his inimitable style:

> I simply taught, preached, and wrote God's Word; otherwise I did nothing. And while I slept or drank Wittenberg beer with my friends Philipp [Melanchthon] and [Nikolaus] Amsdorf the Word so greatly weakened the papacy that no prince or emperor ever inflicted such losses upon it. I did nothing; the Word did everything.[1]

This biblicist assertion that the "Word did everything" actually makes plain a theme that recurs again and again in the history of the Christian faith. Whenever and wherever the church has flourished, the preaching and teaching of the Bible has been central, that Word which lays bare the secrets of human hearts and brings men and women to repentance and

---

[1]Martin Luther, *The Second Invocavit Sermon* in *Karlstadt's Battle with Luther: Documents in a Liberal-Radical Debate*, ed. Ronald J. Sider (Philadelphia: Fortress, 1978), 24. Philipp Melanchthon (1497–1560) and Nikolaus von Amsdorf (1483–1565) were important colleagues of Luther at this time.

conversion.[2] Speaking of this pattern in the history of the church, Iain Murray once put it this way: "The advance of the church is ever preceded by a recovery of preaching [the Word]."[3] The Reformation, a time of great spiritual advance, was no exception.

Further evidence of the centrality of preaching during the Reformation can be culled from the fact that the leading term used by the Reformers to describe leadership in the local church was not the word *priest*, which had been the case in medieval Christendom, nor *pastor*, which only came into regular employ in the eighteenth century, but *preacher*.[4] The main reason for this was the conviction held by all the Reformers that utterly central to ecclesial leadership was the preaching of the Word of God. When Luther singled out the main problem with the medieval church, for instance, he cited the fact that God's Word is not proclaimed; "there is only reading and singing in the churches" and "because God's Word has been suppressed, many unchristian inventions and lies have sneaked into the service of reading, singing, and preaching, and they are horrible to see."[5]

In this analysis, the ultimate failure of the medieval church lay in its refusal to preach the Word of God. And this entailed nothing less than profound religious error and the loss of the gospel. The English Reformer Hugh Latimer (ca. 1490–1555) had a similar critique:

> Preaching is necessary; for take away preaching, and take away salvation. I told you of *Scala coeli* [the ladder of heaven], and I made it a preaching matter, not a massing matter. Christ is the preacher of all preachers, the pattern and the exemplar that all preachers ought to follow. For it was he by whom the Father of heaven said, *Hic est Filius meus dilectus, ipsum audite*, "This is my well-beloved Son, hear him."[6]

---

[2]See Hebrews 4:12-13; James 1:18.

[3]Iain Murray, "Lloyd-Jones: Messenger of Grace," *Banner of Truth* 536 (2008): 32.

[4]Wilhelm Pauck, "The Ministry in the Time of the Continental Reformation," in *The Ministry in Historical Perspectives*, ed. H. Richard Niebuhr and Daniel D. Williams (New York: Harper & Brothers, 1956), 116.

[5]Cited in Pauck, "Ministry in the Time of the Continental Reformation," 111.

[6]Hugh Latimer, "The Fourth Sermon Preached Before King Edward, March 29, 1549," in *The Works of Hugh Latimer*, ed. George Elwes Corrie (Cambridge: Cambridge University Press, 1844), 1:155.

As this English preacher reiterated a week or so after the above statement: "*Scala coeli* is a preaching matter, I tell you, and not a massing matter. God's instrument of salvation is preaching."[7]

For Reformers like Luther and Latimer, there is little doubt that preaching was the central means of grace in ecclesial renewal and revival. For these and other Reformers, hearing was *the* key sense of the Christian man and woman. As the French Reformer John Calvin (1509–1564) stressed, genuine "faith cannot flow from a naked experience of things, but must have its origin in the Word of God."[8] Medieval Roman Catholicism had majored on visual symbols and images as the central means of teaching. The Reformation, coming as it did hard on the heels of the invention of the printing press in the fifteenth century, turned back to the biblical emphasis on words, both spoken and written, as the primary vehicle for cultivating faith and spirituality. As Calvin aptly put it, "the Word is the instrument by which the Lord dispenses the illumination of his Spirit to believers."[9] In the minds of the Reformers, there could be neither true Reformation nor genuine spirituality apart from the Scriptures.[10]

Moreover, for the Reformers, the preaching of the Scriptures was a key mark of a true church. Luther put it thus in 1523: "The certain mark of the Christian congregation is the preaching of the gospel in its purity."[11] Sixteen years later he made the same point when he maintained, "Whenever you hear or see this Word preached, believed, confessed, and acted on, there do not doubt that there must be a true holy catholic church, a

---

[7]Hugh Latimer, "The Fifth Sermon Preached Before King Edward, April 5, [1549]," in *Works of Hugh Latimer*, 1:178.

[8]Cited in Nigel Westhead, "Calvin and Experimental Knowledge of God," in *Adorning the Doctrine: Papers Read at the 1995 Westminster Conference* (London: The Westminster Conference, 1995), 18.

[9]John Calvin, *Institutes of the Christian Religion* 1.9.3, ed. John T. McNeill, trans. Ford Lewis Battles (Philadelphia: Westminster, 1960), LCC 20:96.

[10]Otto Grundler, "John Calvin: Ingrafting in Christ," in *The Spirituality of Western Christendom*, ed. E. Rozanne Elder (Kalamazoo, MI: Cistercian, 1976), 175.

[11]Cited in Sam Chan, *Preaching as the Word of God: Answering an Old Question with Speech-Act Theory* (Eugene, OR: Pickwick, 2016), 62. I am indebted to Dr. Chan for drawing my attention to his work and making it available to me.

Christian, holy people."[12] Similarly, Calvin stated, "Whenever we see the Word of God purely preached and heard, and the sacraments administered according to Christ's institution, it is not to be doubted, a church of God exists."[13]

In what follows, the spotlight is placed on one of the remarkable cadre of preachers raised up during the Reformation, the English preacher Hugh Latimer, whom the Reformation scholar Susan Wabuda has described as the greatest English-speaking preacher of the sixteenth century.[14] J. C. Ryle once provided the following reasons for Latimer's renown: "If a combination of sound Gospel doctrine, plain Saxon language, boldness, liveliness, directness, and simplicity, can make a preacher, few . . . have ever equalled . . . Latimer."[15] Even in the 1560s, it was apparently a common saying in the university town of Cambridge that when "Master [Hugh] Latimer preached, then was Cambridge blessed."[16] And according to Augustine Bernher (fl.1550s–1570s), a Francophone pastor who was mentored by Latimer and later pastored during the reign of Elizabeth I (1533–1603), "If England ever had a prophet, he was one."[17]

---

[12]Cited in Chan, *Preaching as the Word of God*, 63.

[13]Cited in Chan, *Preaching as the Word of God*, 71.

[14]Susan Wabuda, "'Fruitful Preaching' in the Diocese of Worcester: Bishop Hugh Latimer and His Influence, 1535–1539," in *Religion and the English People, 1500–1640: New Voices, New Perspectives*, Sixteenth Century Essays & Studies 45, ed. Eric Josef Carlson (Kirksville, MO: Thomas Jefferson University Press, 1998), 50. See similar descriptions of Latimer as a preacher in *Clare College, 1326–1926* (Cambridge: Cambridge University Press, 1928), 1:135; and Patrick Collinson, *Archbishop Grindal, 1519–1583: The Struggle for a Reformed Church* (London: Jonathan Cape, 1979), 48. According to Michael Pasquarello III, Latimer "was arguably the most popular and persuasive preacher in the realm" of England during this era. See Michael Pasquarello III, *Sacred Rhetoric: Preaching as Theological and Pastoral Practice of the Church* (Grand Rapids: Eerdmans, 2005), 9.

[15]J. C. Ryle, *Five English Reformers* (1890, repr., London: Banner of Truth, 1960), 110.

[16]From Thomas Becon, cited in Marcus L. Loane, *Masters of the English Reformation* (London: Church Book Room Press, 1954), 97.

[17]Cited in John T. McNeill, review of *Hugh Latimer, Apostle to the English*, by Allan G. Chester, *Church History* 24 (1955): 78. The statement is taken from Augustine Bernher, "To the Right Honourable, the Lady Katherine the Duchess of Suffolk" in *The Works of Hugh Latimer*, 1:320-321.

"The Child of Everlasting Joy"[18]

Hugh Latimer's father, also called Hugh Latimer, was a yeoman-farmer in Thurcaston, a small village in Leicestershire. According to his son's witness in a sermon he preached before Edward VI, his father was a "yeoman, who had not lands of his own; only he had a farm of three or four pounds by year at the uttermost."[19] The younger Latimer was the only son among seven siblings, and having profited from his early education, he entered Clare Hall (now Clare College) at the University of Cambridge when he was fourteen, around 1505.[20] He was at Clare for the next twenty-five years or so, until 1530. He received his bachelor of arts degree in 1510 and his master of arts degree four years later.[21] Around the time that he received his MA degree, he was ordained a priest at Lincoln.[22] In 1524 he obtained his bachelor of divinity degree, which proved to be a key turning point in his life.

Up until this time he had been a staunch Roman Catholic. As he stated many years later in 1552, "I was as obstinate a Papist as any was in England."[23] While gifted in Latin, he was typical of many scholars in the Roman Church who were neither deeply conversant with Greek nor the Scriptures. Before his religious conversion, he considered the study of Greek, which at that time was an innovation in the university, with deep suspicion. In fact, on one occasion he

---

[18]For studies of Latimer's life and thought, see Robert Demaus, *Hugh Latimer: A Biography* (London: Religious Tract Society, 1904); Harold S. Darby, *Hugh Latimer* (London: Epworth, 1953); Allan Griffith Chester, *Hugh Latimer, Apostle to the English* (Philadelphia: University of Pennsylvania Press, 1954); Alister McGrath, *Passion for the Gospel: Hugh Latimer (1485–1555) Then and Now* (London: Latimer Trust, 2005); and Michael Pasquarello III, *God's Ploughman. Hugh Latimer: "A Preaching Life" (1485–1555)*, Studies in Christian History and Thought (Eugene, OR: Wipf & Stock, 2014).

[19]Cited in *Clare College, 1326–1926*, 1:132. See also Hugh Latimer, "The First Sermon Preached Before King Edward, March 8, 1549," in *The Works of Hugh Latimer*, 1:101.

[20]For discussion of the date, see *Clare College, 1326–1926*, 1:133. See also Demaus, *Hugh Latimer*, 14-15; and Darby, *Hugh Latimer*, 9-10.

[21]Darby, *Hugh Latimer*, 20.

[22]*Clare College, 1326–1926*, 1:132; P. C.-H. Lim, "Latimer, Hugh," in *Biographical Dictionary of Evangelicals*, ed.Timothy Larsen (Leicester, England: Inter-Varsity Press, 2003), 360.

[23]Latimer, "First Sermon on the Lord's Prayer," in *The Works of Hugh Latimer*, 1:334.

urged his hearers to "study the school divines, and not meddle with the Scripture itself."[24]

On receiving the bachelor of divinity, though, Latimer was expected to deliver a public speech. He used the occasion to deliver a bitter attack on the teaching of Philipp Melanchthon (1497–1560), the German Reformer and coworker of Martin Luther. Among those listening to Latimer was Thomas Bilney (ca. 1495–1531), who was at Trinity College and the earliest of the Cambridge Reformers. Bilney was concerned by what he heard, and after the lecture he went to speak with Latimer, who would later say that he learned more in the space of that conversation than he had in all of the years of his studies at Cambridge.[25] This, then, was his religious conversion, which can be dated to the spring of 1524.[26] As he stated in a sermon years later, "All the Papists think themselves to be saved by the law, and I myself was of that dangerous, perilous, and damnable opinion till I was thirty years of age."[27] More generally, he stated of this great change in his life: "It were too long to tell you what blindness I have been in, and how long it were 'ere I could forsake such folly. . . . [B]ut by continual prayer, continual study of Scripture, and oft communing with men of more right judgment, God hath delivered me."[28] And as he said on another occasion, "I am a Christian man . . . the child of everlasting joy, through the merits of the bitter passion of Christ."[29]

Within a year of these events he was accused of being a Lutheran by his bishop, Nicholas West (1461–1533), the bishop of Ely, who came to hear Latimer preach in Great St. Mary's in Cambridge.[30] With boldness, Latimer took the occasion to set forth Christ as a model for bishops.

---

[24]*Clare College, 1326–1926*, 1:133; "I understand no Greek," he stated at his trial in Oxford in 1555. Demaus, *Hugh Latimer*, 38.

[25]Latimer, "First Sermon on the Lord's Prayer," in *The Works of Hugh Latimer*, 1:334; *Clare College, 1326–1926*, 1:133. See also Darby, *Hugh Latimer*, 26-28.

[26]Demaus, *Hugh Latimer*, 47.

[27]Latimer, "Sermon Preached at Grimsthorpe on Twelfth Day, 1553," in *The Works of Hugh Latimer* (Cambridge: Cambridge University Press, 1845), 2:137.

[28]Latimer, "Letter to Edward Baynton," in *The Works of Hugh Latimer*, 2:333.

[29]Latimer, "Sermons on the Card," in *The Works of Hugh Latimer*, 1:7.

[30]On Nicholas West, bishop of Ely, see Darby, *Hugh Latimer*, 31.

Afterward West asked Latimer if he would refute the views of Martin Luther. When Latimer told him that he could not refute what he did not know (Latimer had not read any of Luther to this point), West said, "Well, Mr. Latimer, I perceive that you somewhat smell of the pan; you will repent this gear one day."[31] In other words, his sermons had the flavor of Lutheran doctrine. Years later, in 1552, after Latimer had read Luther, he described him as a "wonderful instrument of God, through whom God hath opened the light of his holy Word unto the world, which was a long time hid in corners and neglected."[32]

West forbade Latimer to preach in the entire diocese of Ely as well as at the University of Cambridge. A little later, however, Latimer was arraigned before Thomas Wolsey (1473–1530), the papal legate. Latimer made such a favorable impression on Wolsey that the papal legate gave him freedom to preach throughout England and declared, "If the Bishop of Ely cannot abide such doctrine as you have repeated, you shall have my license and shall preach it unto his beard, let him say what he will."[33] And so Latimer was able to continue preaching in Cambridge.

When the matter of King Henry VIII's (1491–1547) marriage came to the fore in the late 1520s—he desired a divorce since it appeared that his wife, the Spanish princess Catherine of Aragon (1485–1536), could not bear him a living son, and Henry was convinced that their marriage was accursed—Thomas Cranmer (1489–1556) suggested that the matter be discussed by the university theologians at Oxford and Cambridge. At Cambridge, Latimer supported Henry in his determination to divorce Katherine and marry Anne Boleyn (ca. 1501–1536), which probably led to his being invited to preach before the king at Windsor on March 13, 1530. Henry VIII continued to favor his preaching so that even after Latimer had been appointed as the parish minister in the pocket village

---

[31]*Clare College, 1326–1926,* 1:133–34.
[32]Latimer, "The Second Sunday in Advent," in *The Works of Hugh Latimer,* 2:52.
[33]Cited in *Clare College, 1326–1926,* 1:134; and Demaus, *Hugh Latimer,* 66.

of West Kington, Wiltshire, for instance, he would be required to preach before the king from time to time.

"TRUE PREACHERS SHOULD BE PERSECUTED AND HATED"

It may have been these opportunities to preach before the king in 1530 that emboldened Latimer to write a courageous letter to the king at the close of that year, pleading with him to allow William Tyndale's (ca. 1494–1536) translation of the New Testament to circulate freely in England.[34] Latimer does not mention Tyndale by name but simply refers to having "the Scripture in English."[35] Since Tyndale's translation was the only one available at this time, the Reformer must be defending his countryman's famous translation.

Latimer began by emphasizing that it was utterly necessary for him to speak truthfully to the king:

> The holy doctor St. Augustine, in an epistle which he wrote to Casulanus, saith, that he who for fear of any power hides the truth, provokes the wrath of God to come upon him, for he fears men more than God. And the holy man St. John Chrysostom saith, that he is not only a traitor to the truth who openly for truth teaches a lie, but he also who does not freely pronounce and show the truth that he knows. These sentences (most redoubted king) when I read now of late, and marked them earnestly in the inward parts of my heart, they made me sore afraid, troubled, and vexed me grievously in my conscience, and at the last drove me to this strait, that either I must show forth such things as I have read and learned in scripture, or else be of those who provoke the wrath of God upon them, and are traitors unto the truth; the which rather than it should happen, I had rather suffer extreme punishment.[36]

Equally strong as this fear of being found a traitor to the cause of God was Latimer's desire to glorify God. As he told Henry:

---

[34]Hugh Latimer to Henry VIII, December 1, 1530, in *Select Sermons and Letters of Dr. Hugh Latimer*, ed. W. M. Engles (London: Religious Tract Society, 1923), 383–92.

[35]Latimer to Henry VIII, December 1, 1530, in *Select Sermons and Letters*, 384.

[36]Latimer to Henry VIII, December 1, 1530, in *Select Sermons and Letters*, 383. Augustine's letter to Casulanus, an African elder, is Letter 36 in his corpus. A perusal of the letter does not reveal any statement similar to the one Latimer attributes to Augustine.

[My] purpose [in writing to you] is, for the love that I have to God principally, and the glory of his name, which is only known by his word, and for the true allegiance that I owe unto your grace, and not to hide in the ground of my heart the talent given me by God, but to chaffer [i.e., speak] it forth to others, that it may increase to the pleasure of God.[37]

Latimer then pleaded with the king not to give way to those who would prevent the free circulation of the Word of God in English. He urged Henry VIII to read various passages from the Scriptures, where he would plainly see that the truth always stirs up opposition, and suffering persecution was one of the marks of a true servant of God:

In the tenth chapter of St. Matthew's gospel, saith our Saviour Christ also, "Lo, I send you forth as sheep among wolves" [Mt 10:16]. So that the true preachers go like harmless sheep, and are persecuted, and yet they revenge not their wrong, but remit all to God: so far are they from persecuting any other but with the word of God only, which is their weapon. And so this is the most evident token that our Saviour Jesus Christ would that his gospel and the preachers of it should be known by, that it should be despised among those worldly wise men, and that they should repute it but foolishness and deceivable doctrine, and the true preachers should be persecuted and hated, and driven from town to town, yea, and at the last lose both goods and life. . . . Wherefore take this for a sure conclusion, that where the word of God is truly preached, there is persecution, as well of the hearers as of the teachers: and where is quietness and rest in worldly pleasure, there is not the truth.[38]

The persecution of those preachers who wanted Tyndale's New Testament available for the common man in England was a mark of their being truly sent by Christ. Since Latimer himself had experienced opposition for preaching God's Word, he was also clearly revealing his conviction that he had been called to be a preacher of the gospel.[39]

---

[37]Latimer to Henry VIII, December 1, 1530, in *Select Sermons and Letters*, 391.

[38]Hugh Latimer to Henry VIII, December 1, 1530, in *Select Sermons and Letters*, 387.

[39]At the close of the letter, Latimer made a remarkable assertion as he prayed for the king. He specifically asked that his sovereign "may be found a faithful minister of his [i.e., God's] gifts, and not a defender of his faith, for he will not have it defended by man or man's power, but by his word only" (Latimer to Henry VIII, December 1, 1530, in *Select Sermons and Letters*, 392). The phrase "defender of his faith" is, of course, an allusion to the title given to Henry by Pope

Latimer's plain speaking in this letter was also typical of his preaching. Although he often used "rhetorical creativity and dynamic delivery" to convey biblical truth, he was never afraid to speak plainly about what he regarded as sin.[40] In the words of Michael Pasquarello III, Latimer's sermons were marked by a "popularizing style," replete with "picturesque imagery, earthly diction, and figures of speech" that enabled him to speak to the common man with "direct, concrete, unadorned, passionate language."[41] Twenty years after this letter to Henry VIII, for example, Latimer penned a description of Jonah's sermon to the inhabitants of Nineveh that can be taken as a summary portrayal of the sort of sermons that he himself sought to deliver: "Here in this sermon of Jonas is no great curiousness, no great clerkliness, no great affectation of words, nor of painted eloquence . . . this was a nipping sermon, a pinching sermon, a biting sermon."[42]

"Meat, Not Strawberries"

In September of 1535 Latimer's preaching gifts led to his being consecrated bishop of Worcester, which was probably the most neglected diocese in England. It had been occupied by Italian bishops for nearly forty years prior to Latimer becoming its bishop, and not one of them had ever set foot in England.[43] Latimer's immediate predecessor, Geronimo de' Ghinucci (1480–1541), had never once been to England. Moreover, there were ministers in the diocese who did not even own a copy of the Latin Bible, and Latimer frequently encountered people who were completely ignorant of the Word of God, for these ministers rarely preached. In his famous "Sermon on the Plough" (1548), Latimer

---

Leo X in 1521 for his *Defence of the Seven Sacraments* (1521) that he wrote in defense of the sacramental system of the Church of Rome.

[40]The quoted words are those of Stewart Holloway, "Past Masters: Hugh Latimer," accessed September 9, 2017, www.preaching.com/articles/past-masters/past-masters-hugh-latimer.

[41]Pasquarello III, *Sacred Rhetoric*, 102.

[42]Hugh Latimer, "A Most Faithful Sermon Preached Before the King's Most Excellent Majesty and His Most Honourable Council," in *The Works of Hugh Latimer*, 1:240.

[43]Loane, *Masters of the English Reformation*, 108.

compared the rarity of such preaching to strawberries that came but in the summer:

> The preaching of the word of God unto the people is called meat. Scripture calleth it meat, not strawberries, that come but once a year, and tarry not long, but are soon gone. But it is meat, it is no dainties. The people must have meat that must be familiar and continual, and daily given unto them to feed upon. Many make a strawberry of it, ministering it but once a year; but such do not the office of good prelates.[44]

As bishop, Latimer sought to preach frequently throughout his diocese.[45] Once he came to a town where he had made arrangements beforehand to preach on the Lord's Day but found the church locked. He waited for half an hour for someone to show up, but no one did, and when he went into the village to find out the reason why no one was at the church, he was told by one of the town's inhabitants, "Sir, this is a busy day with us, we cannot hear you; it is Robin Hood's day." Later, when recounting this incident, Latimer said that this

> is no laughing matter, my friends, it is a weeping matter, a heavy matter; a heavy matter, under the pretence of gathering for Robin Hood . . . to put out a preacher, to have his office less esteemed; to prefer Robin Hood before the ministration of God's Word; and all this hath come of unpreaching prelates. . . . If the bishops had been preachers, there should never have been any such thing.[46]

As Phebe Jensen has noted, Latimer was not opposed to recreation per se. What he did object to were amusements that competed with preaching, and thus he lamented that the people of this village "prefer Robin Hood before the ministration of God's word."[47] To Latimer's way of

---

[44]Latimer, "The Sermon on the Plough," in *The Works of Hugh Latimer*, 1:62. See also Hugh Latimer, "The Sixth Sermon Preached Before King Edward, April 12, [1549]," in *The Works of Hugh Latimer*, 1:202: "The devil . . . hath set up a state of unpreaching prelacy in this realm this seven hundred year."

[45]Wabuda, "Fruitful Preaching," 59.

[46]Latimer, "Sixth Sermon Preached Before King Edward," 1:208; Loane, *Masters of the English Reformation*, 113.

[47]Phebe Jensen, "'Mirth in Heaven': Religion and Festivity in *As You Like It*," in *Shakespeare and Religious Change*, ed. Kenneth J. E. Graham and Philip D. Collington (New York: Palgrave-Macmillan, 2009), 153.

thinking, the great calling of the bishops of England was to be preachers of the Word.[48]

Without preaching, Latimer was assured that there was no hope for England.[49] In his words, "Take away preaching, and take away salvation."[50] Since preaching was central to God's work of salvation, Latimer was not surprised that preaching was "the thing that the devil wrestleth most against: it hath been all his study to decay this office. He worketh against it as much as he can."[51] And there were even some who appealed to the doctrine of election to play down the importance of preaching. When Latimer was faced with the following argument, "What need we preachers then? God can save his elect without preachers," the Reformed bishop replied, "I must keep the way God hath ordained. . . . This office of preaching is the only ordinary way that God hath appointed to save us all by."[52] Similarly, Latimer asserted in a sermon on the Lord's Prayer: "The instrument wherewith we be called to this kingdom [of God] is the office of preaching. God calleth us daily by preachers to come to this kingdom."[53]

Latimer was well aware that it was not merely the act of preaching that saved sinners, but God opening hearts as the Word was preached. To quote from one of Latimer's later sermons, preachers

> can do no more but call; God is he that must bring in; God must open the
> hearts, as it is in the Acts of the Apostles. When Paul preached to the women,
> there was a silk-woman, . . . "whose heart God opened." None could open it

---

[48]Hughes Oliphant Old, *The Reading and Preaching of the Scriptures in the Worship of the Christian Church*, vol. 4, *The Age of the Reformation* (Grand Rapids: Eerdmans, 2002), 142; Wabuda, "Fruitful Preaching," 49-74.

[49]Chester, *Hugh Latimer*, 171. See also Latimer, "The Seventh Sermon Preached Before King Edward, April 19, [1549]," in *The Works of Hugh Latimer*, 1:234: "I am . . . sure that this realm of England . . . is allowed to hear God's word, as though Christ had said a thousand times, 'Go preach to Englishmen: I will that Englishmen be saved.'"

[50]Latimer, "Fourth Sermon Preached Before King Edward," 1:155.

[51]Latimer, "Sixth Sermon Preached Before King Edward," in *The Works of Hugh Latimer*, 1:202.

[52]Latimer, "Residue of the Same Gospel Declared in the Afternoon [at Stamford, November 9, 1550]," in *The Works of Hugh Latimer*, 1:306.

[53]Latimer, "Third Sermon upon the Lord's Prayer," in *The Works of Hugh Latimer*, 1:358.

but God. Paul could but only preach, God must work; God must do the thing inwardly.[54]

Thus, at the outset of a sermon that he preached on the parable of the wedding banquet in Matthew 22, Latimer urged his hearers to pray for him that God would give to both him and them

> his Holy Ghost: unto me, that I may speak the word of God, and teach you to understand the same; unto you, that you may hear it faithfully, to the edification of your souls; so that you may be edified through it, and your lives reformed and amended; and that his honour and glory may increase daily amongst us.[55]

Finally, during his time as bishop of Worcester, Latimer sought to reform the parish churches in his diocese by appointing preachers who would preach scriptural doctrine and be explicitly critical of such false doctrines as praying to the saints, the power of their relics, the spiritual usefulness of pilgrimages, purgatory, and the efficacy of masses celebrated for the dead.[56] Three of the men whom Latimer appointed during this period of time would later be martyred: Thomas Garrard (ca. 1500–1540), Robert Barnes (1495–1540), and Rowland Taylor (1510–1555), who was married to William Tyndale's niece.[57]

Latimer was bishop of Worcester for only four years, however, as he had to retire in 1539 upon the promulgation of the Act of the Six Articles, called by the Protestants at the time "the whip with the six strings."[58] This act represented a swing in Henry VIII's government back to traditional Catholic doctrines, for it affirmed, among other things, transubstantiation, clerical celibacy, the legitimacy of private Masses, and

---

[54]Latimer, "A Sermon Preached at Stamford, November 9, 1550," in *The Works of Hugh Latimer*, 1:285.

[55]Latimer, "A Sermon on the Parable of a King That Married His Son," in *The Works of Hugh Latimer*, 1:455-56. I am indebted to Pasquarello III, *Sacred Rhetoric*, 104, for drawing my attention to this text.

[56]Wabuda, "Fruitful Preaching," 52. For preachers whom Latimer appointed, see Wabuda, "Fruitful Preaching," 59-64.

[57]Wabuda, "Fruitful Preaching," 73.

[58]Hugh Latimer, *Sermon on the Ploughers*, ed. Edward Arber (London: Alex Murray & Son, 1868), 6.

auricular confession.[59] For the next six years, not much is known about Latimer's life.[60] When two of his preachers, Thomas Garrard and Robert Barnes, were martyred in 1540, Latimer was also in prison, expecting to meet a similar fate, for there were some in his diocese calling for his execution.[61] Although he was eventually released, he was forbidden to preach and commanded not to visit Oxford, Cambridge, or his old bishopric of Worcester.

Things radically changed again with the accession of Edward VI in 1547. Latimer was offered back his bishopric in Worcester, which he refused, choosing rather to stay in London with Thomas Cranmer, the archbishop of Canterbury, and assist him in reforming the church. He also spent time at Grimsthorpe Castle in Lincolnshire, where, as the guest of Katherine Willoughby (1519–1580), the Duchess of Suffolk, one of the wealthiest women of her day and an ardent supporter of the Reformation,[62] Latimer generally preached two sermons every Sunday and during weekdays rose in the middle of the night so as to be at his studies by two in the morning.[63] His commitment to the Scriptures and their truth is well seen by a comment he made in 1552 in one of his Grimsthorpe sermons. He was speaking about the Roman Catholic concern for unity and the implicit critique that the Reformation was wrong since it had split the church. Latimer's response was simple: desiring unity was certainly biblical—he referred to the apostle Paul's exhortation to "be united in the same mind" (1 Cor 1:10)—but, he stressed, "We ought never to regard unity so much that we would, or should, forsake God's word for her sake."[64]

---

[59]Lim, "Latimer," 360.

[60]Loane, Masters of the English Reformation, 116.

[61]Wabuda, "Fruitful Preaching," 74.

[62]Willoughby helped finance the publication of a key book by her best friend, Katherine Parr, entitled Lamentation of a Sinner and also supported England's leading Protestant publisher John Day (ca. 1522–1584), who has been called "the master printer of the English Reformation." John N. King, Foxe's Book of Martyrs and Early Modern Print Culture (Cambridge: Cambridge University Press, 2006), 80.

[63]Allan G. Chester, introduction to Selected Sermons of Hugh Latimer (Charlottesville, VA: The University Press of Virginia for The Folger Shakespeare Library, 1968), xxvi.

[64]Latimer, "Second Sermon on the Gospel of All Saints," in The Works of Hugh Latimer, 1:487.

"O WHAT A JOYFUL THING"

Latimer must have preached hundreds of sermons. However, we possess but forty-one, of which twenty-eight were preached at Grimsthorpe to the servants of Katherine Willoughby or to country congregations near her castle in 1552.[65] Latimer did not use a manuscript when he preached, and thus these sermons, along with the others that are extant, were copied down as he spoke. Allan G. Chester has aptly described his preaching as a "torrent of . . . eloquence" and fluency that must have made the task of copying quite difficult, as the copyists struggled to keep up with the preacher.[66] Latimer excelled as an extemporaneous preacher, and the Grimsthorpe sermons especially reveal him as one who was able to adapt himself to his audience: he explains the biblical text ever mindful of its context, stresses points of doctrine arising from the passage, emphasizes moral lessons, warns against the errors of the Roman Catholic Church, and all the while the sermons are suffused with what Chester has rightly described as a "heartfelt earnestness."[67]

Consider this example of Latimer explaining why it is vital to know Christ for salvation in a sermon he delivered on December 27, 1552, the day assigned to St. John the apostle in the liturgical calendar of the Western church:

> By [Christ's] passion, which he hath suffered, he merited that as many as believe in him shall be as well justified by him, as though they themselves had never done any sin, and as though they themselves had fulfilled the law to the uttermost. For we, without him, are under the curse of the law; the law condemneth us; the law is not able to help us; and yet the imperfection is not in the law, but in us: for the law itself is holy and good, but we are not able to keep it, and so the law condemneth us; but Christ with his death hath delivered us from the curse of the law. He hath set us at liberty, and promiseth

---

[65]Chester, introduction to *Selected Sermons of Hugh Latimer*, xxvi-xxvii. On the reliability of the texts of these sermons, see Elizabeth T. Hastings, "A Sixteenth Century Manuscript Translation of Latimer's *First Sermon Before Edward*," *Publications of the Modern Language Association* 60 (1945): 959-1002.

[66]Chester, introduction to *Selected Sermons of Hugh Latimer*, xxviii.

[67]Chester, introduction to *Selected Sermons of Hugh Latimer*, xxvii.

that when we believe in him, we shall not perish; the law shall not condemn us. Therefore let us study to believe in Christ. Let us put all our hope, trust, and confidence only in him; let us patch him with nothing: for, as I told you before, our merits are not able to deserve everlasting life: it is too precious a thing to be merited by man. It is his doing only. God hath given him unto us to be our deliverer, and to give us everlasting life. O what a joyful thing was this![68]

Latimer was thus critical of his Roman Catholic opponents for teaching that salvation could be attained by human merit:

The papists, which are the very enemies of Christ, make him to be a Saviour after their own fantasy, and not after the word of God; wherein he declareth himself, and set out and opened his mind unto us. They follow, I say, not the Scripture, which is the very leader to God, but regard more their own inventions; and therefore they make him a Savior after this fashion. They consider how there shall be, after the general resurrection, a general judgment, where all mankind shall be gathered together to receive their judgment: then shall Christ, say the papists, sit as a judge, having power over heaven and earth: and all those that have done well in this world, and have steadfastly prayed upon their beads, and have gone a pilgrimage, etc., and so with their good works have deserved heaven and everlasting life,—those, say they, that have merited with their own good works, shall be received of Christ, and admitted to everlasting salvation. As for the other, that have not merited everlasting life, [they] shall be cast into everlasting darkness: for Christ will not suffer wicked sinners to be taken into heaven, but rather receive those which deserve. And so it appeareth, that they esteem our Savior not to be a Redeemer, but only a judge; which shall give sentence over the wicked to go into everlasting fire, and the good he will call to everlasting felicity.

And this is the opinion of the papists, as concerning our Savior; which opinion is most detestable, abominable, and filthy in the sight of God. For it diminisheth the passion of Christ; it taketh away the power and strength of the same passion; it defileth the honor and glory of Christ; it forsaketh and denieth Christ, and all his benefits. For if we shall be judged after our own deservings, we shall be damned everlastingly. Therefore, learn here, every good Christian, to abhor this most detestable and dangerous poison of the papists, which go about to thrust Christ out of his seat: learn here, I say, to

---

[68]Hugh Latimer, "Sermon on St. John Evangelist's Day" in *Works of Hugh Latimer*, 2:125-26.

leave all papistry, and to stick only to the word of God, which teacheth thee that Christ is not only a judge, but a justifier; a giver of salvation, and a taker away of sin; for he purchased our salvation through his painful death, and we receive the same through believing in him; as St. Paul teacheth us, saying, . . ."Freely ye are justified through faith" [Rom 3:24]. In these words of St. Paul, all merits and estimation of works are excluded and clean taken away. For if it were for our works' sake, then it were not freely: but St. Paul saith, "freely." Whether will you now believe St. Paul, or the papists?[69]

As these quotations clearly reveal, Latimer was a bold and joyful herald of the Reformation insights of *solus Christus* and *sola fide*. Little wonder that, with the burden of having to win salvation through his own merits lifted, this English Reformer was suffused with joy.

"To Suffer for God's Holy Word's Sake"

During one of the Grimsthorpe sermons that Latimer preached on the petition "Thy kingdom come" from the Lord's Prayer (Mt 6:10), he made a statement that, from the perspective of later events, can be regarded as almost predictive. "Happy is he," he said, "to whom it is given to suffer for God's holy word's sake."[70]

Three years later, during the bloody reign of Mary I (1516–1558), Latimer and his fellow bishop Nicholas Ridley (ca. 1500–1555) were indeed called to suffer death for the sake of their commitment to God's Word and its authority over all of life. Latimer had been committed to the Tower of London in September 1553, and then, in April 1554, he was taken with Ridley to the Bocardo prison in Oxford where they and Thomas Cranmer underwent examination of their theological beliefs. All three were found guilty of heresy and condemned to death. While in the Bocardo, Latimer wrote the following in a lengthy letter dated May 15, 1555:

---

[69]Latimer, "Sermon Preached on the First Sunday After Epiphany," in *The Works of Hugh Latimer*, 2:146-47. Elsewhere ("The Sermon on the Plough," 1:61) Latimer described saving faith as "a faith that embraceth Christ, and trusteth to his merits; a lively faith, a justifying faith; a faith that maketh a man righteous, without respect of works."

[70]Latimer, "The Third Sermon upon the Lord's Prayer," 1:361.

Soap, though it be black, soileth not the cloth, but maketh it clean: so doth the black cross of Christ help us to more whiteness, if God strike with the battledoor. Because you be God's sheep, prepare yourselves to the slaughter, always knowing, that in the sight of God our death is precious. . . .

Die once we must; how and where, we know not. Happy are they whom God giveth to pay nature's debt (I mean to die) for his sake. Here is not our home; let us therefore accordingly consider things, having always before our eyes that heavenly Jerusalem, and the way thereto in persecution.[71]

On October 16, 1555, Latimer and Ridley were taken out of Oxford through the Bocardo Gate, where they were tied to a stake in what is now Broad Street. Wood was piled around the two bishops, and before the fire was lit, Ridley asked if he could say two or three words. He was told that if he was prepared to deny his "erroneous opinions," then he would be allowed to speak. If not, he was told, "you must suffer for your deserts." "Well," replied Ridley, "so long as the breath is in my body, I will never deny my Lord Christ, and his known truth!"[72]

The wood piled around Ridley was freshly cut and thus only smoldered. Ridley was in conscious agony till the very end and at one point was heard to pray: "I cannot burn! Lord have mercy upon me!" Latimer, though, died fairly swiftly, but before he did so he uttered the following words in response to this cry by Ridley. These words, recorded by the English martyrologist John Foxe (ca. 1516–1587), form a fitting conclusion to this study of Latimer as a preacher, for in a sense they have a sermonic quality: "Be of good comfort Master Ridley, and play the man! We shall this day light such a candle by God's grace in England, as I trust shall never be put out."[73]

---

[71]Hugh Latimer, *Letter* LI in *Works of Hugh Latimer*, 2:442, 444.

[72]John Foxe, *The Acts and Monuments of the Church* (1570 ed.), Book 11, page 1976, accessed April 19, 2017, www.johnfoxe.org/index.php?realm=text&gototype=&edition=1570&pageid = 1976.

[73]Foxe, *Acts and Monuments*, Book 11, page 1976, accessed April 19, 2017, www.johnfoxe.org/index .php?realm=text&gototype=&edition=1570&pageid=1976; Peter Newman Brooks, *Cranmer in Context: Documents from the English Reformation* (Minneapolis: Fortress, 1989), 93-94; Andrew Atherstone, *The Martyrs of Mary Tudor* (Leominster, England: Day One, 2005), 93-99; David Horan, *Oxford: A Cultural and Literary Companion* (New York: Interlink Books, 2000), 129-30; Pasquarello III, *God's Ploughman*, 199.

Chapter Four

SCRIPTURE *as* "SACRAMENT" *in* PROTESTANT PASTORAL *and* DEVOTIONAL LITERATURE

RONALD K. RITTGERS

A NUMBER OF YEARS AGO I was conducting research at the Herzog August Bibliothek in Wolfenbüttel, Germany, for a book on the pastoral care of the sick and suffering in the Protestant Reformation.[1] I was seeking to study the Reformation *cura animarum* through the lens of evangelical pastoral and devotional literature. As I made my way through the mountains of such works that are housed in this world-famous library, I came across a couple that included page after page of quotations from Scripture with very little commentary.[2] I remember thinking to myself at the time, "Well these works aren't very valuable; they just list a theme and then quote one relevant Bible verse after the other rather than doing something theologically interesting with Scripture." I was seeking to write a scholarly monograph, after all, and I needed interesting sources. These sources did not seem to qualify. After I waded through a couple

---

[1]See Ronald K. Rittgers, *The Reformation of Suffering: Pastoral Theology and Lay Piety in Late Medieval and Early Modern Germany* (New York: Oxford University Press, 2012).

[2]For examples, see Caspar Huberinus, *Eyn kurtzer außzug der heyligen schrift* (Erfurt, 1525), HAB (=Herzog August Bibliothek, Wolfenbuettel, Germany) QuH 169.15; Caspar Kantz, *Wie man dem krancken vnd sterbenden menschen/ ermanen/ tro[e]sten/ vnnd Gott befelhen soll* (Augsburg, 1539), HAB 917.19 Th. (5); Johann Pfeffinger, *Trostbu[e]chlin Aus Gottes Wort* (Leipzig, 1552), HAB Alv.: Ba 81 (3); Hieronymus Tanneberg, *Trostbu[e]chlein* (Leipzig, 1999), HAB Yv 1209.8° Helmst.

more such Scripture-laden works, I began to move more rapidly through similar ones in my search for stimulating sources.

Of course, at one level I realized that such sources were quite valuable, for they provided eloquent testimony to the centrality of the Word in Protestant pastoral care. Clearly, the Word was the primary source of the consolation that the Protestant authors were seeking to provide for their readers. Scripture contained the truth about God and the human condition that the pastors and theologians wanted to convey to their lay contemporaries who faced affliction. This was an important point, and such sources made it very plainly. But I was still hoping for more.

Then one day it hit me that Scripture might be playing an additional and potentially very interesting role in such sources: perhaps these sources were treating Scripture not simply as a source of doctrinal truth but also, and more profoundly, as a means of divine grace, as a sacrament of sorts. The divinely instituted external sign was missing, of course, so I knew I was dealing with a quasi-sacrament at best, but the more I thought about it the more the category of sacrament seemed to capture, albeit imperfectly, how the authors of these sources were viewing Scripture. The authors appeared to be setting the sacramental Word before their readers so that the Word itself could convey the grace and wisdom that it contained to troubled souls; therefore, no human commentary was necessary. I knew that many Protestants had a sacramental view of the preached Word;[3] here it occurred to me that I might just be encountering a sacramental view of the printed Word in which biblical verses were believed to act as conduits of divine grace for those who had faith. What is more, this sacramental view of the printed Word appeared to cut across confessional lines, providing at

---

[3]On Luther, see Steven Ozment, *The Age of Reform: An Intellectual and Religious History of Late Medieval and Reformation Europe* (New Haven, CT: Yale University Press, 1980), 221; Hughes Oliphant Old, *The Reading and Preaching of the Scriptures in the Worship of the Christian Church*. Vol. 4, *The Age of the Reformation* (Grand Rapids: Eerdmans, 2002), 40-41; and John M. Frymire, *The Primacy of the Postils: Catholics, Protestants, and the Dissemination of Ideas in Early Modern Germany* (Leiden: Brill, 2010), 27. On Calvin (and Beza), see Brian Gerrish, *Grace and Gratitude: The Eucharistic Theology of John Calvin* (Minneapolis: Fortress, 1993), 82-86.

least one case of a unified sacramental theology among Protestants. During the Reformation period, of course, debates about the sacraments—their definition, number, proper administration, and the like—caused much discord among Protestants. One only has to think of Luther and Zwingli's famous disagreement about the Lord's Supper and the deep division between magisterial Protestants and Anabaptists regarding infant baptism.

As I began to reflect on this possible sacramental function of Scripture in Protestant pastoral and devotional literature, and as I learned about the absolute explosion of such works in the Reformation period,[4] I began to wonder about the traditional view of Protestantism as a cause of disenchantment in Western civilization. If I was right about my sources, then I was encountering in them a new and widespread means of access to the divine in the Reformation period. Rather than separating the supernatural from the natural, these sources were combining them as never before and with unprecedented influence. In this chapter I would like to develop this hypothesis about the sacramental view of the Word in Protestant pastoral and devotional literature as part of a larger effort to (1) understand evangelical pastoral care and to (2) revise what one might call the "Disenchantment Thesis" about the Protestant Reformation.

THE DISENCHANTMENT THESIS

First, I would like to make a few comments about this thesis. In his influential work *The Sacred Canopy* (1967), sociologist Peter Berger argued that Protestantism played a decisive role in the disenchantment of Western civilization. When evangelical Reformers sought to sweep the church clean of allegedly superstitious practices like the invocation of saints, the veneration of relics, and the belief in miraculous healing,[5] they

---

[4]See discussion below.

[5]On the Protestant critique of miracles, see Philip M. Soergel, "Miracle, Magic, and Disenchantment in Early Modern Germany," in *Envisioning Magic: A Princeton Seminar and Symposium*, ed. Peter Schäfer and Hans G. Kippenberg (Leiden: Brill, 1997), 215-34; and D. P. Walker, "The Cessation of Miracles," in *Hermeticism and the Renaissance: Intellectual History and the Occult in*

unwittingly took an important first step toward the eventual secularization of Western civilization. Following the lead of Max Weber, who first proposed the disenchantment (*Entzauberung*) thesis in the early twentieth century,[6] Berger maintained that the Reformation effected "an immense shrinkage in the scope of the sacred in reality, as compared with its Catholic adversary."[7] By rejecting the sacramental worldview of the late medieval church, Protestantism "cut the umbilical cord between heaven and earth, and thereby threw man back upon himself in a historically unprecedented manner."[8] Protestants exorcised the demons of pagan superstition only to make room for the more powerful secularizing spirits of rationalism, individualism, and pluralism.

The disenchantment thesis has been very influential in Reformation studies. While most contemporary historians wish to nuance and qualify it at certain points, many agree with Berger's fundamental insight about the connection between Protestantism and disenchantment. Keith Thomas argued in his magisterial *Religion and the Decline of Magic*, "Protestantism thus presented itself as a deliberate attempt to take the magical elements out of religion, to eliminate the idea that the rituals of the Church had about them a mechanical efficacy, and to abandon the effort to endow physical objects with supernatural qualities by special formulae of consecration and exorcism."[9] Steven Ozment once dubbed the early Protestant movement "the first Western enlightenment" and argued that the Reformation removed the *Seelengrund*—the sacred foundation—from both individual souls and human society.[10] The author

---

Early Modern Europe, ed. Ingrid Merkel and Allen G. Debus (London: Associated University Press, 1988), 111-24.

[6]See Max Weber, *The Protestant Ethic and the Spirit of Capitalism* (1905–1906), trans. Talcott Parsons (New York: Charles Scribner's Sons, 1958), 105.

[7]Peter Berger, *The Sacred Canopy: Elements of a Sociological Theory of Religion* (New York: Anchor, 1967), 111.

[8]Berger, *The Sacred Canopy*, 112.

[9]Keith Thomas, *Religion and the Decline of Magic: Studies in Popular Beliefs in Sixteenth and Seventeenth Century England* (New York: Oxford University Press, 1971), 75-76.

[10]Steven Ozment, *The Reformation in the Cities: The Appeal of Protestantism to Sixteenth-Century Germany and Switzerland* (New Haven, CT: Yale University Press, 1975), 116 and 118-19. For an examination of how the Calvinist reform of worship contributed to an extreme divide in

of a widely used Reformation textbook maintains that the Reformation was "a turning point of great significance for universal history" and goes on to observe that "this significance has been described in terms of desacralization and deritualization."[11]

However, a growing number of Reformation scholars have questioned the validity of the disenchantment thesis.[12] Chief among these skeptics has been the late Robert Scribner (d. 1998).[13] Beginning in the early 1990s, Scribner challenged the assumed connection between Protestantism and disenchantment. He argued that the vast majority of early modern Protestants continued to live in a sacralized universe. To make his case, Scribner cited numerous examples of lay Protestants using Bibles, hymnbooks, and catechisms as ersatz sacramentals to access divine power in times of need. Lay people used these evangelical objects as Protestant talismans, believing that the objects themselves—not the theology they contained— would protect them from dark spiritual forces. According to Scribner, there slowly emerged among lay Protestants a "covert evangelical sacramentalism" that signaled an important line of continuity between late medieval and Reformation popular piety.[14] Scribner conceded that by comparison with Catholicism, Protestantism offered the laity a weaker and less well-defined form of sacrality, but there was still a significant

---

Reformed Protestantism between the spiritual and material realms, see Carlos Eire, *The War Against the Idols: The Reformation of Worship from Erasmus to Calvin* (Cambridge: University of Cambridge Press, 1986).

[11]Carter Lindberg, *The European Reformations* (Cambridge, MA: Blackwell, 1996), 379.

[12]It should be noted that there has been a vigorous debate among sociologists about the validity of Berger's secularization thesis in which disenchantment plays such a key role. Berger himself has all but repudiated it. See his chapter "The Desecularization of the World: A Global Overview," in *The Desecularization of the World: Resurgent Religion and World Politics* (Grand Rapids: Eerdmans, 1999), 1-18. However, there are several scholars who continue to argue for the validity of the secularization thesis. See Craig M. Gay, *The Way of the (Modern) World, Or, Why It's Tempting to Live as if God Doesn't Exist* (Grand Rapids: Eerdmans, 1998); and Steve Bruce, *Religion in the Modern World: From Cathedrals to Cults* (Oxford: Oxford University Press, 1996). For a treatment of both sides of the debate, see Steve Bruce, ed., *Religion and Modernization: Sociologists and Historians Debate the Secularization Thesis* (Oxford: Oxford University Press, 1992).

[13]R. W. Scribner, *Religion and Culture in Germany (1400–1800)*, ed. Lyndal Roper (Leiden: Brill, 2001), 275-365.

[14]Scribner, *Religion and Culture in Germany*, 289.

degree of porosity between the natural and supernatural realms, much more so than sociologists like Weber and Berger realized.

Taking Scribner's lead, other historians have found evidence for continuing recourse to saints and folk magic among lay Protestants.[15] Still others have accepted the continuing sacralized nature of the evangelical worldview but have been more impressed with the discontinuities between Catholic and Protestant piety in terms of their respective psychological effects. These scholars maintain that Protestant lay people still wished to access divine power for their lives, especially in the face of suffering, but the Reformation left them with very few resources for doing so. For example, Susan Karant-Nunn has argued that owing to the Protestant rejection of traditional Catholic ritual, "God was not present in the same way as before."[16] Other scholars have maintained that the result of this distancing of the deity was a heightened apocalyptic outlook and fear of the devil among Protestants,[17] an obsession with astrology and various signs and portents,[18] a deep concern with moral discipline as a way of seeking divine favor,[19] and a widespread sense of anxiety and collective guilt for having squandered the gospel that God provided through figures such as Luther.[20]

---

[15]See Carol Piper Heming, *Protestants and the Cult of the Saints in German-Speaking Europe, 1517–1531* (Kirksville, MO: Truman State University Press, 2003), 105; R. Po-Chia Hsia, *Social Discipline in the Reformation: Central Europe, 1550–1750* (London: Routledge, 1992), 153-59; Gerald Strauss, *Luther's House of Learning: Indoctrination of the Young in the German Reformation* (Baltimore: Johns Hopkins University Press, 1978), 284-85, 300-308. See also Thomas, *Religion and the Decline of Magic*.

[16]See Susan C. Karant-Nunn, *The Reformation of Ritual: An Interpretation of Early Modern Germany* (New York: Routledge, 1997), 191.

[17]See Robin Bruce Barnes, *Prophecy and Gnosis: Apocalypticism in the Wake of the Lutheran Reformation* (Stanford, CA: Stanford University Press, 1988). See also Philip M. Soergel, *Wondrous in His Saints: Counter-Reformation Propaganda in Bavaria* (Berkeley: University of California Press, 1993), 142.

[18]See Paola Zambelli, ed., *"Astrologi hallucinati": Stars and the End of the World in Luther's Time* (Berlin: Walter de Gruyter, 1986), 101-51; Soergel, *Wondrous in His Saints*, 147-50; Soergel, "Miracle, Magic, and Disenchantment," 233; and Barnes, *Prophecy and Gnosis*, 87.

[19]Scribner, *Religion and Culture in Germany*, 355-57; Barnes, *Prophecy and Gnosis*, 6.

[20]Barnes, *Prophecy and Gnosis*, 262; Theodore Dwight Bozeman, *The Precisianist Strain: Disciplinary Religion and Antinomian Backlash in Puritanism to 1638* (Chapel Hill: University of North Carolina Press, 2004), 147; Euan Cameron, *The European Reformation*, 2nd ed. (Oxford: Oxford University Press, 2012), 438.

I believe that there is a great deal of truth to the disenchantment thesis, although I am also sympathetic to some of the recent revisions of it. Protestants did seek to remove every hint of the magical and the "superstitious" from Christianity, and they did endeavor to limit the points of contact between the natural and the supernatural to a few biblically approved instances, although there was disagreement about just what these instances were.[21] They were at least partly successful in doing so, and this success has shaped Western culture in important ways. I am also certain that a portion of the laity found evangelical Christianity to be unappealing because it did not provide the kind of access to divine power that traditional Christianity had promised. As Scribner argued, they therefore sought ersatz sacramentals in the material objects available to them, including even images of Luther.[22] I furthermore think that Scribner and others are right to stress that Protestants continued to occupy a sacralized universe even as that universe was undergoing important and unprecedented desacralizing changes.

But I want to locate this sacralization in a different place than Scribner. I want to focus not on how lay Protestants, especially rural lay Protestants, resisted the evangelical campaign against "superstition," which was Scribner's concern. That is, I am not here interested in a "covert evangelical sacramentalism" as a form of lay resistance to the confessionalizing designs of Reformers and their political supporters; rather, I am interested in an "overt evangelical sacramentalism" that was an essential part of the Reformation and its pastoral care. Much of the scholarship that I have briefly cited above emphasizes what the Reformation sought to take away from the laity, especially in terms of methods of coping with

---

[21]Reformation debates about the Lord's Supper are obviously important in this context. So, too, are the respective Protestant attitudes toward images and various cultic objects associated with the Catholic Mass. Regarding the latter, Karant-Nunn has argued that Lutheranism offered a "more diffuse and available sacrality" than Calvinism because of Lutheranism's more permissive attitude toward images and the like. See *Reformation of Ritual*, 133. On Calvinist iconoclasm, see Eire, *War Against the Idols*.

[22]See Robert Scribner, "The Incombustible Luther: The Image of the Reformer in Early Modern Germany," *Past and Present* 110 (1986): 38-68.

suffering. While I value this scholarship and have learned much from it, I do not think that it has explored in sufficient depth what Protestantism attempted to give to lay people by way of positive alternatives to various "superstitious" practices, again, especially in the midst of affliction. This is where I want to focus—on an overt evangelical sacramentalism as an essential part of the intended Reformation. I want to try to demonstrate the existence of this sacramentalism, for while I have come to see it as overt—that is, as readily discernible—I concede that it can be difficult to detect at first sight.

THE POWER OF THE WORD IN PROTESTANT PASTORAL AND DEVOTIONAL LITERATURE

As I have already indicated, I see this sacramentalism in the Protestant pastoral and devotional literature that was so important to evangelical pastoral care. Before I say more about this sacramentalism, I want to underscore something that is a commonplace among Reformation scholars: this literature positively exploded in the Reformation period.[23] It was ubiquitous.[24] Works of devotion were easily the most popular form of printed material in the late medieval and early modern periods.[25] This fact becomes readily apparent if we consider Martin Luther. It was his devotional writings, not his controversial works, that made him into an early modern publishing sensation.[26] Luther's famous (and infamous) Ninety-Five Theses is extant in relatively few editions, while "A Sermon on Preparing to Die" (1519), a vernacular work of devotion, is extant in

---

[23]There was of course a great deal of Catholic pastoral and devotional literature in the later Middle Ages, but Protestants proved to be especially adept at using the printing press in the Reformation period. Their pastoral and devotional literature outpaced that of Catholics.

[24]Portions of the next four paragraphs draw on Ronald K. Rittgers, "The Age of Reform as an Age of Consolation," Church History: Studies in Christianity and Culture 86, no. 3 (2017): 619-26.

[25]Ozment, Age of Reform, 199; Gunter Franz, ed., Huberinus—Rhegius—Holbein. Bibliographische und druckgeschichtliche Untersuchung der verbreitesten Trost- und Erbauungschriften des 16. Jahrhunderts (Nieuwkoop: B. De Graaf, 1973), 215. On the success of printed works of devotion in England, see Alec Ryrie, Being Protestant in Reformation Britain (Oxford: Oxford University Press, 2013), 5, 22.

[26]Mark U. Edwards Jr., Printing, Propaganda, and Martin Luther (Berkeley: University of California Press, 1994), 163-64. On Luther's success as an author, see Andrew Pettegree, Brand Luther (New York: Penguin, 2015), 188.

twenty-four editions; his other devotional writings were likewise "best sellers."[27] Luther was the most popular author of his day,[28] but other clerical authors produced individual works of consolation that outsold his. The Augsburg Lutheran reformer Urbanus Rhegius produced a pamphlet entitled *Soul-Medicine for the Healthy and the Sick in These Dangerous Times* (1529) that went through 121 editions and was translated into nine languages.[29] Scholars have also noted its influence on works of devotion in English.[30] Other important Lutheran works of devotion include Caspar Huberinus's *How One Should Console a Dying Person* (1529; thirty-eight editions) along with his *Concerning the Wrath and Goodness of God* (1529; twenty-one editions), Johannes Spangenberg's *On the Christian Knight* (1541; twenty editions) and his *The Booklet of Comfort for the Sick* (1542; sixteen editions), Michael Bock's *Little Garden of Spices for Sick Souls* (1562; twenty editions), and Johannes Habermann's *Prayer Booklet* (1597; fifty-nine editions).[31]

Reformed Protestants on the Continent did not produce as many works of devotion and pastoral care as Lutherans—here Heinrich Bullinger's *Instruction for the Sick* (1544) is an important exception (six editions)[32]—but we should avoid concluding that the concern was unimportant to Zwingli and Calvin and their followers.[33] Scott Manetsch has demonstrated just the opposite in *Calvin's Company of Pastors.*[34] Reformed Protestantism shared this concern with Lutherans, a fact clearly illustrated by English Protestantism. We have some thirty editions

---

[27]For publication statistics, see Rittgers, *The Reformation of Suffering*, 271.

[28]See Pettegree, *Brand Luther*, 115, 210, 213.

[29]Franz, *Huberinus—Rhegius—Holbein*, 213-24, 266.

[30]See Jonathan Reimer, "The Life and Writings of Thomas Becon, 1512–1567" (PhD diss., Cambridge University, 2016), 145-47.

[31]For publication statistics, see Rittgers, *Reformation of Suffering*, 269-74.

[32]For publication statistics, see Rittgers, *Reformation of Suffering*, 270, 274.

[33]See Bruce Gordon, "Bullinger's Vernacular Writings: Spirituality and the Christian Life," in *Architect of the Reformation: An Introduction to Heinrich Bullinger, 1504–1575*, ed. Bruce Gordon and Emidio Campi (Grand Rapids: Baker Academic, 2004), 117-34.

[34]Scott W. Manetsch, *Calvin's Company of Pastors: Pastoral Care and the Emerging Reformed Church, 1536–1609* (New York: Oxford University Press, 2013), ch. 9 "The Ministry of Pastoral Care," especially 289-98.

of Thomas Becon's *Sick Mans Salve* (1553),[35] while John Norden's *A Pensive Mans Practice* (1623) is extant in forty-four editions,[36] William Cowper's *A Conduit of Comfort* (1606) in twelve editions,[37] and Lewis Bayly's *Practice of Pietie* (1613) in over fifty editions.[38] These works were among the most popular of the day, and they were all intended to enrich devotional life and assist in pastoral care, whether it was carried out by pastors or lay people.

There are fewer extant works of devotion and pastoral care from Anabaptists and spiritualists, but they still contributed to this literature. Caspar von Schwenckfeld authored several letters and works of devotion, two of which appeared together in the late 1530s: *Consolation for One Who Stands Under the Cross* and *A Useful Book of Consolation for All Sick, Afflicted, and Imprisoned People*. This two-part work is extant in eight editions.[39]

As noted above, the centrality and power of the Word is a dominant theme in this literature. Thomas Becon's *Sick Mans Salve* is especially interesting in this regard. It provides an account of how a layman stricken with an unspecified illness seeks and receives consolation from his friends via holy "conferences" in his home. Although Becon was a chaplain to Thomas Cranmer and one of the Six Preachers of Canterbury, he has lay people provide all of this consolation.[40] During the conference, Becon has the sick man and his friends discuss the book of Job. One of the lay consolers strongly protests the decision of Job's friends to sit with

---

[35]For publication statistics, see Christopher Marsh, "'Departing Well and Christianly': Will-Making and Popular Religion in Early Modern England," in *Religion and the English People, 1500–1640: New Voices and Perspectives*, ed. Eric Josef Carlson (Kirksville, MO: Thomas Jefferson University Press, 1998), 204; Mary Hampson Patterson, *Domesticating the Reformation: Protestant Best Sellers, Private Devotion, and the Revolution of English Piety* (Madison, NJ: Fairleigh Dickinson University Presses, 2007), 319.

[36]Ryrie, *Being Protestant*, 22n29.

[37]For publication statistics, see the relevant search on the English Short Title Catalogue, estc .bl.uk/F/?func =file&file_name=login-bl-estc.

[38]According to Ryrie, Bayly's *Practice* was the most successful devotional handbook in early modern Britain. See *Being Protestant*, 22n30.

[39]For publication statistics, see Rittgers, *Reformation of Suffering*, 273.

[40]On the role of such conferences in early modern English piety, see Ryrie, *Being Protestant*, 392.

the afflicted saint for a week in silence (Job 2:13). The lay consoler asserts, "by the space of vii. dayes, [they] spake not one comfortable worde unto hym."[41] Becon has the lay consolers in this work of devotion console their sick friend with "comfortable words" from Scripture as soon as they enter his house. After receiving such consolation from his friends, the sick man asserts that he now knows firsthand what he has heard in sermons:

> That one faithfull preacher, which is able with the sweete promises of the holy Scriptures to comfort the weake and desperate conscience, is better than ten thousand Mumbling Massemongers which promise with their Massing mountains of golde, but performe mole hils of glasse. I have also many times heard it sayd, that though the company of a learned man bee good and profitable at all times, yet chiefly in the time of sicknesse, and when the weake creature is ready to depart from this wicked world, forasmuch as then Sathan is most busie and without ceasing laboureth to disquiet the conscience of the sicke man, that by this meanes he may drive him to desperation, and finally to damnation.[42]

The words of a learned man—not necessarily a pastor—that drew their inspiration from Scripture were essential to the pastoral care that Becon argues will truly console the sick and the suffering.

One finds a similar perspective in John Norden's *A Pensive Mans Practice*. (Norden was a lay cartographer.) As with Becon's *Sick Mans Salve*, this work is organized as a dialogue, here between "Hope" and the "Pensive Man." The latter encourages the former to bear his soul to him and to receive consolation through Scripture. At one point in the dialogue, the Pensive Man exclaims,

> I thanke my GOD, through whose gracious goodnesse my heart is greatly quieted, and my soule comforted: in mine extreme necessities I have received most sweet inward consolation, by my conference with him who is most ready to heare. And now I will wait through faith, which is the evidence of things not seene, for the performance of that which I desire of my God.[43]

---

[41]Thomas Becon, *Sick Mans Salve* (London: John Daye, 1572), EEBO, 33.

[42]Becon, *Sick Mans Salve*, 364.

[43]John Norden, *A Pensive Mans Practice. Or the Pensive Mans Complaint and Comfort* (London, 1623), EEBO, 192b.

A little later in the dialogue Hope provides a list of verses from the Bible with which the sick may console themselves or be consoled by others.[44]

I should pause to note that the prominence of lay people in these works is typical of much of the Protestant pastoral and devotional literature. The authors were well aware of the fact that there were not enough pastors to go around, and so it was necessary for lay people to learn how to console themselves and others. In Becon's *Sick Mans Salve*, a pastor is not even mentioned until the sick man passes away and there is need for someone to preach at his funeral. One reason that such works were so popular is that they were written for lay use. (In the case of the *Pensive Mans Practice*, a lay author writes for lay use.) This was true of Urbanus Rhegius's wildly popular *Soul Medicine* and also of Heinrich Bullinger's more modestly successful *Instruction of the Sick*.[45] Because of the Protestant confidence in the Word as the source of consolation, inviting lay people to engage in pastoral care as ministers of the Word made all the more sense.

Turning to Lutheran sources, we again see that Scripture is the main source of comfort in the evangelical pastoral and devotional literature.[46] The goal of this literature was to convey the Word to afflicted Christians. To cite but one example, the Königsberg preacher Johann Briesmann (1488–1549) states in *A Few Consoling Sayings for Despondent and Weak Consciences* (1525), "It is not possible to revive a disconsolate soul unless this happens through God's word and work."[47] Briesmann urged his readers to hide the Word in their heart so that they could draw on it

---

[44]Norden, *A Pensive Mans Practice*, 215a-b.

[45]See Rhegius, *Seelenärtzney*, in Gunter, *Huberinus—Rhegius—Holbein*, 243; Heinrich Bullinger, *Bericht der krancken* (Zurich: Froshauer, 1544), HAB H: S412.8 Helmst. (5), A iiii r; and Ian Green, "Varieties of Domestic Devotion in Early Modern English Protestantism," in *Private and Domestic Devotion in Early Modern Britain*, ed. Alec Ryrie and Jessica Martin (Farnham, Surrey, England: Ashgate, 2012), 28-29.

[46]The following two paragraphs draw on Rittgers, *Reformation of Suffering*, 150-51.

[47]Johann Briesmann, *Etliche trostspru[e]che fur die blo[e]den/ schwachen gewissen. Von anfechtung des glaubens vnd der hoffnung* (Wittenberg, 1525), HAB H: S149b Helmst. 8° (6), fol. Aii r.

again and again as they faced various trials and tribulations. As in other Lutheran works of devotion, only the Word could rescue suffering Christians from their distress.[48]

This image of the Word being pressed into the heart is a common one in the Lutheran pastoral and devotional literature. Pastors and theologians frequently interpreted suffering as the primary means by which God accomplished this feat. They believed that suffering drove Christians beyond their finite and fallen human abilities to understand and cope with affliction so that they looked beyond all human help, especially their own, and turned to God alone. The evangelical clergy believed that in such cases the Holy Spirit would inwardly apply the assurances of the Word to despondent Christians, helping to call forth faith in its promises, which would provide consolation and certainty. The experience of such deliverance from despair also enabled believers to treasure and understand the Word more fully. Scripture gave them hope in the midst of suffering, and suffering helped them to appreciate the true power and purpose of Scripture. As the Augsburg pastor Caspar Huberinus (1500–1553) explains in *Concerning the Wrath and Goodness of God*,

> God sends you a cross so that the Word of God may also be pressed into your heart and not always remain stuck to your tongue. [The cross] seasons for you His Holy Word so that it begins to taste good to you and thus comes into your heart. You can deal with it properly when you know how to bear and use it. It is not possible for someone to understand the Word of God properly and thus to know how to deal with it unless it has first been pressed into his heart by the cross and suffering. This noble treasure, the Holy Word of God, must always be used with earnestness, otherwise it soon rusts and becomes unappealing.[49]

Luther had argued much the same thing in his early Psalm lectures.[50]

An important Lutheran church order makes a similar argument. In its treatment of the clergy's ministry to the sick and dying, the 1540

---

[48]Briesmann, *Etliche trostpru[e]che fur die blo[e]den/ schwachen gewissen*, fol. Aii v.
[49]Huberinus, *Vom Zornn vnd der Gu[e]tte Gottes* (Augsburg, 1529), HAB M: Th. 1311., fol. Liiii r.
[50]WA 55/2: 55.20-22, 57.5-7; LW 10:49.

Brandenburg Church Ordinance included an elaborate discussion of how pastors should prepare their parishioners to deal with times of affliction. The main author of this church ordinance was Jacob Stratner (d. 1550), a court preacher in Berlin. Stratner provides an evangelical contribution to the late medieval *ars moriendi* literature that instructs pastors to remind the laity of the uncertainty of the hour of death and the ferocity of the adversary. Christians are to look to their spiritual well-being in times of health and calm so that they can be prepared for times of affliction and assault. This preparation consists of being outfitted with "spiritual weapons"—namely, the Word—and especially portions of Scripture that speak of the grace of Christ. Christians are to have such sayings in their hearts, ponder them often, and have recourse to them when faced with temptation and suffering. Believers are also to receive the Word in private confession and the Lord's Supper.[51]

The reference to spiritual weapons in this church ordinance is connected with another important image in the Lutheran pastoral and devotional literature that also illustrates the importance of the Word in Protestant pastoral care. Evangelical pastors and theologians frequently drew on the traditional image of the spiritual knight to express how important the Word was in the Christian life, especially in the midst of tribulation.[52] Lutheran consolers like Caspar Huberinus adopted and adapted the image of the knight from authors such as Erasmus and sought to stress with it the importance of disciplined self-preparation for spiritual battle.[53] As we have seen, Huberinus produced a work entitled *Concerning the Christian Knight*.[54] The General Superintendent of the County of

---

[51]Emil Sehling, ed., *Die evangelischen Kirchenordnungen des XVI Jahrhunderts*, 19 vols. (Leipzig: O.R. Riesland; Tübingen: J.C.B. Mohr (Paul Siebeck), 1902–1913, 1955–), 3:76a.

[52]The following three paragraphs draw on Rittgers, *Reformation of Suffering*, 193-94, 199-203.

[53]Arguably the most famous pre-Reformation work of devotion to employ the image of the knight was Erasmus of Rotterdam's *Enchiridion militis christiani*. It first appeared in 1503 and was first published in Germany in 1515.

[54]Caspar Huberinus, *Vom Christlichen Ritter* (Neuburg an der Donau, 1545), in *Caspar Huberinus, Works* (Zug, Switzerland: Interdocumentation Publications, 1983), Yale Divinity School Library, Fiche B3511.

Mansfeld, Johannes Spangenberg (1484–1550),[55] also utilized the image in his popular *On the Christian Knight* and again in *The Booklet of Comfort for the Sick*, which frequently appeared with *On the Christian Knight*. In *The Booklet of Comfort for the Sick*, Spangenberg advises readers to prepare themselves for death and suffering by seeking to "impress [*einbilden*] some comforting passages from Scripture and the gospel on your memory, passages to use against all temptations. Collect them as provisions [for the journey] and always carry them with you in your heart, just as a soldier carries his arrows in the quiver and has them ready to use whenever he needs them."[56] Spangenberg then proceeds to provide several such passages from Scripture. Scholars have characterized this emphasis on spiritual self-care via sustained meditation on the Word as one of the defining features of the Lutheran care of souls,[57] linking it with exhortations to physical self-care by medical doctors.[58] It should be noted, however, that one can find the same emphasis on spiritual self-care in other versions of Protestantism; we have already seen it in John Norden. In a sense, Protestant devotional literature urged lay people to become this-worldly saints who took over some of the functions of Catholic saints, especially regarding the care of oneself and others in times of suffering.

Of course, Lutherans rejected the cult of saints, arguing that it was unbiblical. They also rejected the miracles associated with the cult of the saints, maintaining that they were false miracles that promoted superstition. But Lutherans did not abandon the category of the miraculous altogether. Especially in their works of devotion they saw that the Word's

---

[55]On Spangenberg, see *A Booklet of Comfort for the Sick, & On the Christian Knight by Johann Spangenberg (1548)*, trans., ed., and introduced by Robert Kolb (Milwaukee: Marquette University Press, 2007), 9-33.

[56]Spangenberg, *A Booklet of Comfort for the Sick*, 60 (German), 61 (English).

[57]See Johann Anselm Steiger, "Die Gesichts- und Theologie-Vergessenheit der heutigen Seelsorgelehre. Anlaß für einen Rückblick in den Schatz reformatorischer und orthodoxer Seelsorgeliteratur," *Kerygma und Dogma* 39 (1993): 75-76.

[58]Johann Anselm Steiger, *Medizinische Theologie. Christus Medicus und Theologia Medicinalis bei Martin Luther und im Luthertum der Barockzeit* (Leiden: Brill, 2005), esp. 106.

ability to console was a true miracle. The Strasbourg theologian Johann Marbach makes this argument in his *On Miracles and Wondrous Signs* (1571),[59] as do other theologians. The Kassell superintendent Johannes Kymaeus argues in his *Passion Booklet* (1539) that while Christ does not work special signs and wonders for Christians, he does intervene miraculously via the Word to free them from doubt and angst regarding their standing before God, who saves them by grace alone.[60] Lutheran pastors and theologians believed that they did not need the kind of miracles attested in the New Testament, because they believed they had access to a greater miracle, consolation for the anxious conscience via the Word of God.[61]

In *The Consoling De Profundis* (1565), the Joachimsthal preacher Johannes Mathesius (1504–1565) relates a story that illustrates the Lutheran belief in the miraculous powers of the Word. Mathesius knew Luther well, having lived under his roof for a time while he studied at the University of Wittenberg in the early 1540s. He experienced firsthand the Reformer's tableside theological quips, publishing the earliest edition of his *Table Talk*; he also wrote the first sympathetic biography of Luther.[62] Mathesius's story is about a pregnant noblewoman who lay bedridden for several days with labor pains. Despite the efforts of those around to provide what assistance they could, the pains continued and yet the infant did not emerge. Everyone feared for the life of mother and child. Then one evening a simple young girl, a student, passed by the woman's house singing a verse from a song based on Psalm 130 (v. 6), completely unaware of the tragedy unfolding inside. She sang, "And even if it endures into the night and again to the next day, my heart shall certainly [wait

---

[59]See Johann Marbach, *Von Mirackeln vnd Wunderzeichen* . . . (s.l. 1571), HAB A: 456.1 Theol. (1), Liii v.

[60]See Johannes Kymaeus, *Passional* (Wittemberg, 1539), HAB H: C 313.2° Helmst. (2), fol. XXXII r.

[61]See Johannes Habermann, *Postilla* (Wittenberg, 1583), HAB S: Alv.: U 45 2°, fol. 272 v, right-hand column.

[62]On Mathesius, see Christopher Boyd Brown, *Singing the Gospel: Lutheran Hymns and the Success of the Reformation* (Cambridge, MA: Harvard University Press, 2005). Brown's book focuses on Joachimsthal and deals with Mathesius throughout.

upon the Lord]." The exhausted noblewoman took great comfort in these words and, according to Mathesius, gave birth to a son within the hour.[63] A simple verse from Scripture sung by a poor unsuspecting *Mädchen* had brought solace to the laboring woman's heart and body, quite literally delivering her of her burden, so great was the miraculous power of the Word.

THE SACRAMENTALITY OF THE WORD IN PROTESTANT PASTORAL AND DEVOTIONAL LITERATURE

The miraculous healing that the Word could effect is closely related, I believe, to the Protestant conviction about the sacramental nature of the Word, which I now need to demonstrate. As far as I know, no Reformation theologian ever explicitly said, "Scripture is a sacrament." Reformation theologians did say that the Holy Spirit inspired Scripture and also illumined human hearts and minds to understand Scripture. Perhaps this view suffices to explain the Scripture-laden sources I encountered in Germany. I have opted for the language of sacrament because I want to emphasize that Protestants viewed Scripture as a means of grace and not just as a source of divine truth, especially in the context of pastoral care. I also want to emphasize that Protestants believed this grace was mediated through a creaturely vehicle, the actual words of Scripture, whether read, sung, spoken, or heard. The finite words of the Bible were capable of bearing the infinite Word of God. The Word, in turn, could be trusted to console troubled hearts and, at least on occasion, to heal afflicted bodies for those who received it by faith. Thus, in the Protestant view of Scripture, I think we are dealing with an especially important evangelical version of sacrality, even enchantment.

As previously mentioned, many Protestants had a sacramental view of preaching—preaching was a means of grace and not simply a source of

---

[63]Johannes Mathesius, *Das tro[e]stliche De Profvndis, Welches ist der CXXX. Psalm Davids* (Nuremberg, 1567), HAB H: C 70b. 4° Helmst., fols. T v–Tii r.

divinely inspired information about God. This is certainly the case with Luther. Hughes Oliphant Old has referred to a doctrine of "kerygmatic real presence" in Luther's view of preaching.[64] Luther's tripartite understanding of the Word as the Word incarnate (Christ), the Word written (Scripture), and the Word proclaimed (preaching) already suggests that Christ is present in and through Scripture, whether preached publicly or proclaimed privately.[65]

As Brian Gerrish has argued, Calvin placed an equally strong emphasis on preaching as a means of grace;[66] preaching was the normal means through which God effected the salvation of the elect by grace.[67] Dawn DeVries has maintained that for Calvin there was an important parallel between Christ's presence in preaching and in the Lord's Supper.[68] In both cases, the Holy Spirit mediated the presence of Christ to the elect. God ruled the church via the Word, and God made use of human beings as his instruments through which to exercise this reign. Like Luther,[69] Calvin could speak of the preacher as a mouthpiece for God or as a tool or instrument used by God,[70] but he maintained that the Holy Spirit was the animating force behind the sacramental quality of evangelical

---

[64]Old, *The Reading and Preaching of the Scriptures*, 4:40-41. See also Fred W. Meuser, "Luther as Preacher of the Word of God," in *The Cambridge Companion to Martin Luther*, ed. Donald K. Kim (Cambridge: Cambridge University Press, 2003), 137; and Beth Kreitzer, "The Lutheran Sermon," in *Preachers and People in the Reformation and Early Modern Period*, ed. Larissa Taylor (Leiden: Brill, 2003), 41.

[65]See Kreitzer, "Lutheran Sermon," 41; O. C. Edwards Jr., *History of Preaching* (Nashville: Abingdon, 2004), 285; and Paul D. L. Avis, *The Church in the Theology of the Reformers* (Atlanta: John Knox, 1981), 82.

[66]Gerrish, *Grace and Gratitude*, 82-86.

[67]See Dawn DeVries, "Calvin's Preaching," in *The Cambridge Companion to John Calvin*, ed. Donald K. McKim (Cambridge: Cambridge University Press, 2004), 109.

[68]DeVries, "Calvin's Preaching," 109. The same parallel existed for Luther, although the two Reformers conceived of Christ's eucharistic presence differently.

[69]See Ronald K. Rittgers, "The Word-Prophet Martin Luther," *The Sixteenth-Century Journal: The Journal of Early Modern Studies* 48, no. 4 (2017 [2018]): 951-76. On the relationship of the Holy Spirit and the Word in Luther's theology, see Paul Althaus, *The Theology of Martin Luther*, trans. Robert C. Schultz (Philadelphia: Fortress, 1966), 35-42; and Jeffrey G. Silcock, "Luther on the Holy Spirit and His Use of God's Word," in *The Oxford Handbook of Martin Luther's Theology*, ed. Robert Kolb, Irene Dingel, and Ľubomír Batka (Oxford: Oxford University Press, 2014), 294-309.

[70]Calvin, *Institutes* 4.3.1. See also Manetsch, *Calvin's Company of Pastors*, 159.

preaching. Preaching has in fact been referred to as a "third sacrament" in Reformed Protestant circles.[71]

My argument is that the sacramental view of Scripture that one finds in magisterial Protestant understandings of the proclaimed Word had a correlate in the Protestant conviction that the Word could also mediate grace in printed works of pastoral care and devotion, including those with very little human commentary.[72] Wherever it was found, Scripture was a Spirit-inspired and Spirit-enabled means of grace for those who had faith, especially for those who suffered in body or soul. God did not simply inform the afflicted of His will in Scripture; God also poured out divine grace to them through Scripture. God was present to them via the Word.

Lutherans and Reformed Protestants also used traditional language associated with the sacraments in their treatments of pastoral care, and this too lends support to the thesis I am advancing about the sacramental nature of Scripture in evangelical and pastoral and devotional literature. Both groups referred to pastors as doctors of souls, a designation that goes back to the early church but which arguably found its most important usage in canon 21 of the Fourth Lateran Council.[73] This canon required annual private confession and provided instructions to priests about how they should act as "a skilled doctor" who seeks to "heal the sick person" through wise counsel, fitting penances, and sacramental absolution.[74] Calvin could refer to preaching as applying "medicine to the patients."[75] The aforementioned Brandenburg Church Ordinance

---

[71]See Pamela Biel, *Doorkeepers at the House of Righteousness: Heinrich Bullinger and the Zurich Clergy, 1535–1575* (Bern, Switzerland: Verlag Peter Lang, 1991), 72.

[72]It is more difficult to find a doctrine of kerygmatic real presence among Anabaptists. See Cornelius J. Dyck, "The Role of Preaching in Anabaptist Tradition," *Mennonite Life* 17, no. 1 (1962): 23.

[73]See Anne T. Thayer, "Judge and Doctor: Images of the Confessor in Printed Model Sermon Collections, 1450–1520," in *Penitence in the Age of Reformations*, ed. Katharine Jackson Lualdi and Anne T. Thayer (Aldershot, England: Ashgate, 2000), 10-29.

[74]See Norman P. Tanner, S. J., ed., *Decrees of the Ecumenical Councils* (Washington, DC: Georgetown University Press, 1990), 1:245.

[75]Manetsch, *Calvin's Company of Pastors*, 168.

exhorted evangelical pastors to immerse themselves in the Scriptures so they could be like "an understanding doctor" who knows how to apply the appropriate medicine to the appropriate wound.[76] An important part of the overall Protestant agenda was to reform and expand pastoral care, which had been focused especially on sacramental confession in the later Middle Ages. We should not be surprised, therefore, when we find Protestants using similar images for the evangelical version of the *cura animarum*. Protestant pastors effectively took on the role of priestly confessors envisioned in canon 21 of the Fourth Lateran Council. In both their sermons and devotional works, they sought to mediate divine grace to their contemporaries via the sacramental Word.[77]

Protestants could also insist that the character of the preacher does not affect the efficacy of the grace that he was offering to his hearers through the preached Word.[78] This was of course a Protestant revision of the ancient Christian teaching that the moral worthiness of the celebrant does not affect the efficacy of the Eucharist. The Word would convey its grace irrespective of the preacher's or the pastor's—or the lay consoler's—moral condition. Again, I wish to extend this view of the Word to printed pastoral and devotional literature.

CONCLUSION

Even as Protestant reformers took away numerous traditional means of accessing the divine, they provided new portals to God and his grace—or rather, they provided new portals through which God could bestow his grace—in the form of Scripture-laden pastoral and devotional works (and also through preaching, new translations of the Bible, and other printed works such as hymnals). These portals could be found throughout

---

[76]Sehling, *Die evangelischen Kirchenordnungen des XVI Jahrhunderts*, 3:77a. See also ibid., 1/II: 18b.
[77]Cf. Rittgers, *Reformation of Suffering*, 175; and Rittgers, "Age of Reform as an Age of Consolation," 630. Lutherans also applied the sacramental Word to troubled souls in a Reformed version of private confession. See Ronald K. Rittgers, *The Reformation of the Keys: Confession, Conscience, and Authority in Sixteenth-Century Germany* (Cambridge, MA: Harvard University Press, 2004).
[78]Avis, *The Church in the Theology of the Reformers*, 92-94.

Protestant Europe in unprecedented quantities. To be sure, these new portals constituted a very different kind of sacrality than was present in traditional Christianity. For one thing, they required the presence of literate persons who could access this grace for themselves or who could mediate it to their illiterate neighbors who could then receive it into their hearts through what Luther once called the most important organs of the Christian, the ears.[79] Thus, Protestants contributed to disenchantment in important ways while simultaneously introducing a new and equally important form of sacrality via their emphasis on the sacramental Word in pastoral and devotional literature (and elsewhere). It is important to take stock of what Protestants both removed and supplied if we are to have a balanced and accurate understanding of how the Reformation and its pastoral care are related to the disenchantment of the West. Protestantism simultaneously contributed to the disenchantment and the re-enchantment of the West.

---

[79]WA 57/3:222.5-9; LW 29:224.

PART THREE

JUSTIFICATION
and the REFORMATION

Chapter Five

NOVUM or *RURSUS*?

JUSTIFICATION *and the* BIBLE
in the REFORMATION

MICHAEL S. HORTON

THIS CHAPTER EXPLORES THE QUESTION OF justification and the Bible at the time of the Reformation. It has long been observed that the Latin Vulgate rendered the verb *dikaioō* (δικαιόω) "to *make* righteous" rather than "to *declare* righteous" and that this mistake was recognized by Erasmus in his *Novum Instrumentum*. This played no small role in the Reformation. Nevertheless, in this essay I challenge the conclusion that Luther's "breakthrough" was a new discovery (*novum*) and attempt to place it in the context of patristic exegesis. Finally, I point out the striking similarities in the exegesis of the Reformers' opponents and the new perspective on Paul, particularly with respect to the meaning of "works of the law."

In examining the earliest commentaries on Paul's epistles for a recent project, I encountered a few surprises. Wary of historical anachronism, I did not want to use the sources as a ventriloquist might, forcing them to say whatever I prefer. There is no greater dishonor to our long-deceased brothers and sisters than to make them teach things that they did not teach, even though they might teach them better now.

So I braced myself for the disappointment that I had experienced before with the patristic sources: namely, that they were immune to my machinations. I knew that there was no monolithic approach, either for or against a doctrine that would be developed a millennium later. My own doctoral supervisor, Alister McGrath, had cautioned against seeing Luther's discovery as anything less than a *novum* in the history of theology.[1]

The surprises arrived at just these very points. First, while Augustine turned out to stand more or less where he always had (viz., part of the disease as well as the cure), I discovered more continuity between a number of early Greek fathers of a more putatively synergistic bent and the Reformation doctrine than I suspected.

Patristic Trajectories in Exegesis of the "Justification" Passages

My main focus will be on the first two commentaries written on Paul's letter to the Romans, that is Origen's and Chrysostom's. However, it is important to observe at the outset that justification was an important theme already in the first century, often treated under the broader rubric of the "marvelous exchange." Already in pre-Christian Judaism there are intimations, as the Qumran community declares, "Surely justification is of God" (1QS 11:9-15).

> If I stumble, God's loving-kindness forever shall save me. If through sin of the flesh I fall, my justification will be by the righteousness of God which endures for all time. Through his love he has brought me near, by his loving-kindness shall he provide my justification . . . and through His exceeding goodness shall he atone for all my sins. By his righteousness shall he cleanse me of human defilement.[2]

Among the earliest post-apostolic Christian writing, the Odes of Solomon speak of being united to the Beloved (Christ) and clothed with a

---

[1]A. E. McGrath, *Iustitia Dei: The History of the Doctrine of Justification*, 3rd ed. (Cambridge: Cambridge University Press, 2005), 188-206.
[2]Michael Wise, Martin Abegg Jr., and Edward Cook, trans., *A New Translation of the Dead Sea Scrolls* (New York: HarperOne, 2005).

garment of righteousness. "For who shall put on Your grace and be rejected?"[3] Besides a robe, we are invited to "put on the wreathed-crown in the true covenant of the Lord," which is "the justification which is for you."[4] "And I was justified by my Lord, for my salvation is incorruptible. . . . And I am not condemned."[5] "And according to His mercy He raised me up . . . He justified me by his grace, for I believed in the Lord's Messiah."[6] "Grace is for the elect ones. And who will receive it, but they who trusted in it from the beginning?"[7] "And I became mighty in Your truth and holy in Your righteousness. . . . And I was justified by His kindness, and His rest is for ever and ever."[8] "Hearken unto Me and be saved, for I am proclaiming unto you the grace of God. And through Me you will be saved and become blessed. I am your judge. And they who have put Me on will not be rejected, but they will possess incorruption in the new world. My elect ones have walked with Me. And I shall promise them My name."[9] In short, "Grace has been revealed for your salvation. Believe, and live, and be saved. Hallelujah."[10] The congregation cries out to Christ, "May we also be saved with You, because You are our Savior," to which Christ replies, "Then I heard their voice and placed their faith in My heart. And I placed My name upon their head, because they are free and they are mine."[11]

In what is apparently the earliest reference to the "marvelous exchange," the Epistle to Diognetus praises God the Father for sending his Son,

---

[3]"God's Sanctuary," in *The Earliest Christian Hymnbook: The Odes of Solomon*, trans. James H. Charlesworth (Eugene, OR: Wipf & Stock, 2009), 7. Hereafter *Odes*. Scholars date the *Odes* variously to the first three centuries of the Christian era.

[4]"The Wreathed-Crown of the True Covenant," in *Odes*, 25.

[5]"My Wreathed-Crown Is Living," in *Odes*, 49.

[6]"The Lord Is My Hope," in *Odes*, 87.

[7]"Joy Is for the Elect Ones," in *Odes*, 67.

[8]"My Helper," in *Odes*, 76.

[9]"The Perfect Virgin Is Judge," in *Odes*, 98. The Virgin here is Wisdom, "Who was preaching and summoning" (97).

[10]"The Simple Heart," in *Odes*, 100.

[11]"The Righteous One Our Savior," in *Odes*, 123.

the holy one for the lawless, the guiltless for the guilty, the just for the unjust . . . *For what else but his righteousness could have covered our sins?* In whom was it possible for us, *the lawless and ungodly,* to be *justified,* except *in the Son of God alone?* O sweet exchange, O the incomprehensible work of God, O the unexpected blessings, that *the sinfulness of many should be hidden in one righteous person,* while *the righteousness of one should justify many sinners!*[12]

With the great second-century bishop Irenaeus we have a more fully developed soteriology in which Christ recapitulates all that was lost in Adam and fulfills the trial that leads all who are united to him into everlasting glory. Given this emphasis on recapitulation (reheadship-ing), it is not surprising that Irenaeus underscores Christ's fulfillment of the law in his life and cancellation of our debts in his passion and that in his resurrection he becomes the source of justification and glorification for his new humanity.[13] Similarly, the third-century bishop Cyprian counsels, since "we neither please God with good deeds nor atone for our sins . . . [l]et us of our inmost heart and of our entire mind ask for God's mercy."[14] He adds, "Believe and live," for "[t]he approach to God's mercy is open, and the access is easy to those who seek and apprehend the truth."

This grace Christ bestows; this gift of his mercy he confers upon us, by overcoming death in the trophy of the cross, by redeeming the believer with the price of His blood, by reconciling man to God the Father, by quickening our mortal nature with a heavenly regeneration. If it be possible, let us all follow him; let us be registered in his sacrament and sign. He opens to us the way of life; he brings us back to paradise; he leads us on to the kingdom of heaven. [We are] made by him the children of God, [therefore] we shall ever live with Him rejoicing.[15]

---

[12]The Epistle to Diognetus, ch. 9 (ANF 1: 28), emphasis added. Scholars date this epistle from AD 125 to the late second century.

[13]Irenaeus, *Against Heresies* 3.18.7; 5.16.3; 5.9.3 (ANF 1:448, 1:544, 1:535).

[14]Cyprian, Epistle 7.2 (ANF 1:286).

[15]Cyprian, Epistle 7.2 (ANF 1:286).

At least with respect to these early theologians, I am convinced that modern contrasts between the Christian East and West are greatly exaggerated. A deeper divide emerges between Irenaeus and Origen of Alexandria. Due in part to different contexts and locations, these ancient writers represent two distinct trajectories that weave in and out of each other in church history. I have documented elsewhere their approaches to key points relative to our topic.[16] For our purposes, it is sufficient to point out that while Origen opposed the Gnostics, he was profoundly shaped by the Alexandrian milieu that gave rise to Philo's Middle Platonism, Neoplatonism (Origen was a pupil of Ammonius Saccas, Plotinus's master), and Gnosticism. This broader worldview presupposed an exit-return cosmology, with spiritual beings cascading down the ladder from the One to the lowest rungs of earthly matter. Origen's tripartite anthropology governs his entire theology, from the three levels of biblical interpretation to his soteriology and eschatology. Especially in his controversy with the Gnostics, Irenaeus stresses the believer's redemption *with* creation and history, not *from* it. Furthermore, while the thrust of Origen's Christian Neoplatonism is the contemplative and moral ascent of the soul, Irenaeus focuses on the deliverance of sinners through the incarnation, life, death, resurrection, and bodily ascent of Christ as our representative head. The contrast with Irenaeus's *Against Heresies* is most evident in Origen's *On First Principles,* but a few points are worth noting concerning Origen's commentary on Romans, the first of its kind.

I examine Origen's Romans commentary at considerable length in a forthcoming work.[17] A few important points may be mentioned here. What especially stands out is the tension between Origen the first-class exegete who recognizes the revolutionary force of Paul's

---

[16]Michael Horton, "Atonement and Ascension," in *Locating Atonement: Explorations in Constructive Dogmatics*, ed. Oliver Crisp and Fred Sanders (Grand Rapids: Zondervan Academic, 2015), 226-50.

[17]Michael Horton, *Justification*, 2 vols. New Studies in Dogmatics (Grand Rapids: Zondervan Academic, 2018), chapters 1–3.

arguments and Origen the theologian who is keen to explain away the more controversial parts, especially with regard to God's grace in election and justification. For Origen, justification is being "made just through the indwelling Christ, who is justice."[18] "Thus," Thomas Scheck observes, "because Origen conceives justification to be an effective sanctification in which sin is expelled and grace is established in the believer's soul, it cannot be attributed to faith alone."[19] "On the other hand, there are striking statements in Origen's *Commentary* where Origen insists that justification is by faith alone."[20] His overwhelming concern is to discourage indifference toward good works. "For the gift of forgiveness is not a license to sin, since forgiveness applies to past sins, not future ones."[21] For him, the Pauline phrase "works of the law" refers to boundary markers.[22] In contrast with the merely "saved," he conjectures that "those who are saved through 'the election of grace' are shown to have more perfect souls." They have added "works of virtue" to "the gift of grace."[23] When Paul adds, "But if grace, it is no longer on the basis of works," Origen again pushes back: *works* means the ceremonies separating Jews from Gentiles (circumcision and food laws), not works in general. "These, then, and works of this nature are the ones on the basis of which he says no one can be saved."[24]

Origen also launched the first argument in favor of purgatory and different levels of being based on merits—views that were rejected in the Christian East and West until the high Middle Ages. The Reformers (especially Peter Martyr Vermigli and John Calvin)

---

[18]Thomas P. Scheck, "Introduction to Origen," in *Commentary on the Epistle to the Romans, Books 1–5*, trans. Thomas Scheck (Washington, DC: Catholic University of America Press, 2001), 26.

[19]Scheck, "Introduction to Origen," 37.

[20]Scheck, "Introduction to Origen," 39.

[21]Scheck, "Introduction to Origen," 41.

[22]Scheck, "Introduction to Origen," 41-42.

[23]Origen, *Commentary on the Epistle to the Romans*, 158.

[24]Origen, *Commentary on the Epistle to the Romans*, 159.

appealed to Irenaeus frequently, while they were sharply critical of Origen as the source of many of the interpretive missteps of later medieval theology.[25]

A half century after Origen, John Chrysostom, patriarch of Constantinople, preached a series of homilies on Romans. Origen had stressed that justification—the initial infusion of grace—had sufficed to wipe away the guilt and corruption of sins committed to that point, but after this a strict regimen of penance was required. By contrast, Chrysostom says,

> For it was not as much as we must have to do away the sin only, that we received of His grace, but even far more. For we were at once freed from punishment and put off all iniquity and were also born again from above (John 3:3) and [we] rose again with the old man buried, and were redeemed, justified, led up to adoption, sanctified, made brothers of the Only-begotten, and joint heirs and of the one Body with Him, and counted for His Flesh, and even as a Body with the Head, so were we united unto Him![26]

Chrysostom even distinguishes justification and sanctification here. Elsewhere he rhapsodizes on the great exchange: a grace that

> has allowed Him that did no wrong to be punished for those who had done wrong . . . Him that was righteousness itself, "He made sin," that is allowed Him to be condemned as a sinner, as one cursed to die . . . so that we also might become not just "righteous," but "righteousness," indeed "the righteousness of God." For this is the righteousness of God, when we are justified not by works, in which case it would be necessary that not even a spot should be found, but by grace, in which case all sin is done away. And this, at the time that it does not allow us to be lifted up (for it is entirely the free gift of God), teaches us also the greatness of what is given. For what came

---

[25]Scheck observes, "In the *Commentary* Origen uses the expression, or an approximation of the expression, 'justification by faith alone,' on numerous occasions, both approvingly and disapprovingly. These passages were hotly disputed during the age of the Reformation. The magisterial Protestants (Luther, Melanchthon, Calvin, Beza) cited the texts in which Origen repudiated the 'formula' of 'justification by faith alone' to show that Origen was no true Christian but a Pelagian or even a pagan." "Introduction to Origen," 33.

[26]Chrysostom, *The Epistle to the Romans*, in NPNF, vol. 11, *Saint Chrysostom* (repr., Edinburgh: T&T Clark, 1989), 403.

before was a righteousness of the law and of works, but his is the righteousness of God.[27]

As early as his comments on Romans 1:17, Chrysostom says that justification is a "righteousness not thine own, but that of God . . . For you do not achieve it by toilings and labors, but you receive it by a gift from above, contributing one thing only from your own store, 'believing.'"[28] The apostle's whole argument in Romans 1–3 is to lay all people low that "they might with much earnestness run unto Him who offered them the remission of their sins, and accept grace through faith."[29] The "declaring of His righteousness" is not only a manifestation of the righteousness that belongs to God "but that He doth also make them that are filled with putrefying sores of sin *suddenly righteous*. . . . Doubt not then: for it is *not of works, but of faith*; and shun not the righteousness of God, for it is a blessing in two ways: because it is easy and also open to all men."[30] He adds that Paul returns in Romans 3:27 yet again to the contrast between the law and the gospel. "For since all were convicted, He therefore saves by grace." The apostle has carefully and patiently built up his argument to this conclusion, "that it was not possible to be saved by the Law and by our own labors and well-doings . . . so that after they were by every argument clearly convinced of inability to help themselves, He then saved them by His grace."[31]

In contrast with Origen's reduction of Paul's "works of the law" to boundary markers, Chrysostom understands law/works as encompassing all human efforts to attain salvation apart from grace: "our own labors and well-doings," as he says above.

---

[27]Chrysostom, *Homilies on 2 Corinthians* 11.5, cited in Nick Needham, "Justification in the Early Church Fathers," in *Justification in Perspective: Historical Developments and Contemporary Challenges,* ed. Bruce McCormack (Grand Rapids: Baker Academic, 2006), 35.

[28]Chrysostom, *The Epistle to the Romans,* 349.

[29]Chrysostom, *The Epistle to the Romans,* 376.

[30]Chrysostom, *The Epistle to the Romans,* 378, emphasis added.

[31]Chrysostom, *The Epistle to the Romans,* 378.

> But what is the "law of faith"? It is being saved by grace. Here he shows God's power, in that He has not only saved, but has even justified and led them to boasting, and this too without needing works, but looking for faith only. . . . Do you see how great faith's preeminence is? How it has removed us from the former things, not even allowing us to boast of them?[32]

Paul is no longer speaking of Jews and Gentiles, but of everyone.[33] "For when a man is once a believer, he is straightaway justified." Chrysostom adds, "since after this grace whereby we are justified there is need also of a life suited to it."[34] Notice the logical priority: justification by grace through faith, apart from works, with works as the fruit.

Chrysostom connects Paul's argument thus far with chapter 4:

> He had said that the world had become guilty before God and that all had sinned, and that boasting was excluded, and that it was impossible to be saved otherwise than by faith. He is now intent upon showing that this salvation, so far from being a matter of shame, was even the cause of a bright glory and a greater than that through works. . . . For a person [Abraham] who had no works, to be justified by faith was nothing unlikely. But for a person richly adorned with good deeds *not* to be made just from them but from faith, this is the thing to cause wonder, and to set the power of faith in a strong light.[35]

Here the apostle "pitches the battle for faith against works. . . . For there are two 'gloryings,' one of works and one of faith. . . . For he that glories in his works has his own labors to put forward, but he that finds his honor in having faith in God has a much greater ground for glorying to show in that it is God that he glorifies and magnifies."[36]

Chrysostom even distinguishes between justification and sanctification.[37] Chrysostom emphasizes this point that "grace alone through faith alone" is the basis not only for the beginning but for the continuation of salvation. "For it was not only that we might have simple remission of

---

[32]Chrysostom, *The Epistle to the Romans*, 379.
[33]Chrysostom, *The Epistle to the Romans*, 379.
[34]Chrysostom, *The Epistle to the Romans*, 380.
[35]Chrysostom, *The Epistle to the Romans*, 385.
[36]Chrysostom, *The Epistle to the Romans*, 386.
[37]Chrysostom, *The Epistle to the Romans*, 395.

sins that we were reconciled; but that we might receive also countless benefits. . . . For this is the nature of God's grace. It has no end, it knows no bound, but evermore is on the advancement to greater things, which in human things is not the case."[38] This is why we can glory even in our tribulations because God is using them to work out his saving purposes toward us.[39] "For there is no one else that will save us, except He who so loved us when we were sinners, as even to give Himself up for us. Do you see what a ground this topic affords for hope?" That God is *willing* can hardly be in dispute, since he gave up his Son. But he is also *able* to save, "from the very fact of His having justified men who were sinners. What is there then to prevent us anymore from obtaining the things to come? Nothing!"[40]

The unabashed emphasis on assuring believers of the surpassing greatness of God's grace in Christ contrasts with Origen's repeated interjections and disclaimers. Rather than make final justification conditional on works, Chrysostom teaches, "For the righteousness of the Law, that one should not become liable to its curse, *Christ has accomplished for you*."[41] Throughout, Chrysostom is stirred by Paul's emphasis on the "superabundance of grace." If he "'spared not His own Son' for you, and elected you, and justified you, why be afraid anymore?"[42]

Augustine wrestled with Paul's letter to the Romans, never completing his commentary on it. This turns out to be a happy providence because only two years later the great bishop of Hippo shuddered in horror to think that he had written so erroneously about justification and grace. With his anti-Pelagian period (from about 396), the mature Augustine became the great defender of God's unconditional grace in election and justification. Ironically, however, while he is more "monergistic" than Chrysostom (especially in affirming unconditional election), Augustine

---

[38]Chrysostom, *The Epistle to the Romans*, 396.
[39]Chrysostom, *The Epistle to the Romans*, 396-97.
[40]Chrysostom, *The Epistle to the Romans*, 398-99.
[41]Chrysostom, *The Epistle to the Romans*, 433, emphasis added.
[42]Chrysostom, *The Epistle to the Romans*, 455.

is less convinced that justification is a declaration "all at once" (as Chrysostom says) that a sinner is righteous for the sake of Christ. Instead, along with Jerome, he introduces the idea that justification is a process of becoming righteous and that faith is completed by love in this process.[43]

The Pauline Renaissance

The fourteenth century saw a sharp confrontation between Augustinians and Semi-Pelagians who were associated especially with the Nominalist School. In his treatise *Against the New Pelagians* (1344), Thomas Bradwardine, the fourteenth-century archbishop of Canterbury, sounded the alarm that medieval theology had veered from sound teaching. Another representative of the *via Augustini moderna*, Gregory of Rimini (ca. 1300–1358), spent his labors against Semi-Pelagian Nominalism.[44] Johann von Staupitz (ca. 1460–1524), vicar general of the Augustinian order in Germany, wrote moving treatises on predestination, grace, and justification.[45] Luther considered Gregory a major forerunner, and although he regarded Staupitz as the one who set him on his path, his mentor did not embrace the Reformation. But we can regard these figures as "forerunners of the Reformation" only in a qualified sense. While they were staunch advocates of the priority of grace and the centrality and sufficiency of Christ, and while they emphasized the role of faith in receiving Christ with all of his benefits, they regarded justification as a process of conversion from sinner to saint. In other words, they were Augustinians.

---

[43]The best (and most recent) work on Augustine's doctrine of justification is Jairzinho Lopes Pereira, *Augustine of Hippo and Martin Luther on Original Sin and the Justification of the Sinner* (Gottingen: Vandenhoek & Ruprecht, 2013). See also Friedrich Loofs, *Leitfaden zum Studium der Dogmengeschichte*, 4th ed. (Halle, 1906); John Burnaby, *Amor Dei* (London: Hodder & Stoughton, 1938); B. B. Warfield, "Introductory Essay on Augustine and the Pelagian Controversy," in *Nicene and Post-Nicene Fathers: First Series, Volume 5. St. Augustine: Anti-Pelagian Writings* (1887), ed. Philip Schaff, ii-xxi; David F. Wright, "Augustine and Justification by Faith," in *Justification in Perspective*, 50-60; and McGrath, *Iustitia Dei*, 1:1-24.

[44]See James L. Halverson, *Peter Aureol on Predestination: A Challenge to Late Medieval Thought* (Leiden: Brill, 1998).

[45]Johann von Staupitz, "The Eternal Predestination of God," in *Forerunners of the Reformation: The Shape of Late Medieval Thought*, ed. Heiko A. Oberman (Philadelphia: Fortress, 1966), 151-64.

The resurgence of Augustinianism was not limited to the north. There were similar circles in Italy, especially among Benedictine monasteries. The movement grew out of a fascination with biblical and patristic scholarship and attracted some of the best and brightest young minds of Italy. About the same time that Luther was preparing his Ninety-Five Theses and had not himself come to his mature understanding of justification, a network of monks associated mainly with the Benedictine Order in Italy were delving into the New Testament, especially Paul, as well as the church fathers. While some were drawn especially to Bernard of Clairvaux (as Luther and Calvin were as well), this Pauline renaissance focused especially on the writings and sermons of John Chrysostom, whom Calvin would identify as his favorite patristic commentator.

Some were members of the so-called *spirituali,* evangelically minded reformers who would become sympathetic to the concerns of the Protestant reformers. Tracing the movement in detail, Barry Collett unearths a distinct kind of piety and theology that emphasized the "benefits of Christ" and salvation by grace alone through faith alone.[46]

This circle included Cardinal Gasparo Contarini (1483–1542), who in 1536 was commissioned by Pope Paul III to head a committee for church reform. The result was his *Consilium de Emendanda Ecclesia,* which nevertheless fell on deaf ears when Paul III was succeeded by Pope Paul IV, who even placed the work on the *Index Librorum Prohibitorum* in 1539. Contarini continued his labors at the Colloquy of Regensburg in 1541, attended by Luther, Bucer, Melanchthon, and briefly by Calvin, but his concessions (especially on justification through faith alone) made him suspect thereafter. Another important member of the *spirituali* was Peter Martyr Vermigli (1499–1562), abbot of several monasteries, chapter general of the Lateran Congregation, and prior of the basilica in Lucca. The pope's fear that Lucca, an independent republic, would embrace the Reformation provoked the institution of the Inquisition in

---

[46]See Barry Collett, *Italian Benedictine Scholars and the Reformation: The Congregation of Santa Guistinia of Padua,* Oxford Historical Monographs (Oxford: Clarendon Press, 1985).

1542. In Lucca, Vermigli founded a college where Hebrew and Greek as well as Latin were taught and its most prestigious professors—Immanuel Tremellius, Paolo Cacizi, Celio Secundo Curione, and Girolamo Zanchi—all eventually became Reformed Protestants. Bernardino Ochino, vicar general of the Capuchins, had embraced the Reformation and fled the approaching Inquisition for Geneva after being warned off by Cardinal Contarini as he himself lay dying.[47] A few days later, Vermigli fled for Strasbourg and later to England with Bucer. However, the majority of these Benedictine monks, though sympathetic to the Reformation, did not embrace its distinctive doctrines and remained loyal to the Roman Church. As Collett observes: "For them the split in Latin Christendom was the product of Latin theology, and they held the remedy—taken from the Greek Fathers—in their hands."[48] The greatest product of this movement was the *Beneficio di Christo* by Benedetto da Mantova, published in Venice in 1543. At first hailed even by some leading churchmen, the book was suspected of "Lutheran heresy," was burned in Naples, and placed on the *Index*.[49] Entire sections of Calvin's 1536 *Institutes* were incorporated into the text, perhaps as additions by his friend and humanist poet, Marcantonio Flamino. The content reveals the influence also of the Spanish humanist and biblical scholar Juan de Valdés. The tract argues that only by the imputation of Christ's righteousness can we be justified.[50]

---

[47]Collett notes, "The year 1542 was a time of crisis for Italian evangelicals. The flight of Ochino, followed a few days later by that of Peter Martyr, was a sign of the dilemma being forced upon them. The work of reconciliation was no longer a virtue, and began to carry the smell of treachery: Contarini told Ochino that even he believed himself to be in danger because he had not opposed the Protestants strongly enough on the article of justification" (*Italian Benedictine Scholars*, 153). Ochino fled over the Alps to Geneva, then to Augsburg, and on to Canterbury under the protection of Edward VI. After the accession of Mary, he fled to Zurich, where he was made a pastor of the Italian congregation but was expelled for controversial views on the Trinity. He lived out the rest of his life in Poland, under suspicion from Protestants as a freethinker.

[48]Collett, *Italian Benedictine Scholars*, 154.

[49]Collett, *Italian Benedictine Scholars*, 157.

[50]Benedetto da Mantova, *Il Beneficio di Christo: con le version del secolo xvi, documenti e testimonianze*, ed. S. Caponetto, Corpus Reformatorum Italicorum (Dekalb: Northern Illinois University Press and The Newberry Library, 1972), 38, lines 281-89 and 467, lines 513-20, quoted in Collett, *Italian Benedictine Scholars*, 176.

THE REFORMERS AND THE NEW PERSPECTIVE ON PAUL

Few texts have been pored over with such interest and erudition as Paul's epistles. The Reformation cannot be reduced to a rediscovery of Paul; the Reformers were expositors of the whole Bible and found the doctrine of justification anchored in passages from Genesis to Revelation. Nevertheless, Paul's letters stand out as having an obvious primacy in the debates. What is noteworthy from the survey thus far is the relatively limited scope of possible interpretations that can be derived from these texts. In particular, we see that many of the perspectives on Paul that today are considered "new" are in fact to be found among ancient commentators, especially Origen. There are many points at which I find striking similarities between Origen and the interpretations of Sanders and other new perspective scholars. Here I will conclude merely by identifying one key similarity: the reduction of "works of the law" to boundary markers.[51]

In his Romans commentary, Peter Abelard (ca. 1079–1142) continued Origen's approach. Notice the prevaricating moves in his comment on Romans 3:20:

> *Because by the works of the law,* that is, its bodily observances . . . , for example, circumcision, sacrifices, the observance of the Sabbath and the other figural commandments of this kind, *no one,* that is, no one who fulfills those things carnally only, and not spiritually, *shall be justified in his sight* . . . that is, those figurative commandments that the natural law does not know. But *now,* that is, in the time of grace, *the righteousness of God,* that is, what God approves and through which we are justified with God, that is, charity, *is made manifest,* namely through the teaching of the Gospels, *without the law,* that is, those carnal and particular observances of the law.[52]

---

[51]See, for example, the defense of the view by James D. G. Dunn, "The New Perspective on Paul: Whence, What, and Whither?" in James D. G. Dunn, *The New Perspective on Paul: Collected Essays* (Grand Rapids: Eerdmans, 2005), 22-26.

[52]Peter Abelard, *Commentary on the Epistle to the Romans*, in *The Fathers of the Church: Mediaeval Continuation*, trans. Steven R. Cartwright (Washington, DC: Catholic University of America Press, 2011), 12:161, emphasis added.

It is love—charity, "not external works"—that justifies.[53] At Romans 3:25
he comments,

> *To demonstrate his righteousness,* that is, his charity which, as was said, justifies
> us with him, that is, to show us his love or to teach us how much we ought to
> love him. . . . *In the forebearance of God* [Rom 3:26], that is, on account of the
> patience of God, who does not immediately punish the guilty and destroy
> sinners but waits long that they may return through penance and cease from
> sin, and thus they may obtain leniency.[54]

Throughout Abelard's *Commentary* we encounter the familiar interpretation of "the works of the law." In effect, the law by which we are
not justified is the external ceremonial commands, while the law by
which we *are* justified is the inward and spiritual command to love.
It was just such interpretations—as much qualified rebuttals as
commentary—that came to dominate late medieval theology on the
eve of the Reformation.

Peter Martyr Vermigli writes, "First, they acknowledge that as often
as the Holy Scriptures take away the power of justifying from works,
they do so only with regard to the ceremonies of the old law and not
with regard to just and upright works, which they commonly call moral
works." It is true, of course, that Paul "says many things that seem to
refer both to the rites and the ceremonies of the law, yet in his other
discussions he wrote a great deal where he speaks not only of ceremonies, but also of the other laws of righteousness and uprightness.
Indeed, to sum up, these things pertain to conduct as well as to the
Decalogue."[55] Vermigli confirms this point by a cursory inventory
chapter by chapter. In the beginning of Romans, Paul "sets their [the
Gentiles'] works in front of their eyes, namely idolatry and shameful
lusts. Toward the end of the chapter he reviews a very long catalogue

---

[53] Abelard, *Commentary on the Epistle to the Romans,* 12:162.

[54] Abelard, *Commentary on the Epistle to the Romans,* 12:163, emphasis added.

[55] Peter Martyr Vermigli, "Locus on Justification," in Frank A. James III, introduction to *Peter
Martyr Vermigli: Predestination and Justification,* The Peter Martyr Library 8, trans. and ed. Frank
A. James III (Kirksville, MO: Sixteenth Century Essays & Studies, 2003), 115.

of vices with which they were afflicted, but says nothing about the ceremonies of Moses."[56]

> In chapter 2 he reproves the Jews for the same kind of sins, for he says, "You who teach others, do you not teach yourself? You who teach that a man should not steal, do you steal? That a man should not commit adultery, do you commit adultery? Indeed, you who detest idols, do you rob God of his honor?" Who does not see that these things are contained in the law of the Decalogue?[57]

So, by chapter 3, Paul concludes, "no one does good, not even one." "If the apostle wanted to speak only of ceremonial laws, he would never have mentioned these matters."[58] And in Romans 4:15 Paul says, "The law brings wrath." But how do the ceremonies do this? The ensuing argument contrasts reward and gift, not ceremonies and moral works. "It is also written in chapter 5 that 'law came in to increase the trespass. Now where sin increased, grace abounded all the more.' These things also cannot be derived from ceremonies alone."[59]

In chapter 6, clearly baptism into Christ purges us of *all sins*, not of a failure to be circumcised, and we are called to righteousness—moral purity.[60] Vermigli adds that in Romans 7:5 "the passions in our members were aroused by the law to bear fruit for death. . . . But what are those passions except desires, lusts, anger, hatred, and envy, which are recounted to the Galatians in that catalogue where the works of the flesh are distinguished from the works of the Spirit? There is no doubt that all these things pertain to the Decalogue."[61] What is Paul struggling with in Romans 7? Is he finding it hard to remain circumcised or to keep the dietary laws?[62] Commenting on Romans 8:3, Vermigli notes:

> These words, I say, cannot be explained as dealing with the law of ceremonies; still less can those words that follow in the same chapter: "We are debtors, not

---

[56]Vermigli, "Locus on Justification," 115.
[57]Vermigli, "Locus on Justification," 116.
[58]Vermigli, "Locus on Justification," 116.
[59]Vermigli, "Locus on Justification," 116.
[60]Vermigli, "Locus on Justification," 116-17.
[61]Vermigli, "Locus on Justification," 117.
[62]Vermigli, "Locus on Justification," 117.

to the flesh, that we should live according to the flesh, for if you live according to the flesh you shall die. But if by the Spirit you mortify the deeds of the flesh, you shall live." This cannot refer to ceremonies any more than what is written to the Galatians: "The law was given because of transgression, for where there is no law there is no transgression." It is certain that boasting cannot be excluded, nor can the promise be firm if our justification depends on observing the Decalogue and moral precepts. This is the case no matter how much you take away the rites and ceremonies of Moses.[63]

Finally, in Romans 11:6, Paul says that if it is by works, then not grace. "This is a universal antithesis," as it is in Ephesians 2:9 and Philippians 3:6, 2 Timothy 1:9 and Titus 3:5.[64]

In a similar fashion, Luther pointed out that if we cannot be justified through the law of Moses, then certainly this must be true of all works.[65] It is the "argument from greater to lesser," Michael Allen notes. Luther "notes that the Judaizers require the best of all possible additions to faith (law observance that was at one time required by God), yet they are still rebuked as gospel repudiators; Luther sees the medieval Romans of his day as worse, requiring not divinely mandated obedience, but that rendered toward their own human traditions."[66] Allen continues:

[Luther] is most straightforward in his commentary on Galatians 3:10, where he states: "Paul might have said, by a general proposition, whatsoever is without faith, is under a curse. He saith not so, but he taketh that which, besides faith, is the best, the greatest, and most excellent among all corporal blessings of the world; to wit, the law of God. . . . Now if the law of God do bring men under a curse, much more may the same be said of inferior laws and blessings." Here and elsewhere in his later lectures on Galatians, Luther plainly shows his awareness of contingent differences between the Judaizers in Galatia and the flaws he perceived in late medieval Roman Catholic piety. It will not do for New Testament scholars to continue suggesting that Luther

---

[63]Vermigli, "Locus on Justification," 118.

[64]Vermigli, "Locus on Justification," 118.

[65]Martin Luther, *Galatians 1535*, in LW 26:139-41, 407.

[66]Michael Allen, *Justification and the Gospel: Contexts and Controversies* (Grand Rapids: Baker Academic, 2013), 108, quoting Luther, *Lectures on Galatians,* on Gal 1:7, 14-17; 2:1, 3; 3:10; 4:27.

simply read the Pharisees or the Judaizers as ancient appearances of his own opponents. Clearly, he did not. Yet Luther does show that engagement with the Judaizers can connect with battles in his own day by extension.[67]

The Reformers knew that the best of the medieval tradition was not Pelagian and the specific part of Aquinas they were rejecting. "Luther summarized Rome in this way: 'We must believe in Christ, and that faith is the foundation of our salvation, but it justifieth not, except it be furnished with charity.'"[68]

Calvin was even more precise in his criticisms. Of course, the pope teaches that Christ saves us by his grace (but poured into us so that we may obtain it finally by the merit of works) and that faith justifies (but only if it is transformed by love into good works). "The principal cause of obscurity, however, is that we are with the greatest difficulty induced to leave the glory of righteousness entirely to God *alone*." Calvin argues that the position of Trent is not Pelagian but Semi-Pelagian. They preface their statement by extolling Christ but then leave him behind, repeating the line of the schools: "that men are justified partly by the grace of God and partly by their own works; thus only showing themselves somewhat more modest than Pelagius."[69] This is hyperbole in the heat of battle. Calvin is not making a point as a historical theologian but as a Reformer. For all the magisterial Reformers, it is an all-or-nothing gamble: all of our righteousness is found in Christ or somewhere else. There simply is no mediating position, a place where merit is shared between Christ and sinners, including Mary and the saints, much less ordinary believers. Quotations from scholastics defending a robustly Augustinian doctrine of grace will not suffice any more than would a syllabus of grace-affirming citations from Second Temple Judaism. What *else* is deemed necessary besides the merit of Christ?

---

[67] Allen, *Justification and the Gospel*, 108.

[68] Allen, *Justification and the Gospel*, 110, from Luther, *Lectures on Galatians* (1535).

[69] John Calvin, *Acts and Antidote*, in *Selected Works of John Calvin: Tracts and Letters*, ed. Henry Beveridge and Jules Bonnet, trans. Henry Beveridge (repr., Grand Rapids: Baker, 1983), 3:108.

This was why Luther, Bucer, Vermigli, Cranmer, Knox, Calvin, and the rest of the magisterial Reformers believed that the justification of the ungodly is "the main hinge on which religion turns."[70] Numerous biblical passages promise all believers this assurance. Who is to deprive believers of that which Christ purchased and promised? Calvin asks.[71] But there is no assurance from the law. Peter spoke of the law "as that which none of their fathers could bear." At the heart of the Council of Trent's errors, Calvin argues, lies the confusion of law and gospel. Paul "calls the gospel, rather than the law, 'the doctrine of faith.' He moreover declares that the gospel is 'the message of reconciliation.'"[72]

"For the words of Paul always hold true, that the difference between the Law and the Gospel lies in this, that the latter does not like the former promise life under the condition of works, but from faith." Calvin asks, "What can be clearer than the antithesis" that we find in such passages as Romans 10:5:"For Moses writes about the righteousness that is based on the law, that the person who does the commandments shall live by them."

In Calvin's view, Paul's contrast between works of the law and faith is absolute. "Grace" is not sufficient. It must be *sola gratia*. But even this is not adequate. God is not singularly merciful; he is also just. He must be "just and justifier of the ungodly." Salvation cannot be by grace alone unless it is *solo Christo*.

> It were long and troublesome to note every blunder, but there is one too important to be omitted. They add, "that when catechumens ask faith from the Church," the answer is, "If you will enter into life, keep the commandments," (Matt 19:17). Woe to their catechumens, if so hard a condition is laid upon them! For what else is this but to lay them under an eternal curse, since they acknowledge with Paul that all are under the curse who are subject to the law (Gal 3:10)? But they have the authority of Christ! I wish they would observe to what intent Christ thus spoke. This can only be ascertained from the

---

[70]Calvin, *Institutes* 3.11.1 (LCC 20:726).
[71]Calvin, *Acts and Antidote*, 3:126.
[72]Calvin, *Acts and Antidote*, 3:154.

context, and the character of the persons. He to whom Christ replied had asked, What must I do to have eternal life? Assuredly, whoever wishes to merit life by works has a rule prescribed to him by the law, "This do, and thou shalt live." But attention must be paid to the object of this as intimated by Paul, viz., that man experiencing his powers, or rather convinced of his powerlessness, may lay aside his pride, and flee all naked to Christ. There is no room for the righteousness of faith until we have discovered that it is in vain that salvation is promised us by the law. . . . But so preposterous are the Fathers of Trent that while it is the office of Moses to lead us by the hand to Christ (Gal 3:24), they lead us away from the grace of Christ to Moses.[73]

Calvin is not imposing an abstract principle on the biblical texts at this point. Rather, he recognizes the difference between law and gospel, the covenants with Moses as mediator and Christ as mediator. The new covenant is *not* a renewal of the Sinai pact, and Jesus is not another Moses. The confusion of law and gospel, of Moses and Christ, of the covenants of law and grace, is the heart of the problem. It is not abstraction, to say the least; the argument is based on *Paul's* antitheses.

As Pelagius had once argued against Augustine, so the Tridentine fathers insist that God cannot command something that we cannot fulfill. Yet, as Calvin notes, "if we are to debate about a word, the very thing was expressed by Peter (Acts 15) when he spoke of the yoke of the law as that which none of their fathers could bear. It is an error to suppose that this refers only to ceremonies: for what so very arduous was there in ceremonies as to make all human strength fail under the burden of them?"[74] To be sure, John says "his commandments are not burdensome" (1 Jn 5:3). "I admit it, provided you exclude not the doctrine of remission of sins, which he places before all the commandments."[75]

Hence, too, it is that Christ's yoke is easy and his burden light because the saints feel an alacrity in their liberty while they feel themselves no longer under the law. Paul applies to them this best stimulus of exhortation

---

[73]Calvin, *Acts and Antidote*, 3:119-20.
[74]Calvin, *Acts and Antidote*, 3:131.
[75]Calvin, *Acts and Antidote*, 3:131.

(Rom 6:12). And David also teaches, "With thee is forgiveness, that thou mayest be feared" (Ps 130:4). Take that hope of pardon from me, and the least commandment of the law will be a heavier load than Aetna.[76]

If we do not come to terms with *these* arguments, which are entirely exegetical and biblical-theological, then we cannot understand properly the contentions of the "old perspective."

I am convinced that Chrysostom was (like Origen) reacting against the fatalism of Greek religious philosophy, which influenced the Gnostics. Yet he recognized the clarity of Paul's argument and was willing to embrace it in ways that eluded Origen. "For He pursued us when we fled from Him with all speed," Chrysostom recognizes.[77] It is difficult to imagine any similar comment in Origen, much less Pelagius. In Homily VI on Colossians, Chrysostom says, "Do you speak even of the Law? Henceforth it is but a doctrine of men, after the time is come," along with "the Gentile institutions. The doctrine, he says, is altogether of man."[78] Not only remarkably astute, this comment is surprisingly (for the period) sensitive to Paul's eschatological-apocalyptic view of the law-gospel distinction. The law is a *time*, he realizes with the apostle, that has become past with the arrival of Christ. The problem, says Paul, is not with the law itself. But "the law" is an era.

No one was ever justified under the Sinai covenant (it did not even promise justification), so one can hardly be justified by the terms of the law after Christ has come, Chrysostom continues:

> He wiped them [our sins] out; He did not scratch them out merely, so that they could not be seen. . . . It is enough to believe. He has not set works against works, but works against faith. . . . Nowhere has he spoken in so lofty a strain. . . . We were all under sin and punishment. He Himself,

---

[76]Calvin, *Acts and Antidote*, 3:132.

[77]Chrysostom, *Homilies on Philippians*, in NPNF, vol. 12, *Saint Chrysostom* (repr., Edinburgh: T&T Clark, 1988), 237, commenting on Phil 3:12.

[78]Chrysostom, *Homilies on Colossians*, in NPNF, vol. 12, *Saint Chrysostom* (repr., Edinburgh: T&T Clark, 1988), 289, commenting on Col 2:21-22.

through suffering punishment, did away with both the sin and the punishment, and He was punished on the Cross. To the Cross then He affixed it; as having power, He tore it asunder. What bond? He means either that which they said to Moses, namely, "All that God has said we will do and be obedient" (Ex 24:3), or, if not that, this, that we owe to God obedience; or if not this, he means that the devil held possession of it, the bond which God made for Adam, saying, "In the day you eat of the tree, you shall die" (Gen 2:17). This bond then the devil held in possession. And Christ did not give it to us, but Himself tore it in two, the action of one who remits joyfully . . . There death received his wound, having met his death-stroke from a dead body.[79]

Chrysostom also contrasts a bond with a covenant:

For that is "a bond" whereby one is held accountable for debts, but this is a covenant. It has no penalty, nor does it say, If this be done, or if this be not done: what Moses said when he sprinkled the blood of the covenant, by this God also promised everlasting life. All this is a covenant. There, it was slave with master; here, it is a friend with a friend. There, it said, "In the day that you eat of it you shall die" (Gen 2:17), an immediate threatening; but here there is nothing of the kind. God arrives and here is nakedness, and there was nakedness; there, however, one that had sinned was made naked because he sinned, but here, one is made naked that he may be set free. Then, man put off the glory which he had; now, he puts off the old man and before going up (to the contest) puts him off as easily as it were his garments . . . He took dust from the earth and formed man (Gen 2:7), but now, dust no longer, but the Holy Spirit. With this Spirit he is formed, with this harmonized, even as Himself was in the womb of the Virgin . . . [This heaven where we are raised and seated with Christ] has no tree with knowledge of good and evil, but the Tree of Life only. No more shall woman be formed from your side, but we all are one from the side of Christ.[80]

By this point, hopefully, we have seen that the contemporary debates over works of the law are by no means modern, even as understood to encompass the sixteenth-century debates. It is significant that the great exegetes of the church, for whom Greek was the mother tongue, differed

---

[79]Chrysostom, *Homilies on Colossians*, 286, commenting on Col 2:13-15.
[80]Chrysostom, *Homilies on Colossians*, 287.

on these questions. It would be understandable if exegetes like Chrysostom simply followed Origen, but they did not.

The differences between the Origenist and Irenaean trajectories becomes quite clear. In spite of his preference for conditional election, Chrysostom (like Irenaeus) really understood Paul's antithesis between *all works of the law* and *faith*. In this light, it is not surprising that Calvin considered the patriarch of Constantinople his favorite preacher. Chrysostom writes, "For to have received the Spirit came not of the poverty of the Law, but of the righteousness which is by Faith, and to preserve it when obtained came not from Circumcision but from Grace."[81] He adds that one does not despise the ladder you used to climb onto the roof, even though you no longer need it. So too the law. Paul considers it a loss. "How? Not because it is a loss, but because grace is far greater . . . For when the sun hath appeared, it is loss to sit by a candle."[82]

> If he who had righteousness ran to this other righteousness because his own was nothing, how much rather ought they who have it not to run to Him? And he well said, "a righteousness of my own," not that which I gained from labor and toil, but that which I found from grace. If then he who was so excellent is saved by grace, much more are you. For since it was likely they would say that the righteousness which comes from toil is the greater, he shows that it is dung in comparison with the other. For otherwise I, who was so excellent in it, would not have cast it away and run to the other. But what is that other? That which is from the faith of God, i.e., it too is given by God. This is the righteousness of God; this is altogether a gift. And the gifts of God far exceed those worthless good deeds, which are due to our own diligence.[83]

In conclusion, I have demonstrated that the narrative that Luther introduced a novel doctrine of justification, unheard of in previous centuries, proves to be untenable. Of course, we should remain aloof to exaggerated claims about precedents. It is certainly true that Augustinianism

---

[81]Chrysostom, *Commentary on Galatians* in Schaff, vol. 12, *Saint Chrysostom* (repr., Edinburgh: T&T Clark, 1988): 47-48, commenting on Gal 6:18.

[82]Chrysostom, *Homilies on Philippians*, 235, commenting on Phil 3:7-10.

[83]Chrysostom, *Homilies on Philippians*, 235.

did not teach imputation of an alien righteousness. Yet there are crucial components and Latin writers who anticipate Luther to some extent. What is surprising is the extent to which scholarship has decided this question by basically ignoring the Christian East, deciding the case for or against continuity exclusively within an Augustinian frame of reference. Focusing especially on Chrysostom, this chapter has shown that a broader search will yield remarkable support for the conclusion that the doctrine of justification (at least in many of its components) enjoyed a long and fruitful place in the church's proclamation of the "great exchange."

Chapter Six

JUSTIFICATION *for* TODAY

KEVIN DeYOUNG

"JUSTIFICATION IS AN ACT OF GOD'S free grace, wherein he pardoneth all our sins, and accepteth us as righteous in his sight, only for the righteousness of Christ imputed to us, and received by faith alone."[1] That is the definition of justification given in the Westminster Shorter Catechism. We'll come back to that later in this chapter and see why the Reformation understanding of justification is exactly what the world needs (even if it doesn't realize it yet). But before we get to the doctrine itself, I want to start with a story and an article. First, the story.

A SERMON FOR THE AGES

When my older kids were younger, they went through a short-lived phase where they liked to play church. I promise you I didn't make them do it, and it's not what they do now as teenagers. But when the older children were around two, four, six, and eight they would sometimes go into the basement and have a pretend church service. It was actually a good advertisement for having children with you in worship because they had, almost by osmosis, picked up what the main elements were in a church service.

---

[1] Westminster Shorter Catechism (Question-Answer 33), in *The Creeds of Christendom,* ed. Philip Schaff, vol. 3, rev. ed. (Grand Rapids: Baker, 1985), 683.

So one child was in charge of the offering. Another one picked some songs. Another one turned a trash can upside down and played the drums. They would offer short little prayers and sing a verse of "Jesus Loves Me" or "Come, Thou Fount." They even tried to serve Communion, which I thought was going a bit too far. When it came time for the sermon, my second son, maybe about six at the time, volunteered to do the preaching. I was curious what the sermon was going to be like, especially since the only preacher they had ever really heard was me. My six-year-old looked around, cleared his throat, and gave his first sermon: "You are all sinners. Let's pray." It was a little light on gospel—more like Jonah preaching to Nineveh, with a firm accent on the bad news side of the equation. I'm not sure what that says about the preaching he was hearing at his church, but at least it was theologically accurate. We *are* all sinners. And as long as there are sinners, the doctrine of justification will remain powerfully needed and surprisingly relevant.

THAT STAIN THAT REMAINS

And now the article. Earlier this year, in a periodical called *The Hedgehog Review*, there was a fascinating and important piece written by Wilfred McClay, a professor at the University of Oklahoma. The article was entitled "The Strange Persistence of Guilt." Here's the opening paragraph:

> Those of us living in the developed countries of the West find ourselves in the tightening grip of a paradox, one whose shape and character have so far largely eluded our understanding. It is the strange persistence of guilt as a psychological force in modern life. If anything, the word *persistence* understates the matter. Guilt has not merely lingered. It has grown, even metastasized, into an ever more powerful and pervasive element in the life of the contemporary West, even as the rich language formerly used to define it has withered and faded from discourse, and the means of containing its effects, let alone obtaining relief from it, have become ever more elusive.[2]

---

[2] Wilfred M. McClay, "The Strange Persistence of Guilt," *The Hedgehog Review* 19, no. 1 (2017), accessed April 18, 2017, www.iasc-culture.org/THR/THR_article_2017_Spring_McClay.php.

McClay argues that despite the best efforts of secular prophets like Friedrich Nietzsche and Sigmund Freud, guilt has not been eradicated. Nietzsche believed that by the "death" of God, humans would no longer carry around a sense of indebtedness, while Freud tried to "demoralize" guilt by explaining it away as a subjective and emotional pathology. But now, well into the twenty-first century, we see that Nietzsche's aggressive secularism and Freud's therapeutic revolution have proven no match for the nagging sense most of us feel that we aren't doing enough and that what we are doing is not good enough.

Now at this point you may stop and think, "Wait a minute, most of the people I know seem to live quite happily with an untroubled conscience. Are you sure guilt is still a problem?" McClay notes at least two pieces of evidence to suggest that it is.

First, he points to the "infinite extensibility of guilt." In our massively connected world—where we can fly anywhere, phone anywhere, get the news from anywhere, and see pictures from anywhere—we cannot help but feel weighed down by suffering on a global scale. With increased capability comes increased culpability. It used to be that we were largely ignorant of the troubles that beset billions of people on the planet. But now when there is a hurricane or an earthquake or a homicide or a traffic accident or a shooting spree or an act of terrorism, we all know about it. And as *School House Rock* taught us, "Knowledge is Power." Consequently, we feel like there is always more we can do. We could give another dollar or send another teddy bear or purchase another goat. The circle of obligation feels limitless.

Second, McClay perceptively points to our preoccupation with "stolen suffering." Of course, we don't want to deny that millions of people in the world suffer every day from intense pain and hardship. In fact, all of us struggle with suffering on some level. That always has been and always will be. What seems new is the propensity for comfortable and privileged people to position themselves as victims. And even more than that, what's new is the extraordinary prestige conferred on victims.

The honor we heap on sufferers is so pervasive we hardly notice it anymore. My family loves watching the Olympics when they come around every two years. I like watching for the competition. My wife wants to get everyone's backstory, which inevitably highlights some family member with an incurable disease, or a loved one who just died, or an athlete who has battled tremendous setbacks just to make it this far. Our heroes are those who have been hurt the most. We see this with politicians all the time. They are all on a race to the bottom to prove that they grew up more impoverished and more hardscrabble than their opponents. Even when we celebrate the military, it is usually as sufferers and victims, not as warriors and conquerors.

Why are we so fixated on victims? McClay explains:

> I believe the explanation can be traced back to the extraordinary weight of guilt in our time, the pervasive need to find innocence through moral absolution and somehow discharge one's moral burdens, and the fact that the conventional means of finding absolution—or even of keeping the range of one's responsibility for one's sins within some kind of reasonable boundaries—are no longer generally available. Making a claim to the status of a certified victim, or identifying with victims, however, offers itself as a substitute means by which the moral burden of sin can be shifted, and one's innocence affirmed.[3]

McClay is not trying to "blame the victim" or discount genuine human suffering. But his larger point is insightful. "As a victim," he writes, "one can project onto another person, the victimizer or oppressor, any feelings of guilt we might harbor, and in projecting that guilt lift it from his own shoulders." The result is a profound sense of moral release, of recovered innocence. Whatever imperfections I may have, my role in this human drama is not as a selfish, sinful person, but as a victim, as a sufferer, as one who has been put upon by others. And when you multiply this on a worldwide scale, it produces a widespread grievance culture in which all of us are constantly jockeying for position so that our group, our race,

---

[3]McClay, "The Strange Persistence of Guilt."

our party, our tribe are the innocent ones, and the people in that group over there or that race or that party or that tribe are guilty.

THE JUDGMENT DAY(S)

I would say that we live in a puritanical age, but I don't want to give the Puritans a bad name. Even if the Puritans were as bad as people think—with their witch trials and scarlet letters—at least they had a well-articulated offer of redemption. They may have talked a lot about sin, but they also talked a great deal about a Savior. The same cannot be said about today's secular puritans. It is all law and no gospel.

When I was in college I remember talking a lot about moral relativism. I read books with that term. I taught a Sunday school class on the subject. The debate was about *absolute* truth. The secular edge of the culture and the academy was pushing for tolerance and permissiveness. They wanted Christians to accept that "you'll have your truth and I'll have mine." But that's decidedly *not* the issue today, and Christians who still bewail moral relativism are fighting yesterday's battles. If anything, Christians are now the ones asking for permission to believe what they want and be left alone. The world we now inhabit is fundamentalist in its understanding of right and wrong. People may still quote Matthew 7:1 to your face, "Hey man, judge not lest ye be judged," but then they go online and come down on you with the force of an Old Testament prophet.

Think of all the areas in contemporary life where we face increasing judgment and guilt. Take *food*, for example. Until fairly recently, Westerners had a lot of rules about sex but were pretty laissez-faire about food. Now the situation is reversed. We keep track of calories and keep away from trans fats and MSG. Big cities want to ban Big Gulps. Lunch lines are getting rid of standard kids fare like pizza and French fries in favor of vegetable sticks and low fat yogurt. And it's not just a matter of eating healthy and losing weight.

Anyone who thinks we live in an age of moral relativism has never tried to feed the neighbor kids sugar cereals. I've been a picky eater my whole life with decidedly lowbrow tastes. People are shocked, and more than a little dismayed, when they see me eating Lucky Charms or find out that I'd gladly eat at Applebee's. There are some young people who would feel less shame being caught with pornography than being caught at McDonald's. Our food choices face constant scrutiny from friends, free rangers, and foodies. There is good reason to consider what we eat and how we treat our bodies, but there is really no question that many of us feel guilty about the foods we eat.

We are also made to feel guilty about the *environment*. I'm not wanting to adjudicate disputes about climate change or global warming. I simply want to note how environmental concerns have added a new layer of guilt in the West. Now when hurricanes come, it's not preachers blaming the weather on abortion, it's secular prophets warning about the impending doom if we don't beat our Styrofoam into plowshares and our SUVs into pruning hooks. We are to blame for deforestation, the hole in the ozone, and the plight of the polar bears. And even if we shrug our shoulders at some extreme claims, most of us still feel a tinge of guilt if we throw the milk gallon into the trash instead of the recycling bin. Yes, we should consider what it means to be good stewards of God's creation, but environmentalism can become a surrogate religion whereby the infallible oracles of science demand austerity and obedience in order to atone for the original sin of spoiling our pristine Garden and the continuing sins of selfish consumption.

And that's not to mention all the *isms* and *phobias* we are said to be guilty of in the West: colonialism, imperialism, capitalism, racism, sexism, Islamophobia, homophobia, and all the rest. Again, there is no doubt that some of these concerns are warranted, but the fact remains that we are often told how bad we are and how bad we have been. In fact, it is a measure of social standing in some circles to see who can protest the loudest about all of our sins in the Western world.

If we take seriously what mainstream voices tell us, we are a compromised people through and through, deeply complicit in centuries of guilt. And keep in mind, this sort of indictment is coming often from those who completely reject any traditional notions of sin and salvation. The same culture that says it does not believe in original sin or total depravity is awash in statements of universal corruption and moral culpability.

And I haven't even mentioned the area in which most people older than thirty feel guilty all the time. There is a group of people who roam this planet with a never-ending, debilitating, nearly ubiquitous sense that they aren't doing things right. They're called *parents*. There is immense social pressure to feed your kids the right food, get them to the right doctors, put them in the right schools (whether inside or outside the home). Moms especially can feel as though they have too many kids, or not enough, or they should nurse, or they should use formula, or they should put kids on their stomachs, or they should never ever think about putting babies on their tummies under any circumstances, or they should put their kids to bed whether they cry or not, or they should never let a child cry himself to sleep. Parents feel pressure to get kids piano lessons at three years old, and soccer at four, and watercolor painting at five. Some of the pressure is self-imposed, but some of it is simply the air we breathe. And if you think I'm exaggerating, you haven't been a parent with access to Facebook.

In short, we are people loaded with guilt—sometimes we are conscious of it, more often it's a low-level sense that we are not doing enough, that we have way more than other people on the planet, that the problems in the world could be our fault, and that we're not living up to our own expectations. McClay's summary is apt:

> Notwithstanding all claims about our living in a post-Christian world devoid of censorious public morality, we in fact live in a world that carries an enormous and growing burden of guilt, and yearns—sometimes even demands—to be free of it. Indeed, it is impossible to exaggerate how many of the deeds of individual men and women can be traced back to the powerful and inextinguishable need of human beings to feel morally justified, to feel themselves "right with the world."[4]

---

[4]McClay, "The Strange Persistence of Guilt."

THE CURE WE DON'T KNOW WE NEED

Which brings us back to justification. Here again is the definition from the Westminster Shorter Catechism: "Justification is an act of God's free grace, wherein he pardoneth all our sins, and accepteth us as righteous in his sight, only for the righteousness of Christ imputed to us, and received by faith alone." This is precisely the doctrine our world needs. It's the cure people desperately need for the disease they don't even know they have. Let me give you three reasons why this Reformation understanding of justification is the good news we've been waiting for.

First, it is personal. The Christian understanding of justification moves in a vertical direction. It's about our offenses against God and God's right to be angry at our rebellion. That may sound harsh to modern ears, but besides being biblical, it has the advantage of being savable. If ultimately it's against God only that we have sinned (Psalm 51:4), then at least we know where to turn for salvation.

We have a psychologized understanding of guilt, which leads to therapeutic notions of forgiveness. Guilt is seen as a subjective state of consciousness. It may not be what we are, but it is what we feel. So forgiveness is about emotional acceptance. It's about learning to live with ourselves. That sounds nice and soft and easy to manage, until you try to work out the details. Secular notions of "justification" are either internal and subjective or cosmic and impersonal, which means we are either getting right with ourselves or right with the universe. But how can we really be sure we are right with ourselves? And how does the universe let us know that we are right with it? Who or what is in the place to pronounce definitive absolution for our moral failings?

A few years ago a book titled *Making Gay Okay* was published.[5] Although the title might make you cringe, it was a serious book that examined the push for the acceptance of homosexual behavior in politics, in education, in medicine, and in every area of life. One of the central

[5]Robert R. Reilly, *Making Gay Okay: How Rationalizing Homosexual Behavior Is Changing Everything* (San Francisco: Ignatius Press, 2014).

theses of the book is that victory for the sexual revolution *must* be total and complete because the mere tolerance of rival viewpoints undermines the quest for moral legitimacy. In other words, you cannot make "gay okay" unless all dissenting viewpoints of ethical judgment are effectively sidelined or silenced. It's a provocative argument, but it does fit the anthropology of Romans 1 and 2, which says we all have a conscience and we all know something about the truth, but we exchange the truth for a lie and suppress the truth in unrighteousness. Rather than screaming against the culture with fear and loathing, we should realize, somewhat sympathetically, that aggressive opposition to traditional sexual norms is one expression of the innate human longing for moral approbation.

But if there is no God to sin against, then there is no God who can say, "I forgive you." And without personal pardon from a personally offended God, it's hard to see how we can really know lasting peace. Years ago, as part of my training for pastoral ministry, I had to work at a detox center in the Boston area. It was a thoroughly secular environment with strict rules against bringing the Bible or religion into the seminars. I was tasked with leading a quasi-counseling session with more than a dozen men and women detoxing from heroin. As I worked through the material provided for me, I could tell there was a profound disconnect with the people in front of me. The problem they faced, among several problems, was guilt. They all felt a sense of shame and failure. They had let people down. They had hurt people, sometimes literally. They had made a mess of their lives and lived with never-assuaged guilt. Yet they were constantly told the drug was to blame, not them. They were told they were good people deep down. They were told they needed to move on and forgive themselves. It was all nonsense. And they knew it.

I remember after one session asking them what they felt like and what should be done to them. One man took the piece of paper in front of him, forcefully crumpled it into a ball and threw it on the ground. "That's what should be done," he said. From there I tried as best I could to talk about the parable of the prodigal son. Here was a man who knew he was guilty of sin, yet he didn't know the personal God he had offended and the personal God who could pardon him.

Our world may not think it's interested in Reformation dogma, but it is searching for justification. So many people are at a point of despair precisely because they have done away with a big God—a God big enough to judge and big enough to acquit. We are left with Judeo-Christian instincts without a spiritual framework to make sense of the conscience. We have all the vestiges of inhabiting a moral universe of right and wrong but no way, other than the dead end of therapeutic self-talk, for dealing with the wrongs we know we have committed. It's the worst of all worlds: an abiding sense of guilt for which there is no effective atonement and no coherent plan of redemption.

Second, we need the doctrine of justification because it is gracious. The Westminster definition begins and ends with mercy. Justification is an act of grace alone (*sola gratia*) that we receive by faith alone (*sola fide*). The world's way to be justified is by strenuous effort and exacting asceticism. That may sound strange at first. Don't we live in a culture that is easygoing to a fault? Not really. To eat correctly requires a casuistry and a precision that would make the Levites blush. To appease Mother Earth we must embrace the strictest asceticism. And to deal with the burdens of affluence in a world racked with disease and starvation demands a treasure of humanitarian merit that no non-governmental organization and no amount of fair trade coffee can provide.

Because we have so much and know so much we have no choice but to *do* so much. We all suffer from Spider-Man syndrome. With our great power in the West comes great responsibility. But no matter how responsible we are, there is always more we can do. We may laugh at Martin Luther ascending the staircase on his knees in order to merit an indulgence for sin, but plenty of our middle-class neighbors practice the same rigorous self-denial, not in fear of God but in fear of unwanted pounds, unrefined flour, and the untold evils we haven't yet addressed in the world.

But of course, even this sad state of affairs presumes that effort and asceticism can win us at least some moral good will, when we all know this is often not the case. Not only is the world's "grace" earned grace (if there could be such a thing), in plenty of contexts there is no grace at all. Case in point: the internet. Woe be to the poor soul that uses a word from the cultural *Index Librorum Prohibitorum* or links to the wrong post or retweets the wrong tweet. Hell hath no fury like a blogger with too much time on his hands. Nathaniel Hawthorne's *The Scarlet Letter* has nothing on the never-ending shame that can be doled out on Twitter. If you spend any time on social media, you know that it deals with offenses through a potent combination of abject humiliation, public ridicule, and demands for retribution.

And there is no real forgiveness. The best you can hope for is that most people forget about your errant word or your misplaced opinion and go about their normal lives. Social media specializes in accusations without corrections and in condemnation without any hope of pardon. The internet offers no act of grace whereby we can be pardoned of our cultural sins and accepted by the world based on faith alone. There is no removing of our transgressions as far as the east is from the west (Psalm 103:12), only a fearful and permanent marking of our iniquities that we may never stand (Psalm 130:3).

Finally, we need the doctrine of justification because it is forensic. The Christian doctrine of justification is a legal declaration of innocence based on the imputation of Christ's righteousness. Romans 4:25 says Christ was delivered up for our trespasses and raised for our justification. We usually link justification to Christ's death on the cross, but here the link is based on his resurrection from the grave. Why? Because the resurrection is God's loud declaration that justice has been satisfied.

In Romans 1:4 we read that Christ "was declared to be the Son of God in power according to the Spirit of holiness by his resurrection from the dead." The resurrection speaks. It declared that Christ is the Son of God. According to Romans 1:4, the fact that he came back to life said something about the *person* of Christ. In Romans 4:25 we see that the resurrection also says something about the *work* of Christ. It tells us that justice has been satisfied and we have been justified. That is what it means that Christ was raised for our justification.

Here is the main point I want to make: *we were saved not by the removal of justice but by the satisfaction of it.* It's easy for people to think the cross was where love conquered holiness. It's easy to think we are saved because God, out of his great love, woke up one day and decided he wouldn't count our sins against us. But that's not how justification works. We are not justified because mercy obliterated justice. We are justified because, in divine mercy, God sent his Son to the cross to satisfy divine justice.

Consider this astounding statement in Acts 2:24: "God raised him up, loosing the pangs of death, because *it was not possible* for him to be held by it." Why was it impossible for Jesus to remain dead? Because God is more powerful than death and the devil? Absolutely. But there is another reason. The grave could not hold the Son of God because it had no claim on him. The wages of sin is death. So when sin is paid for, there is no obligation to pay the wages of sin. The resurrection is the declaration that there is nothing left to pay.

Here is how Charles Hodge puts it: "Our sins were the judicial ground of the sufferings of Christ, so that they were a satisfaction of justice; and his righteousness is the judicial ground of our acceptance with God, so *that our pardon is an act of justice.*"[6] Think of the wording in 1 John 1:9: "If we confess our sins, he is faithful and just to forgive us our sins and to cleanse us from all righteousness." We might expect John to say "merciful" or "gracious," but he says God is *just* to forgive us our sins. Justification is not an act of legal fiction but an act of justice. God would be unjust if he did not pardon those who belong to Christ. We don't wash away guilt by positive self-talk or by a renewed sense of our self-worth.

---

[6]Charles Hodge, *An Exposition of the Second Epistle to the Corinthians* (New York: Robert Carter and Brother, 1876), 151.

Guilt is an objective reality, and as such it must be dealt with by an objective satisfaction.

Many of us have not begun to grasp just how good the good news is, just how secure our salvation is, just how completely and unalterably justified we are through faith in Christ. The world is settling for subjective shame displacement when the Bible offers objective guilt removal. God did not set aside the law in judging us. He fulfilled it. But Christ bore the curse of the law so that in him we might become the righteousness of God (2 Cor 5:21), not because you possess this righteousness but because God credits it to your account. By the imputation of our sin, Christ "deserved" death, and by the imputation of his righteousness, we now "deserve" eternal life.

Justice is shot through the entire plan of redemption. People go to hell because God is just, and people go to heaven because God is just. Brothers and sisters, you are not forgiven and justified because God waved his magic wand and decided to overlook your faults. He has not overlooked the smallest speck of your sin. He demands justice for all of your iniquities. He demands justice for every last lustful look and proud thought and spiteful tongue. He demands justice for all of it. But praise God: the resurrection of the crucified Son of Man tells us all the demands of justice have been met for those who are trusting in Christ.

The resurrection is not a sentimental story about never giving up or the possibility of good coming from evil. It is not first of all a story about how suffering can be sanctified or a story of how Jesus suffered for all of humanity so we can suffer with the rest of humanity. The gospel is not a story about a good man dying a sad death and coming back to life so we can have hope. The cross is about the atoning sacrifice for our sins. And the resurrection is the loud declaration that Jesus is enough to atone for your sins, enough to reconcile you to God, enough to present you holy in God's presence, enough to free you from the curse of the law, enough to assure you that there is now no condemnation for those who are in Christ Jesus.

PART FOUR

THE CHRISTIAN LIFE
in the REFORMATION

Chapter Seven

THE SAINTHOOD *of* ALL BELIEVERS

THE BIBLE *and* SANCTIFICATION

THOMAS H. McCALL

AS EVANGELICAL PROTESTANTS—which is to say as catholic Christians who are heirs of the Reformation—we should give thanks for the insights and advances of the Reformers. But we should also, where appropriate, continue learning from them. And it may be that their most important contributions concern the doctrine of sanctification, and they may have a great deal to teach us. Paying attention to both the magisterial Reformers and some of the Protestant scholastics, in this chapter I shall try to help us retrieve some insights from the major traditions. We will look at what the Reformers say about the reality and necessity of sanctification, and we will look more closely at the function of the Word in sanctification. I shall conclude with a few brief reflections on the importance of their views for the contemporary context.

HOLINESS AND SALVATION: SOME KEY REFORMATION INSIGHTS

The Lutheran theological tradition. We begin with the Lutheran tradition, and, indeed, with Martin Luther. We do so not only because this is a natural place to begin but also because the Lutheran doctrine of sanctification has been the subject of no little confusion and misunderstanding.[1] There is a fairly popular understanding of "the Lutheran view"

---

[1]See further Carl R. Trueman, *Luther on the Christian Life: Cross and Freedom* (Wheaton, IL: Crossway, 2015); Carl R. Trueman, "Martin Luther," in *Christian Theologies of Salvation:*

that goes along these lines: Martin Luther's great theological discoveries taught us that we need not be overly concerned with sanctification—indeed, if we take his insights seriously, we will understand that we *must* not worry about sanctification. Did not Luther teach us that we are always sinful—but that even our most grievous sins are no match for the justifying grace of God as it is given to the elect? Did not he teach us the all-important truth of *simul iustus et peccator* (at the same time righteous and a sinner)? And is not a focus on sanctification at best a distraction from our celebration of the great and beautiful doctrine of justification? Isn't the Reformation—and particularly Lutheranism—all about *sola gratia* and *sola fide*? And isn't it wrong—not only in the sense of being mistaken but also in the sense of being wrong-headed or dangerous—to turn our attention away from the celebration of the truth that God justifies *sinners* to a morbid focus on holiness?

A well-known and forceful proponent of this popular view is the Lutheran theologian Gerhard Forde. Seizing the Lutheran banner and waving it proudly, Forde asserts that sanctification is merely the "art of getting used to justification."[2] Justification is the central truth of the gospel, and sanctification is what happens to us spontaneously—as "God's secret"—when we relax and accept our justification. In his words, justification by faith alone "is, after all, *the* dogma of the Protestant Reformation," and anything that might distract us from that is a cause for concern.[3] Talk about sanctification is thus "dangerous."[4] It is dangerous, and sometimes even a "disaster," for it tempts us to think that we can add something to the salvation gained for us by Christ.[5] Forde insists that to

---

A Comparative Introduction, ed. Justin S. Holcomb (New York: New York University Press, 2017), 191-207; Bernhard Lohse, *Martin Luther's Theology: Its Historical and Systematic Development*, trans. Roy A. Harrisville (Minneapolis: Fortress, 2006); and Oswald Bayer, *Martin Luther's Theology: A Contemporary Interpretation*, trans. Thomas H. Trapp (Grand Rapids: Eerdmans, 2008).

[2]Gerhard Forde, "The Lutheran View," in *Christian Spirituality: Five Views*, ed. Donald L. Alexander (Downers Grove, IL: InterVarsity Press, 1988), 3.

[3]Gerhard Forde, "The Christian Life: Introduction," in *Christian Dogmatics*, ed. Carl Braaten and Robert W. Jenson (Minneapolis: Fortress, 1984), 2:397.

[4]Forde, "The Lutheran View," 15; and Forde, "The Christian Life: Introduction," 2:396.

[5]Forde, "The Lutheran View," 15.

allow *any* room for "cooperation" means that "*everything* eventually depends on the human contribution"—and to allow this is to undercut the truth of justification.[6] To allow that good works accompany and demonstrate justification is to lose the battle.[7] Instead, Forde insists that Luther was right in his teaching that we are *simul iustus et peccator*, and he calls us to appreciate Luther's advice to Philipp Melanchthon to "be a sinner and sin boldly, but believe even more boldly and rejoice in Christ."[8]

As widespread and popular as this view may be, however, it simply isn't the case that it is *the* Lutheran view. It may or may not be acceptable as *a* Lutheran view (I happily leave that debate to Lutheran intramural tussles), but it simply isn't right to claim that it is *the* Lutheran position, for it does not cohere with the classical Lutheran theology that is exemplified in the Lutheran scholastics.[9] And it does not come close to representing the depth and complexity of Luther's own thought. Consider this statement from Luther's Smalcald Articles (1537):

> I do not know how I can change what I have heretofore constantly taught on this subject, namely, that by faith (as St. Peter says) we get a new and clean heart and that God will and does account us altogether righteous and holy for the sake of Christ, our mediator. Although the sin in our flesh has not been completely removed or eradicated, he will not count or consider it.[10]

Here we see familiar Lutheran themes; the notions of forensic righteousness and imputation are at work. But we should also note that Luther insists that we in fact *do* acquire a "new and clean heart." And there is more. Luther continues by saying,

---

[6]Forde, "The Christian Life: Justification," 2:406-7.

[7]Forde, "The Christian Life: Justification and Sanctification," in *Christian Dogmatics*, 2:427.

[8]LW 48:282. See Forde, "The Christian Life: Justification and Sanctification," 438-39; cf. Forde, "The Lutheran View," 23-27.

[9]Forde surely knows that his view differs quite radically from the Lutheran scholastics. He consistently polemicizes against those who do theology "after the manner of Aristotle," and he explicitly rejects the third use (*tertius usus*) of the law. See "The Christian Life: Justification and the World," 2:449.

[10]"The Smalcald Articles," in *Martin Luther's Basic Theological Writings*, ed. Timothy Lull (Minneapolis: Fortress, 1989), 534.

Good works follow such faith, renewal, and forgiveness. Whatever is still sinful or imperfect in these works will not be reckoned as sin or defect for the sake of the same Christ. The whole man, in respect both of his person and of his works, shall be accounted and shall be righteous and holy through the pure grace and mercy . . . if good works do not follow, our faith is false and not true.[11]

Note here that when he refers to what is sinful or imperfect, he is not talking about sinful acts *simpliciter*. Instead, he is talking about what is sinful or imperfect in our *good works*. He is aware that our best efforts to follow Christ will fall short, and he insists that these are not accounted as sin against us and do not incur God's wrath. But he also insists that the "entire man"—both person and works—are both called to be righteous and holy and indeed are changed by God's "pure mercy and grace" so that we indeed *are* righteous and holy. And he makes it plain that if this does not happen, then "faith is false and not true." For "the Holy Spirit does not permit sin to rule" in the life of the Christian; if sin does have dominion and does "what it wishes," then we can conclude nothing else than that "the Holy Spirit and faith are not present, for St. John says, 'No one born of God commits sin . . .'" (1 John 1:9)."[12]

Luther excoriates those "Antinomians" who "speak beautifully and (as I cannot but think) with real sincerity" about the forgiveness of sins and justification but then "ignore the third article" of sanctification.[13] Such people, he says,

think one should not frighten or trouble the people, but rather always preach comfortingly about the grace and forgiveness of sins in Christ, and under no circumstances use these or similar words: "Listen! You want to be a Christian and at the same time remain an adulterer, a whoremonger, a drunken swine, arrogant, covetous, a usurer, envious, vindictive, malicious!" Instead they say, "Listen! Though you are an adulterer, a whoremonger, a miser, or other kind

---

[11]"The Smalcald Articles," 534.
[12]"The Smalcald Articles," 527.
[13]Luther, "On the Councils and the Church," LW 41:113.

of sinner, if you but believe, you are saved and you need not fear the law. Christ has fulfilled it all!"[14]

Such preachers, Luther thunders, "may be fine Easter preachers, but they are very poor Pentecost preachers, for they do not preach concerning the sanctification and vivification of the Holy Spirit (*de sanctificatione et vivificatione Spiritus sancti*)."[15] There "is no such Christ that died for sinners who do not, after the forgiveness of sins, desist from sins and lead a new life."[16] For a proper understanding of Christ and his benefits is much more full-orbed, much more robust, and indeed much more beautiful than the counterfeit offered by such sincere preachers. A proper understanding of Christ knows that he "did not only earn *gratia* for us, but also *donum*, 'the gift of the Holy Spirit,' so that we might have not only forgiveness of, but also cessation of, sin. Now he who does not abstain from sin, but persists in his evil life, must have a different Christ."[17] This so-called Christ is a fake, a fraud, and the person who relies on this Christ "must be damned with this, his new Christ."[18]

To know Christ truly is to know that the incarnate Son has sent his Holy Spirit, and it is to know further that the ministry of the Holy Spirit is to make people truly holy as they are transformed into the image of the Son. Those who are filled with the Holy Spirit are those who are rightly called the *"sancta catholica Christiana*, that is, 'a Christian holy people.'"[19] Those who are rightly called "Christians" are those who "have the Holy Spirit" who "sanctifies them daily, not only through the forgiveness of sins acquired for them by Christ, but also through the abolition, the purging, the mortification of sins, on the basis of which they are called a holy people."[20] Thus true "Christian

---

[14]Luther, "On the Councils and the Church," LW 41:113-14.
[15]Luther, "On the Councils and the Church," LW 41:114.
[16]Luther, "On the Councils and the Church," LW 41:114.
[17]Luther, "On the Councils and the Church," LW 41:114.
[18]Luther, "On the Councils and the Church," LW 41:114.
[19]Luther, "On the Councils and the Church," LW 41:143.
[20]Luther, "On the Councils and the Church," LW 41:143-44.

holiness . . . is found where the Holy Spirit gives people faith in Christ and sanctifies them."[21]

I have cited Luther at some length here, partly because the common misunderstanding is so widespread and deep that I feel that we need to hear Luther's own voice to grasp fully the reality of his thought, and partly because his words are so forceful and convicting. I could go on. But it should be clear that Luther's own doctrine of sanctification is very far removed from the pervasive—and pernicious—misunderstanding. Of course Luther resolutely believes in justification by grace alone through faith alone; Christ's righteousness is imputed to us, and we are to be comforted by that reality. But he also believes just as resolutely in the sanctifying work of the Holy Spirit who renews us, radically transforms us, and makes us actually righteous and holy. And we are to be both challenged and comforted by that reality as well.[22]

This isn't merely Luther. The Lutheran confessional statements also proclaim the truth of sanctification. For instance, the Formula of Concord (1577) insists that

> it is no less necessary to admonish the people to Christian discipline and good works and to remind them how necessary it is that they practice good works as a demonstration of their faith and their gratitude to God than it is to admonish them that works not be mingled with the article on justification.[23]

In other words, while it is true that we must always be watchful to avoid thinking that our good works contribute to our justification, so also must we beware thinking that they do not matter. For while we are

---

[21]Luther, "On the Councils and the Church," LW 41:145.

[22]See further David Yeago, "Martin Luther on Renewal and Sanctification: *Simul Iustus et* Revisited," *Sapere teologico e unita' della defe: studi in onore del Prof. Jared Wicks* (2004): 655-74. See also David Yeago, "Gnosticism, Antinomianism, and Reformation Theology: Reflections on the Costs of a Construal," *Pro Ecclesia* (1993): 37-49; and David Yeago "A Christian, Holy People: Martin Luther on Salvation and the Church," in *Spirituality and Social Embodiment*, ed. L. Gregory Jones and James J. Buckley (Oxford: Wiley-Blackwell, 1997), 101-20.

[23]"The Formula of Concord," in *The Book of Concord: The Confessions of the Evangelical Lutheran Church*, ed. Robert Kolb and Timothy Wengert (Minneapolis: Fortress, 2000), 499.

justified *sola fide* (in the instrumental sense), nonetheless we should also remember that "faith is never alone but is always accompanied by love and hope."[24]

Important theologians of Lutheran scholasticism agree. They carefully distinguish sanctification from justification (and sometimes from regeneration), for justification deals with the legal status of sinners (through the imputation of Christ's righteousness), and regeneration refers to the beginning of the life of inherent holiness or righteousness that is continued in the process of sanctification.[25] For instance, Johann Baier (1647–1695) uses the language of new creation (*nova creatio*), vivification (*vivificatio*), and spiritual resuscitation (*spiritualis resuscito*) to refer to God's work in sanctification.[26] The principal efficient cause of our sanctification is the triune God,[27] and the ultimate goal of God's work in sanctification is the salvation of humanity to the glory of God.[28] In no sense can sanctification be considered a soteriological "option" for the Lutheran dogmaticians; those whom God declares righteous through the imputed righteousness of Christ are also truly *made* holy by the sanctifying work of the Holy Spirit.

The Reformed tradition. John Calvin is perhaps the best-known proponent of Reformed theology.[29] The entire point of regeneration is to bring the heart and life of the believer into line with God's righteousness, and such a life of holy concord with God's will is the confirmation of our adoption as God's children.[30] In the work of sanctification, an

---

[24]"The Formula of Concord," 496.

[25]See the discussion in Heinrich Schmid, *The Doctrinal Theology of the Evangelical Lutheran Church* (Minneapolis: Augsburg, 1899), 486-91.

[26]Johann Baier, *Compendium theologiae positivae* (1685), 587.

[27]Baier, *Compendium* III.IV.VI, 592.

[28]Baier, *Compendium* III.IV.XIII, 597.

[29]On Calvin's relation to the broader Reformed tradition, see Richard A. Muller, "John Calvin and Late Calvinism: The Identity of the Reformed Tradition," in *The Cambridge Companion to Reformation Theology*, ed. David Bagchi and David Steinmetz (Cambridge: Cambridge University Press, 2004), 130-49; Richard A. Muller, *Calvin and the Reformed Tradition: On the Work of Christ and the Order of Salvation* (Grand Rapids: Baker Academic, 2012); Richard A. Muller, *After Calvin: Studies in the Development of a Theological Tradition* (Oxford: Oxford University Press, 2003).

[30]Calvin, *Institutes*, 3.6.2 (LCC 20:685-86).

authentic "love of righteousness" is "instilled and established" within God's people.[31] This holiness, which is the gift of God to us (and never something that we can either achieve or use as merit), is the "bond" of our union with God.[32] We are made holy by virtue of our union with Christ, and this same union truly makes us temples of the Holy Spirit.[33] It changes our affections at the deepest and innermost levels, and—as it moves from "heart" to "daily living"—it results in lifestyles that are radically transformed in love of God and neighbor.[34] This sanctification, which is always and only by God's Holy Spirit, cultivates in the believer "blamelessness and purity of life."[35] This transformation "in the soul itself" is afterward seen in "the renewal by the fruits that follow from it."[36]

Although the holiness of redeemed persons is not yet perfect, nonetheless it is real.[37] It is also vitally important; indeed, there is a sense in which it is necessary. It can—and surely must—be distinguished from justification, but it cannot be *separated* from justification. For while we are "justified by faith alone," nevertheless "actual holiness of life, so to speak, is not separated from free imputation of righteousness."[38] "[D]o we not see," Calvin asks, "that the Lord freely justifies his own in order that he may at the same time restore them to true righteousness and sanctification by his Spirit?"[39] Indeed, the Lord's promise is to "bring us, purged of all uncleanness and defilement, into obedience to God's righteousness."[40] Those who are saved *cannot* "wallow" in the "wickedness and pollution" from which they have been

---

[31]Calvin, *Institutes*, 3.6.2 (LCC 20:685-86).

[32]Calvin, *Institutes*, 3.6.2 (LCC 20:686).

[33]Calvin, *Institutes* 3.6.3 (LCC 20:687). On the theme of union with Christ, see J. Todd Billings, *Calvin, Participation, and the Gift: The Activity of Believers in Union with Christ* (Oxford: Oxford University Press, 2007).

[34]Calvin, *Institutes* 3.6.4 (LCC 20:688).

[35]Calvin, *Institutes* 3.11.1 (LCC 20:725).

[36]Calvin, *Institutes* 3.3.6, 8 (LCC 20:598, 600).

[37]Calvin, *Institutes* 3.3.11 (LCC 20:603-4).

[38]Calvin, *Institutes* 3.3.1 (LCC 20:593).

[39]Calvin, *Institutes* 3.3.19 (LCC 20:613).

[40]Calvin, *Institutes* 3.3.14 (LCC 20:520).

rescued.[41] Those who live otherwise are guilty of nothing less than insulting God.[42]

Subsequent generations of Reformed theologians largely agree (although, in comparison to Lutheran theology and the views of Martin Luther, without the direct dependence on and degree of deference toward, the theology of John Calvin).[43] For instance, the Swiss theologian Johannes Wollebius (1589–1629) recognizes the distinction between justification and sanctification as vitally important. He insists that justification deals with issues of "legal" righteousness and sanctification with "evangelical" righteousness.[44] But while they are distinct, they are also inseparable, for sanctification accompanies justification as light follows the sun.[45] Where justification declares us righteous, sanctification actually transforms us so that we are righteous. The efficient cause is the entire Trinity, the internal impulsive cause is God's free and bountiful grace, the external impulse is Christ, the external instrumental cause is the Word (the law and gospel), and the internal instrumental cause is faith.[46] Notably, sanctification demands our cooperation; the Holy Spirit is the "chief agent," and nothing happens without the prior work of the Spirit, but it is also true that sanctification does not take place apart from our cooperation with the Spirit. The subject of sanctification is the entire or whole human person: intellect, will, and affections (*intellectus, voluntas,* and *affectus*).[47] Through sanctification, the Holy Spirit produces righteousness that is rightly said to be *inherent* (*inherens nobis infunditer*).[48] Wollebius

---

[41]Calvin, *Institutes* 3.6.2 (LCC 20:686).

[42]Calvin, *Institutes* 3.6.4 (LCC 20:688).

[43]See the discussion by Michael Allen, "Sanctification, Perseverance, and Assurance," in *Reformation Theology: A Systematic Summary*, ed. Matthew Barrett (Wheaton, IL: Crossway, 2017), 558.

[44]Johannes Wollebius, *Christianae Theologiae Compendium* (Basel, 1634), I.xxx.1, 245. An older English translation is *An Abridgement of Christian Divinity,* trans. Alexander Ross (London, 1660), 256.

[45]Wollebius, *An Abridgement of Christian Divinity,* 269.

[46]Wollebius, *Christianae Theologiae Compendium* I.xxi.3-6, 258-59.

[47]Wollebius, *Compendium* I.xxxi.9, 259.

[48]Wollebius, *Compendium* I.xxxi.13, 261.

is far from idiosyncratic on these points. The German theologian Amandus Polanus (1561–1610), for instance, agrees on virtually all points.[49] He celebrates the work of the Spirit, for the work of sanctification renews humanity (*novus homo*) through mortification and vivification.[50] Notably, he insists that sanctification happens only by grace, and he distinguishes between different aspects of grace: grace is rightly understood as prevenient, preparing, operating, cooperating, and perfecting—and all are vital to the process of sanctification. Notably, operating grace (*gratia operans*) initiates the renovation of our minds, will, and affections (*mentes, voluntas,* and *affectiones*)—and this produces obedience that is acceptable to God.[51] But while operating grace is necessary, so also is cooperating grace (*gratia cooperans*), for God not only enables our cooperation but also demands it. Other witnesses could be called: German Reformed theologian Zacharias Ursinus (1534–1583) insists that we can never have justification without also being sanctified.[52] Swiss theologian Johannes Heidegger (1633–1698) goes so far as to say that sanctification is our greatest need (*sanctificationis summa necessitas est*).[53] Reformed theologian Peter von Mastricht (1630–1706) holds that sanctification is a gift—it is a gift that is now inherent within God's children. It is never their possession or something of which they can boast; it is always and ultimately a gift. But it is not a gift that is an entity somehow exterior to them; it is an "infusion" into them, and it truly changes them.[54] Sanctification is rightly said to be *necessary*—not necessary for gaining or earning salvation (which we cannot do) but necessary for the reception of

---

[49]E.g., Amandus Polanus, *De Partibus Gratuitae Iustificationis Nostrae Coram Deo: Theses Theologica* (Basel, 1598); and Amandus Polanus, *Syntagma Theologiae Christianae* (Basel, 1609), 2:2933-3030. On the importance of Polanus, see Robert Letham, "Amandus Polanus: A Neglected Theologian?" *Sixteenth Century Studies* (1990): 463-76.

[50]Polanus, *Syntagma* VI.xxxvii, 3015-16.

[51]Polanus, *Syntagma* VI.xxxvii, 3019.

[52]See the discussion in Heinrich Heppe, *Reformed Dogmatics: Set Out and Illustrated from the Sources* (London: George Allen and Unwin, 1950), 566.

[53]Johannes Heidegger, *Corpus Theologiae Christianae* (Zurich, 1700), XXIII.vii, 314.

[54]Peter von Mastricht, *Theoretico-Practica Theologica,* 2nd ed. (1698), VI.viii.7, 735.

it.[55] These theologians are representative in many respects, and, by my judgment, their views are right in the mainstream of historic Reformed theology.[56]

Seen in this light, it is not at all surprising that the major Reformed confessional statements are decisive about the reality and necessity of sanctification. As the Second Helvetic Confession (1566) puts it, "Wherefore, in this matter we are not speaking of a fictitious, empty, lazy, and dead faith, but of a living, quickening faith. It is and is called a living faith because it apprehends Christ who is life and makes alive, and shows that it is alive by living works."[57]

The Anglican tradition. Briefly turning our attention to the Anglican Reformation, we see a strong and pronounced emphasis on the doctrine of sanctification. The English Reformer Thomas Cranmer (1489–1556), for example, holds to the doctrine of justification by grace alone through faith alone. He makes a case that it is to be found not only in Scripture but also in patristic theology.[58] He denies that good works are meritorious.[59] And he is sure that all that is within us remains imperfect.[60] But he also insists that the doctrine of *sola fide* is not meant to imply that justifying faith *is* alone; to the contrary, such faith is always accompanied by "true repentance" and renewed holiness.[61] "Faith" that does not issue in repentance but instead brings "either evil works, or no good works, is

---

[55]von Mastricht, *Theoretico-Practica Theologica* VI.viii.xxvii, 745.

[56]See further, e.g., Lucas Trelcatius Jr. (one of the primary opponents of Jacobus Arminius in the theological controversy at Leiden), *Disputatio theologica de justificatione hominis coram Deo,* XX (Leiden, 1604); and Lucas Trelcatius Jr., *Opuscula theologica omnia, duorum catalogum, prima edita* XIII (Leiden), 348-78. Trelcatius insists that sanctification is *necessary* for salvation, e.g., *Opuscula theologica omnia,* XIV, 386. See also Francis Turretin, *Institutio Theologiae Elencticae, XVII* in *Opera Tomus I* (Edinburgh, 1847). Turretin clearly distinguishes sanctification from justification (e.g., 609-12) but also insists that sanctification and the good works that flow from it are necessary for salvation (620-23).

[57]Cited in Michael Scott Horton, *The Christian Faith: A Systematic Theology for Pilgrims on the Way* (Grand Rapids: Zondervan, 2011), 655.

[58]Thomas Cranmer, "Homily of Salvation," in *The Works of Thomas Cranmer* (Cambridge: Cambridge University Press, 1846), 130.

[59]Cranmer, "Homily of Salvation," 131.

[60]Cranmer, "Homily of Salvation," 133.

[61]Cranmer, "Homily of Salvation," 133.

not a right, pure, and lively faith, but a dead, devilish, counterfeit, and feigned faith."[62]

Cranmer is exercised to show that a truly biblical doctrine of salvation will encompass the breadth of God's work in Christ and the Spirit.[63] Salvation includes justification, but it can never be reduced to it. For the "infinite benefits of God" actually

> move us to render ourselves to God wholly, with all our will, hearts, might, and power, to serve him in all good deeds, obeying his commandments during our lives, to seek in all things his glory and honor . . . [and] move us for his sake also to be ever ready to give ourselves to our neighbors, and as much as lieth within us, to study with all our endeavor to do good to every man.[64]

For the faith that truly justifies is genuine faith; it is "good and lively faith." And such "good and lively faith" issues in works of charity.[65]

Cranmer is aware that sanctification is a process, and he is also keenly aware that even our best efforts are not untainted. But true faith not only changes our legal standing before God, it changes *us* as well—and this change is exhibited in our affections and behaviors. The view that justifying faith sets us "at liberty from doing all good works" is a "phantasy," and those who teach this "trifle with God and deceive themselves."[66]

Other important Anglican theologians are in substantial agreement. For instance, Richard Hooker (1554–1600) takes a line that is similar in many important respects. Like Cranmer (and many others), he holds resolutely to a distinctly Protestant account of justification; God justifies *sinners*. God justifies those who are "full of iniquity"; it is those who are full of sin who are pardoned.[67] But the sinners who are justified by God

---

[62]Cranmer, "Homily of Salvation," 133.

[63]On Cranmer's soteriology more generally, see Ashley Null, *Thomas Cranmer's Doctrine of Repentance: Renewing the Power to Love God* (Oxford: Oxford University Press, 2007).

[64]Cranmer, "Homily of Salvation," 134.

[65]Thomas Cranmer, "A Short Declaration of the True, Lively, and Christian Faith," in *The Works of Thomas Cranmer*, 135.

[66]Cranmer, "A Short Declaration," 136.

[67]Richard Hooker, *Golden Words: The Rich and Precious Jewel of God's Holy Word* (Oxford, 1863), 290.

are those sinners who are repentant and who *hate* their sin.[68] Sanctification is as real as is justification; it is "the baptism with heavenly fire which both illumineth and inflameth. This worketh in man that knowledge of God and that love unto things divine whereupon our eternal felicity endureth."[69] And it is necessary: "Pelagius urged labor for the attainment of eternal life without necessity of God's grace; if we teach grace without the necessity of man's labor, we use one error as a nail to drive out the other."[70] Similarly, the bishop of Salisbury, John Davenant (1572–1641), denies that our sanctification results in good works that are perfect, and he furthermore denies that such works are meritorious.[71] He protests that Cardinal Robert Bellarmine misunderstands and misrepresents the authentically Protestant doctrine, and in doing so he insists that sanctification is *necessary*. It is necessary as a concomitant of justifying faith, for the faith of repentance comes with the faith of justification. It is also necessary "downstream" of justification, for those who are justified are also regenerate and are being sanctified. Thus Davenant argues from Scripture, and he cites patristic authorities in support of his position.[72] His views cohere well with other Protestant theologians, and together they insist on the reality and necessity of sanctification.

Summary. Much more could be said on the topic of sanctification among sixteenth- and seventeenth-century Protestants. We could call on many witnesses from the various church traditions and listen all day to the Puritans and the voices of the Dutch "Second Reformation" (*nadere reformatie*). Even from this brief sketch, however, we should be able to see significant agreement and continuity within Protestantism. There are areas of disagreement, of course, and I do not mean to elide or erase such differences. For instance, the Lutherans and the more "Arminian" of the Anglicans (and, of course, the Remonstrants) part ways with the more

---

[68]Hooker, *Golden Words*, 290.
[69]Hooker, *Golden Words*, 268.
[70]Hooker, *Golden Words*, 289.
[71]John Davenant, *A Treatise on Justification*, trans. Josiah Allport (London, 1844), 328-42.
[72]Davenant, *A Treatise on Justification*, 280-81.

confessionally Reformed over the status of those who claim to be justified but who do not grow in sanctification; the Lutherans and "Armin-
ians" think that some of these people may have been genuine believers
who were regenerate, while the Reformed deny that they were ever truly
Christian. Lutheran theologians think that there is a legitimate distinction between mortal and venial sin, while (most) Reformed theologians
do not find this distinction helpful or appropriate.[73] Some Protestants,
such as Jacob Arminius (1560–1609), follow the teaching of the mature
Augustine in holding that it is possible that sanctification be completed
in this life; other major theologians are quite skeptical about this.[74] Theologians differ on the proper interpretation of the seventh chapter of
Romans and even somewhat more broadly on the implications of that
passage (and others) for our expectations of sanctification in the
Christian life.

Such areas of disagreement, however, pale in comparison to the
significant concord on the doctrine of sanctification. Without denying the differences between traditions (and between theologians
within the various traditions), we can summarize some of the most
important points of agreement. The relation of justification to sanctification is vitally important. Justification is instantaneous; sanctification is instantaneous in the sense that it begins at the moment of
the new birth, but it is a process that continues throughout the Christian life. Justification concerns imputed righteousness; it is "alien"
righteousness that is credited to us. Sanctification is real righteousness that is given to us and imparted in us. Justification and sanctification are always to be distinguished, for they are logically distinct in

---

[73]On this distinction, see David Hollatz, *Examen Theologicum Acromaticum* (1763; repr. Darmstadt: Wissenschaftliche Buchgesellschaft, 1971), 547-51, and Quenstadt, *Theologica* II, 147-51.

[74]On Arminius, see Keith D. Stanglin and Thomas H. McCall, *Jacob Arminius: Theologian of Grace*
(New York: Oxford University Press, 2012), 170-72; and Keith D. Stanglin, *Arminius on the Assurance of Salvation: The Context: Roots, and Shape of the Leiden Debate, 1603–1609* (Leiden, Brill:
2007), 120-30. For background, see, for example, Augustine, *De Natura* 37, *PL* 44:265; *De Natura*
41, *PL* 44:267, *De Natura* 52, *PL* 44:272; *De Natura* 68-72, *PL* 44:281-82; *De Perfectione* 3-4, *PL*
44:295-96; *De Perfectione* 20, *PL* 44:315-16.

ways that really matter. At the same time, however, they can never be *separated*. Both justification and sanctification are benefits of our union with Christ: neither can be had apart from that union with Christ. Nor can one be had apart from the other. As Michael Scott Horton puts it, "The Reformers saw 'Christ for us' and 'Christ in us,' the alien righteousness imputed and the sanctifying righteousness imparted, as not only compatible but necessarily and inextricably related. Those who are justified through faith are new creatures and begin then and there to love God and their neighbor, yielding the fruit of good works."[75]

The Reformation doctrine of sanctification is thoroughly biblical in form; the Reformers make every effort to ground their teaching in Scripture, and their work is replete with appeals to both Testaments. It is from Scripture that we learn what holiness is, it is from Scripture that we learn the depths of our unholiness, and it is from Scripture that we learn that God has made provision for our holiness and calls us to it. More pointedly, Scripture teaches us that genuine holiness takes expression in love of God and love of neighbor, as articulated in the two tables of the Decalogue and the great commandments of Jesus. Notably, they concur on the so-called third use of the law: it is given not only to restrain evil and convict of sin but also to instruct believers in true righteousness as they walk in the way of holiness. Accordingly, Protestants in the age of the Reformation are convinced that we should be grateful to God for this gift. And they are resolutely convinced that Scripture teaches that God not only calls his people to holiness of heart and life but also has made provision for it.

The Reformation doctrine of sanctification is thoroughly trinitarian in substance. As we are reminded by such Lutheran theologians as Johann Baier and Johannes Quenstadt (1617–1688) and Reformed theologians such as Johannes Wollebius, the efficient cause of sanctification

---

[75]Horton, *The Christian Faith*, 648-49.

is the whole (*tota*) Trinity.[76] The triune God whose essence is holy love has formed creatures in his image to know that love and to reflect that holiness, and this God is active in the sanctification of those creatures. As a deeply trinitarian doctrine, it is christologically oriented in (at least) two senses. At one level, it is Christocentric in the sense that Christlikeness norms our account of holiness, and indeed Christ is an example to us. As Luther puts it, "This righteousness follows the example of Christ in this respect and is transformed into his likeness. It is precisely this that Christ requires."[77] At another level, God sanctifies his people by uniting them to the incarnate Son; the same Christ who offers us the wonderful gift of imputed righteousness also offers to us the resplendent gift of actual righteousness. This actual righteousness is rightly said to be ours as it is imparted to us and thereby inherent in us, but it is also the gift of the triune God that we receive—only and always—through our union with Christ. Union with Christ, by faith, both justifies us and sanctifies us. And as there is one Christ rather than two, so it is that to be united to the one and whole Christ is to enjoy the benefits of the one and whole Christ. In other words, to be united with Christ is to be both pronounced righteous (in a forensic sense) and truly made holy. This union with Christ occurs by the work of the Spirit, and Protestant doctrines of sanctification had a profoundly pneumatological element as well. It is the Spirit—the Spirit *of Christ* (against the "enthusiasts")—who makes us holy. This is the mission of the Spirit, and it is the relentless work of the triune God as it reaches its *terminus* in the person of the Spirit. In other words, the Holy Spirit unites us to Christ and thus brings us home to the Father (cf. Rom 8), and in doing so he transforms us so that we truly belong in this home.

This may sound abstract, but for the Protestant reformers the doctrine of sanctification is intensely personal and pervasively ethical in

---

[76]See, for example, Baier, *Compendium* III.iv.6, 592; Wollebius, *Christianae theologiae compendium* I.xxxi.3, 258-59; Trelcatius, Jr., *Disputatio* XIII.
[77]Martin Luther, "Two Kinds of Righteousness," in LW 31:300.

expression. It cannot be reduced to moralism or another version of legalism, for there is no sense in which sanctification is "our part" of the order of salvation—as if God does the work of justification but then demands that we become holy and throws us back on ourselves to do so. It cannot be reduced to behavior modification. To the contrary, it is the work of God. Make no mistake, it is the work with which we are called to cooperate, but it is God's work nonetheless. It is God's work at the innermost part of the sinner; it is God's work of renovation and re-creation that cleanses the sinner of sin. It is God's work of healing and rescue, and it takes place in the "heart," the will, the mind, and the "affections." This results in outward change, and this change is exhibited in good works of justice and charity.

Accordingly, such good works are vitally important; indeed, they are rightly said to be *necessary* (in the appropriate sense). In Luther's memorable and powerful words, "A Christian should either have the Holy Spirit and lead a new life, or know that he has no Christ."[78] And it is for all believers. There is no sense in which we should entertain any notion that sanctification and holiness are somehow reserved for a distinct order or class or group. Sanctification is not only for an elite class of "super-saints." To the contrary, it is intended for all God's people. As Timothy George puts it, "All who believe in Christ are saints."[79] And, by the gracious provision of Christ and the work of the Holy Spirit, it is available to all. God now calls us to know him and walk with him in holiness, and he invites us to this new life. It is no wonder, then, that Hooker exults in the hopefulness and beauty of this doctrine: "To make a wicked and sinful man most holy through his believing is more than to create a world from nothing. Our faith most holy!"[80]

---

[78]Luther, "On the Councils and the Church," 115.
[79]Timothy George, *Theology of the Reformers* (Nashville: B & H, 1988), 96.
[80]Hooker, *Golden Words,* 255.

HOLY SPIRIT AND HOLY SCRIPTURE

To this point, however, we have not been very specific about *how* this sanctification occurs. To be sure, the answers of the Protestant traditions are complex, and there is some variegation within and between the traditions. But there is also significant agreement. Many theologians share the conviction that the Holy Spirit works through the sacraments, through the discipline of the church, and through divine providence (including suffering). They also are convinced that the Spirit sanctifies *through the Word*, and this will be our focus here.[81]

The convictions of the Reformers. For the Reformers, sanctification takes place by the work of the Holy Spirit (or, more precisely, the work of the triune God with the Holy Spirit as the *terminus*). Sanctification is always by the Spirit, and sanctification is only by the Spirit. It is not ultimately about us or what *we* do; it is not "our part" of salvation. As Luther puts it, "Christian holiness . . . is found where the Holy Spirit gives people faith in Christ and sanctifies them."[82] Hooker makes the point with clarity and force: "What we have and what we shall have is the fruit of His goodness, and not a thing which we can claim by right or title of our own worth . . . let Him alone have the glory by whose grace we have our whole ability and power of well-doing."[83] So we always look to the Holy Spirit as the source of our holiness and goodness.[84] Indeed, we should do so especially when we think that we are advancing in godliness: "Our very virtues may be snares. . . . There is no man's case so dangerous as when Satan hath persuaded him that his own righteousness shall present him pure and blameless before God."[85]

The Holy Spirit is the agent of sanctification, and the Holy Spirit works through the Word. As Luther says, God's Word is the "holiest of all

---

[81]For a helpful overview of pneumatology, see Graham A. Cole, "The Holy Spirit," in *Reformation Theology: A Systematic Summary*, ed. Matthew Barrett (Wheaton, IL: Crossway, 2017), 393-421.

[82]Luther, "On the Councils and the Church," 145.

[83]Hooker, *Golden Words*, 289.

[84]von Mastricht observes that even our mortification is only possible by the work of the Holy Spirit, *Theoretico-Practica Theologica* 6.8.9, 736.

[85]Hooker, *Golden Words*, 292.

possessions," for "the Holy Spirit administers it and anoints or sanctifies the Church with it."[86] Sanctification is the work of the Holy Spirit—it is not something that the Bible does on its own. At the same time, however, the Holy Spirit works in and through the written Word of God to sanctify and cleanse. This insight, fundamental to Protestant theology, fuels Luther's rejection of Thomas Müntzer's claim to be a "scribe of the Holy Spirit" rather than a "scribe of Scripture" (which was his term for the Wittenberg theologians).[87] Instead, as Michael Allen notes, "Luther inextricably tied sanctification to Scripture."[88] Similarly, Calvin insists that Word and Spirit go together. Thus "we must come," Calvin says, "to the Word," for it is the light of guidance in the "labyrinth" of human finitude and fallenness.[89] For the Holy Spirit so works through the Word that we may be changed by its divine energy, for "his divine majesty lives and breathes there," and by "this power we are drawn and inflamed, knowingly and willingly, to obey him."[90]

Scholastic refinements. For the Reformers, we are sanctified by the work of the Holy Spirit in and through Holy Scripture. We are not sanctified by the Bible itself—as if the book itself has some power or ability to act as a causal agent in the purification of a holy people. But neither are we sanctified by the Holy Spirit apart from the written Word. This much is basic to Reformation teaching.

Further development of this teaching is worked out by the scholastic theologians of the Lutheran and Reformed traditions. Using the conceptual tools inherited from the medieval traditions, they specify that while the triune God (and more particularly the Holy Spirit) is the *efficient* cause of sanctification, the written Word is the *instrumental* cause.[91] The Holy Spirit is the principal and primary cause, and Scripture is a kind of

---

[86]Luther, "On the Councils and the Church," 149.

[87]Luther, "On the Councils and the Church," 170.

[88]Michael Allen, "Sanctification, Perseverance, and Assurance," 555.

[89]Calvin, *Institutes* 1.6.3 (LCC 20:72-73).

[90]Calvin, *Institutes* 1.7.5 (LCC 20:80).

[91]See, for example, the Leiden Synopsis, in Heppe, *Reformed Dogmatics,* 569; and Polanus, *Syntagma,* 3019, 3022.

secondary cause. Together, they produce "the one effect by one and the same action."[92] Accordingly, the written Word has properties of power and efficacy, but it has these only dependently and derivatively (rather than essentially).[93] Accordingly, in the words of the Lutheran theologian Johannes Quenstadt, "The divine Word is not the principal agent in the work of conversion, regeneration, and salvation, but it is only a suitable means or organ which God ordinarily uses."[94] The basic lines of this teaching cross confessional lines and are held by theologians in the Reformed tradition as well. There is some disagreement on points of higher-resolution detail (e.g., the Lutheran dogmaticians use sacramental language that is distinctive to their tradition and deny that the grace that comes through the Word is irresistible, while matters are not so straightforward for the Reformed).[95] But overall, there is broad continuity and agreement: it is the Holy Spirit who sanctifies, and the Holy Spirit does so through the written Word.[96]

THE FAITH ONCE DELIVERED: LESSONS FROM THE REFORMERS FOR TODAY

The Protestant reformers and their scholastic children have much to teach their descendants. Perhaps what we really need to hear is the powerful and resounding emphasis on the reality and beauty of the sanctifying grace of the triune God.

Those of us who are children of the Protestant Reformation and who are tempted by the disastrous but prevalent misunderstanding of Luther's soteriology might benefit from the classical Protestant message of sanctification. Those of us who are tempted to think that the Reformers'

---

[92]Johannes Andreas Quenstadt, *Theologica didactico-polemica*, I, 183, as cited in Schmid, *Doctrinal Theology*, 505. Quenstadt here adds that the Holy Spirit is "in, with, and through" the written Word (*Theologica* I, 170).

[93]See the discussion in Schmid, *Doctrinal Theology*, 505.

[94]Quenstadt, *Theologica* I, 172, cited in Schmid, *Doctrinal Theology*, 506.

[95]On the resistibility of grace, see the discussion in Schmid, *Doctrinal Theology*, 477-79, 504-5.

[96]Although, again, not *only* through the Word; the Spirit also uses the Eucharist, suffering in providence, etc.

doctrine of justification is the only or the ultimate teaching of the Reformation need to hear their insistence on the reality and necessity of sanctification. We need to be reminded that sanctification is real, and we need to see again that it is radiant and beautiful. We need to hear again the message that God loves us too much to leave us as he finds us—even though *we* might be content to wallow in the sin in which he finds us, the triune God who is the Holy One isn't willing to leave us in our filth and folly. The Holy One calls us to himself, and he cleanses us and renews us and fills us with his blessed Holy Spirit as we are transformed more and more into the image of the Son.

We need to see that sanctification is not limited to an elite class of super-saints who are other-worldly. Instead, we need to see that God's will and provision for holiness is meant for all of us, and that the vilest, meanest sinner can be radically transformed by God's grace. We need to see again that the holy life is life lived in community, shaped by the rhythms of family and ecclesial life, and oriented ever more toward love of God and neighbor. We need to see again that we were created, re-created, and cleansed "to do good works" from a heart that is holy (Eph 2:10).

Those of us who are tempted toward a privatization and individualization of holiness would do well to see again the vitally important place of good works in the Christian life. Those who are tempted, on one hand, to pursue visions of social reform that may not be adequately formed by the biblical prescriptions of justice and charity, as well as those on the other hand who pursue vague notions of "spirituality" that are divorced from Word and sacrament, stand to benefit from the classical Protestant insistence that the Holy Spirit sanctifies God's people by God's Word.

It may be that the signal contribution of the Reformation for us today—at least for those of us in the contemporary, all-too-comfortable world of Western Christianity—is the doctrine of sanctification. For, truly, "our God is a consuming fire" (Heb 12:29). And this, brothers and sisters, is good news indeed—the "purest gospel."

Chapter Eight

LUTHER *and the* GENERAL PRIESTHOOD

AN EMBEDDED ACCOUNT

DAVID J. LUY

THE DOCTRINE OF THE GENERAL PRIESTHOOD is undoubtedly a signature theme of Luther's reformation theology. It appears in each of the three well-known "Reformation treatises" of 1520, which set forth the marrow of Luther's vision for the reform of the church. It also surfaces rather frequently elsewhere in texts from across the span of Luther's lifetime.[1] In his treatise *The Freedom of a Christian*, Luther writes, "Christ has made it possible for us, provided we believe in him, to be not only his brethren, co-heirs and fellow-kings, but also his fellow priests."[2] Again, commenting on Psalm 110 in the late 1530s, Luther explains, "In his own person Christ is indeed the only High Priest between God and us all. Nevertheless, He has bestowed this name upon us, too, so that we who believe in Him are also priests, just as we are called Christians after

---

[1]The three Reformation treatises of 1520 to which I refer include *The Freedom of a Christian*, *To the Christian Nobility of the German Nation*, and *The Babylonian Captivity of the Church*. For a helpful catalog of Luther's most substantive expositions of this doctrine, see Hank Voss, *The Priesthood of All Believers and the* Missio Dei: *A Canonical, Catholic, and Contextual Perspective*, Princeton Theological Monograph Series 223 (Eugene, OR: Pickwick, 2016), 130n1.

[2]LW 31:355.

Him."[3] What does it mean for Luther to insist that all Christians are priests?

Secondary studies have often focused on the deconstructive ecclesiological significance of this doctrine. From this vantage point, Luther's concept of a general priesthood is understood primarily in polemical rather than constructive terms.[4] It is regarded essentially as a critique of hierarchical, sacerdotal clericalism with minimal implications for the positive, spiritual significance of the Christian community. On the strongest versions of this view, to say that all Christians are priests is effectively to dislocate each individual Christian from any sort of necessary relation to the visible church.[5]

It is certainly true that Luther regularly deploys the priesthood of all believers as a fulcrum point for leveraging criticism against late medieval understandings of church office.[6] Yet the doctrine is not deconstructive at its root. Underneath and alongside its critical deployments, the priesthood of all believers conveys a genuinely constructive account of the church as an indispensable locus of God's sanctifying action in the

---

[3]LW 13:329.

[4]B. A. Gerrish "Luther on Priesthood and Ministry," *Church History* 34, no. 4 (1965): 406.

[5]In other words, the significance of the priesthood of all believers is thought to reside primarily in its *displacement* of the church as an institution essential for Christian faith and life. This view is represented, for instance, in an interview with Joseph Ratzinger in 1983, quoted in David Yeago, "'A Christian, Holy People:' Martin Luther on Salvation and the Church" *Modern Theology* 13 (1997): 102. It is paralleled by prominent appropriations of the priesthood of all believers within certain strands of the baptistic theological tradition. See, for instance, Timothy George, "The Priesthood of All Believers and the Quest for Theological Integrity," *Criswell Theological Review* 3 (1983): 283-94; and Mark Rogers, "A Dangerous Idea? Martin Luther, E. Y. Mullins and the Priesthood of All Believers," *Westminster Theological Journal* 72 (2010): 119-34. See also Gerrish "Luther on Priesthood and Ministry," 404-5.

[6]He objects repeatedly to the idea that ministerial ordination confers an elevated status, which is distinct from the worldly estate occupied by the laity. With respect to status (or "walk of life," as Timothy Wengert renders the idea), Luther is insistent: "There is no true, basic difference between laymen and priests, princes and bishops, between religious and secular." On the contrary, Luther argues, "All Christians are truly of the spiritual estate, and there is no difference among them except that of office." "To the Christian Nobility of the German Nation Concerning the Reform of the Christian Estate" (1520) in LW 44:129, 127. See Timothy Wengert's helpful discussion in *Priesthood, Pastors, Bishops: Public Ministry for the Reformation and Today* (Minneapolis: Fortress, 2008), 4-16. The term depicted here as "estate" or "status" is the German word *Stand*, which is distinct from classifications according to office (*Amt*).

world.[7] Far from encouraging modern notions of spiritual autonomy, Luther's account of the general priesthood underscores precisely the inextricability of Christian existence from the corporate life of the church community.[8]

Luther's positive conception of the priesthood of all believers is intelligible, however, only in relation to a particular set of complementary theological themes. Because this is so, my goal in this chapter will be to provide an embedded interpretation, that is a construal of the general priesthood, which is situated within the context of Luther's doctrinal theology. In the end, I will suggest that the doctrine of the priesthood of all believers conveys Luther's conception of the church as a spiritual community within which Christians mediate Christ one to another through the corporate sharing of benefits and burdens, especially through the mutual administration of God's efficacious Word.

THE CASE FOR AN EMBEDDED INTERPRETATION

There has been a general tendency within scholarship to locate the significance of Luther's doctrine of the general priesthood in relation to some interpretive lens *other* than Luther's own theology. In this first section, I will suggest that dis-embedded accounts of this sort tend to distract from important aspects of the positive significance Luther himself attaches to the idea. One source of the distraction has already been mentioned—namely, the tendency to interpret the general priesthood primarily, if not solely, in relation to what it opposes. This

---

[7]It would, of course, be a mistake to act as though we could extract the entirety of Luther's doctrine of the church from this one solitary strand in his thought. Indeed, an entire family of receptions of this theme in Luther's theology appears indebted to precisely this sort of mistake. See, for instance, Wengert, *Priesthood, Pastors, Bishops* and the instructive comparison and contrast in Rogers, "Dangerous Idea?"

[8]By asserting this point, I make common cause with a number of recent voices who seek likewise to recover the positive content of Luther's account of the general priesthood. See, for instance, Voss, *Priesthood of All Believers and the* Missio Dei; Yeago, "A Christian, Holy People"; Gerrish, "Priesthood and Ministry," 410-11; George, "The Priesthood of All Believers and the Quest for Theological Integrity;" and Hans-Martin Barth, *Einander Priester sein: allgemeines Priestertum in ökumenischer Perspektive* (Göttingen: Vandenhoeck & Ruprecht, 1990).

methodological prioritization of the polemical is understandable for a variety of reasons (Luther certainly *is* a polemicist!) but inadvertently leaves one with the impression that the priesthood of the baptized is little more than an oppositional slogan.[9] In this case, it is abundantly clear what Luther is *against* but less obvious what Luther is *for*. As a consequence, the underlying substance of Luther's constructive outlook tends to be eclipsed or ignored.

The same sort of occlusion can also take place as the result of an eagerness to locate the significance of the general priesthood for the developmental history of late modern religion and culture.[10] Within this interpretive frame of reference, the general priesthood will understandably often be presented as a prelude to characteristics typical of late modern culture in the West: for instance, its emphasis on the right of private judgment, its religious principle of spiritual autonomy, its destabilization of institutional authority, its burgeoning secularity, and so forth.[11] An emphasis on what are perceived in retrospect to be the long-term aftereffects of the general priesthood tends likewise to obstruct Luther's own constructive vision because the focus of interpretation does not rest on the contents of Luther's theology per se but rather on Luther in relation to subsequent realities he did not anticipate.

Finally, scholarship surrounding the doctrine of the general priesthood has often been overwhelmingly preoccupied with issues of church polity.[12] Here again, the preoccupation is an understandable one. Luther's

---

[9]For an example of this general approach to Luther on the general priesthood, see Douglas A. Campbell, "'The Priesthood of All Believers': A Pauline Perspective," *The Journal of the Christian Brethren Research Fellowship* 129 (1992): 14-24. Campbell argues that Luther's use of the slogan is defined entirely by its opposition to varieties of clericalism prominent within the sixteenth century and thus has no positive contribution—as such—for the church today.

[10]See, for instance, Charles Taylor, *Sources of the Self: The Making of the Modern Identity* (Cambridge: Cambridge University Press, 2012), 217-18.

[11]For a presentation of individualist antiministerial appropriations of this theme, see B. A. Gerrish, "Priesthood and Ministry," 404-5; and Timothy George, "The Priesthood of All Believers and the Quest for Theological Integrity."

[12]Tom Greggs, for instance, suggests that Luther remains captive to the late-medieval affiliation of priesthood with polity and fails to consider the priesthood of the church in more corporate terms. See Tom Greggs, "The Priesthood of No Believer: On the Priesthood of Christ and His

discussion of the ordained ministry is notoriously complicated, and the doctrine of the general priesthood does indeed appear to exercise some sort of important role in relation to his official view. The critical question among scholars is whether Luther's emphasis on the universal priesthood of the baptized carries with it an egalitarian reconstruction of the ministerial office (itself derived from the universal priesthood), as it sometimes seems, or whether Luther retains a conception of the ordained ministry, which, in Brian Gerrish's words, is a "special institution of Christ . . . prior to the common priesthood in time and rank."[13] As important as this question is, it is still important to remember that Luther's theology of the general priesthood is not concerned primarily with issues of church office. To focus predominantly on polity is once again to eclipse the substance of the doctrine on its own positive terms. In each of these three cases, it would be easy to overstate the nature of my concern. The point is not to suggest that any of these various interpretive tendencies is illegitimate or unimportant. It is rather more modestly to suggest that an exaggerated preoccupation with these various topics threatens to obscure Luther's own substantive account of the general priesthood by way of inadvertent neglect.

What is generally missing or underdeveloped in these sorts of modern accounts is a sustained exposition of what Luther actually thought

---

Church," *International Journal of Systematic Theology* 17 (2015): 386-90. Greggs is right to observe that Luther does indeed draw connections between the general priesthood and issues of church polity, but he is wrong, in my view, to set this in opposition to non-polemically defined ecclesiological interests. For Luther, these issues are all interrelated and should not be treated as mutually exclusive objects of concern (e.g., *because* he attends to polity, he neglects the priesthood of the church). Greggs's account is ironic because Luther actually affirms most of what Greggs presents as an *alternative* to Luther's view.

[13]Gerrish, "Priesthood and Ministry," 408. In my view, although Luther's position on this issue is something of a moving target, the latter option has the stronger case to make. For a helpful discussion of these issues, see Jonathan Mumme, *Die Präsenz Christi im Amt: am Beispiel ausgewählter Predigten Martin Luthers, 1535–1546*, Refo500 Academic Studies 21 (Göttingen: Vandenhoeck & Ruprecht, 2015); Wengert, *Priesthood, Pastors, Bishops*; Robert Kolb, "Ministry in Martin Luther and the Lutheran Confessions," in *Called and Ordained: Lutheran Perspectives of the Office of the Ministry*, ed. Todd Nichol and Mark Kolden (Minneapolis: Fortress, 1990), 49-66; Yeago, "A Christian, Holy People;" Wilhelm Brunotte, *Das geistliche Amt bei Luther* (Berlin: Lutherisches Verlagshaus, 1959); and Hellmut Lieberg, *Amt und Ordination bei Luther und Melanchthon* (Göttingen: Vandenhoeck & Ruprecht, 1962).

about the priesthood of all believers on its own terms. Prior to each of these focal points (i.e., polemical application, reception history, polity) there resides Luther's positive conception of the general priesthood as conditioned by the particularities of his own theological framework. To neglect this positive conception is to encourage descriptive distortions. A dis-embedded version of the doctrine of the priesthood of all believers easily becomes a plastic abstraction, taking on a life of its own. It becomes capable of applications that would have appeared strange and probably even grotesque to Luther himself. Of course, it could be argued that Luther is nevertheless responsible in some manner even for the *inadvertent* aspects of his reception history, but it is not our present purpose to consider questions of this speculative variety.[14] It is rather to turn attention to Luther and to pursue an embedded account of the general priesthood, which is governed by the dogmatic structure of Luther's own theological vision and not by peripheral interests, effects, and applications.

THE GENERAL PRIESTHOOD IN THEOLOGICAL PERSPECTIVE

Luther "lays the theological foundations" for his doctrine of the priesthood of all believers in his celebrated treatise of 1520, *The Freedom of a Christian*. So argues Hans-Martin Barth, the author of an important, ecumenical study of the general priesthood.[15] In this brief treatise, Luther explains "the whole of Christian life in a brief form."[16] Included within the overview is an explicit treatment of the general priesthood, situated and framed by an intricate doctrinal architecture. In this, the main section of my paper, I call attention to two main themes from within this treatise, each of which stands out also in an

---

[14]In my view, treatments of this question would generally benefit from a more specific delineation of modal concepts. Is one "responsible" (1) for contributing to the conditions necessary for x, (2) for creating the conditions necessary for x, (3) for creating the conditions sufficient for x, or must one (4) create the conditions *entailing* x?

[15]Barth suggests that this is so even beyond the scope of those particular passages in which Luther mentions the general priesthood in explicit terms. Barth, *Einander Priester sein*, 36.

[16]LW 31:343.

assortment of other writings as especially important for the delineation of Luther's positive account of the general priesthood. The first is Luther's concept of the "wondrous exchange," which presents the mystical union between Christ and the Christian through faith. The second is Luther's emphasis on the efficacy of the mediated Word as the special means through which God operates in, on, and among human beings. These themes are significant for our topic because each intersects in an explicit manner with the doctrine of the general priesthood. Perhaps more important, each of these two themes also contributes to the theological infrastructure within which Luther's positive conception of the general priesthood makes sense. We consider each theme now in turn.

Wondrous exchange. The concept of a wondrous exchange is a pervasive motif across Luther's soteriological writings.[17] Its principal purpose is to describe the intimate communion and fellowship that exists between Christ and the Christian through faith. Within this mystical union, the believer receives a share in all that belongs to Christ, and Christ receives from the believer all that belongs to him or her. Christ assumes sin, death, corruption, and the curse. The Christian receives righteousness, life, victory, blessings, and so on. Luther describes this redemptive exchange in especially vivid terms in his treatise *The Freedom of a Christian.* "The third incomparable benefit of faith," Luther writes, "is that it unites the soul with Christ as a bride is united with her bridegroom. By this mystery, as the Apostle teaches, Christ and the soul become one flesh [Eph 5:31-32]."[18] "And if they are one flesh," Luther continues,

---

[17] For an in-depth documentation of this motif, see Uwe Rieske-Braun, *Duellum mirabile: Studien zum Kampfmotiv in Martin Luthers Theologie*, Forschungen zur Kirchen- und Dogmengeschichte 73 (Göttingen: Vandenhoeck & Ruprecht, 1999); Walter Allgaier, "Der 'froehliche Wechsel' bei Martin Luther; eine Untersuchung zu Christologie und Soteriologie bei Luther unter besonderer Beruecksichtigung der Schriften bis 1521" (PhD diss., University of Erlangen-Nürnberg, 1966); Theobald Beer, *Der fröhliche Wechsel und Streit: Grundzüge der Theologie Luthers* (Leipzig: St. Benno-Verlag, 1974); Raymund Schwager, *Der wunderbare Tausch: zur Geschichte und Deutung der Erlösungslehre* (München: Kösel, 1986); and Erwin Iserloh, "Luther's Christ-Mysticism," in *Catholic Scholars Dialogue with Luther* (Chicago: Loyola University Press, 1970), 37-58.

[18] LW 31:351.

and there is between them a true marriage . . . it follows that everything they have they hold in common, the good as well as the evil. Accordingly the believing soul can boast of and glory in whatever Christ has as though it were its own, and whatever the soul has Christ claims as his own. Let us compare these and we shall see inestimable benefits. Christ is full of grace, life, and salvation. The soul is full of sins, death, and damnation. Now let faith come between them and sins, death, and damnation will be Christ's, while grace, life, and salvation will be the soul's; for if Christ is a bridegroom, he must take upon himself the things which are his bride's and bestow upon her the things that are his.[19]

As Walter Allgaier and others have rightly observed, Luther's conception of the wondrous exchange is essentially a dramatic enactment of two-nature Christology.[20] The salvific exchange of properties described in this text presupposes the hypostatic union of divinity and humanity in Christ.[21] Christ is only able to assume the defects pertaining to the sinful human condition on account of His true humanity, and He is only able to conquer and eradicate sin, death, and the devil on account of His true divinity.[22] In his well-known commentary on the book of Galatians, Luther stresses the fact that the righteousness and life of Christ are divine and eternal properties and thus cannot be overtaken even by all the dreadful powers that assault sinners in this mortal flesh.[23]

> Christ, who is the *divine* Power, Righteousness, Blessing, Grace, and Life, conquers and destroys these monsters—sin, death, and the curse—without weapons or battle, in His own body and in Himself, as Paul enjoys saying (Col. 2:15): "He disarmed the principalities and powers, triumphing over them in Him." Therefore they can no longer harm the believers.[24]

---

[19]LW 31:351.

[20]Allgaier, "Der 'froehliche Wechsel,'" 2, 8.

[21]For more on the anatomy of this pattern, see David Luy, "A Wondrous Strife: Luther's Baroque Soteriology," in *Savior and Lord: The Work of Jesus Christ*, ed. Paul R. Hinlicky and R. David Nelson (Delhi, NY: American Lutheran Publicity Bureau, forthcoming).

[22]I do no not mean to imply here that the humanity of Christ does not exercise any positive, salvific role for Luther (an interpretation often associated with the work of Gustav Aulen).

[23]See LW 26:281-82.

[24]LW 26:282, emphasis mine. Luther sometimes expresses this point by utilizing the image of a scale. Weighed against the perfections of God himself, even the mighty powers of sin, death, and hell are simply no match. See also LW 41:103-4 (WA 50:590).

As these excerpts illustrate, the primary significance of the wondrous exchange is soteriological in a vertical sense. Through union with Christ, the Christian is definitively reconciled to God and is also efficaciously renewed in soul and body through the lavish bestowal of Christ's own life-giving properties. Luther summarizes:

> Thus, the believing soul by means of the pledge of its faith is free in Christ, its bridegroom, free from all sins, secure against death and hell, and is endowed with the eternal righteousness, life, and salvation of Christ its bridegroom.... Who then can fully appreciate what this royal marriage means? Who can understand the riches of the glory of this grace? Here this rich and divine bridegroom Christ marries this poor, wicked harlot, redeems her from all her evil, and adorns her with all his goodness. Her sins cannot now destroy her, since they are laid upon Christ and swallowed up by him.[25]

Luther's depiction of the wondrous exchange provides an important framework for the doctrine of the general priesthood in several respects. First, its description of the saving work of Christ serves to a large extent as the underlying foundation for Luther's understanding of Christ as the one true priest. The convergence between Luther's view of the wondrous exchange and his description of Christ as priest is especially palpable in a commentary on Psalm 110 from the late 1530s, where he considers what it means for the psalmist to say that Christ is a "Priest forever after the order of Melchizedek." Luther's exposition presupposes the same christological substructure as previously outlined.

> Because He is our Priest and Mediator between God and us (1 Tim. 2:5), He must also be a man of our nature; He must be flesh and blood, just as Hebrews 5:1 says: "For every high priest chosen from among men is appointed to act on behalf of men in relation to God." On the other hand, because He is called an "eternal Priest," one who possesses in His person the quality of eternity, He must also be true God.[26]

---

[25]LW 31:352.
[26]LW 31:323.

Notice further that particular aspects of Christ's priestly work depend for Luther directly on one or the other of his distinct but inseparable natures. As a human being, Christ is able to assume our abject estate and to make vicarious restitution for sin through his perfectly atoning death. Christ does this as our priestly representative, despite the fact that he lived a blameless life. Indeed, as the ideal priest and ideal sacrificial victim, he is himself spotless and pure, "conceived and born without sin."[27] Yet because Christ is also fully divine, neither death nor sin could triumph finally over him. Luther explains: "But since the true divine nature was in Him and His priestly office was eternally established, He could not remain in death or in the grave. He had to rise again and enter into another life, an eternal life, where He can function as our Priest forever in the presence of the Father."[28]

In addition to this shared christological substructure, Luther's exposition of the priesthood of Christ mirrors the wondrous exchange by centralizing a lavish communication of goods. As priest, Christ assumes what belongs to us and bestows on us what belongs to him. Salvation consists essentially in a generous bestowal of the *benefitia Christi*.[29] Luther writes:

> Since this Person is eternal and lives as Lord of all creation, possessing total power, He must bestow His eternal gifts on us, whose Priest He is. These gifts are our redemption from sin, from death, and from all the power of the devil and of evil. He must create an entirely new nature and being in us, so that we may also rise from the dead, in body and soul, and live with Him in eternal glory, in purity and perfection. This is the reason why He became our High Priest. Everything He did was designed to achieve and obtain this for us.[30]

Luther's emphasis on communicative exchange climaxes in another passage emphasizing the sheer uniqueness of Christ's eternal priesthood.

---

[27]LW 31:323.
[28]LW 31:323.
[29]Luther himself uses this phrase in a sermon from 1528. See WA 27:158.
[30]LW 31:323-24.

Christ alone is true priest, for Luther, because only he possesses and imparts those communicative goods, which are needful for salvation.

> No other priestly office can, or ever could, achieve this, not even the office which God established through Moses! Still less is it within the possibility of any other person, act of worship, holiness, wisdom, power, and might on earth. Such a person and his possessions are temporal and perishable; he must die and cease to be. Consequently he cannot achieve or bestow something that is eternal. In this text the very idea is made irrelevant! All glory which God recognizes in this matter is concentrated upon this one Person, so that we may cling only to Him in faith and obtain from God everything that pertains to everlasting righteousness and everlasting life.[31]

Luther's emphasis on the exclusivity of Christ's priesthood may seem to undercut the main focus of this essay. After all, if Christ alone is the true priest, what sense can it make to say that Christians also are priests, even if only in some subsidiary manner? Here again, the concept of communicative exchange provides a helpful framework. In an important statement from *The Freedom of a Christian* (1520), Luther explains that priestliness is *itself* one of the benefits or goods that Christ imparts to the believer through the wondrous exchange.

> Now just as Christ by his birthright obtained these two prerogatives [i.e., prerogatives pertaining to true kingship and true priesthood], so he imparts them to and shares them with everyone who believes in him according to the law of the above-mentioned marriage [i.e., the wondrous exchange, which Luther likens to earthly marriage], according to which the wife owns whatever belongs to the husband. Hence all of us who believe in Christ are priests and kings in Christ.[32]

In other words, Christians are not priests *in themselves* but priests by way of participation. They have been made priests as the result of communicative fellowship in the One who truly is priest. Christians are priests, for Luther, but only in an explicitly derivative sense. "In his own person Christ is indeed the only High Priest between God and us all.

---

[31]LW 13:324.
[32]LW 31:354.

Nevertheless He has bestowed this name on us, too, so that we who believe in Him are also priests."[33] The participatory priesthood consists in two different aspects, both presupposing the underlying reality of wondrous exchange. The first aspect pertains to the *appropriation* of Christ's benefits and has to do with the status of the believer *coram Deo*.[34] The second aspect pertains to the *enactment* of communicative exchange and focuses especially on the horizontal obligations and relations of dependency that obtain among believers. When Luther says that Christians are priests, he encompasses both aspects.

From the perspective of appropriation in the vertical sense, the priesthood of all believers refers principally to issues of status and access. To be a priest, as Luther explains at one point, is to be "the kind of person whose proper office it is to deal with God, to be closest to God, and to be concerned with nothing but divine things."[35] Priestly status, in other words, implies close proximity to God, and Luther wants to insist that all Christians enjoy privileged access because of their participation in Christ's atoning work. On account of their communicative union with him, all Christians occupy the spiritual estate and are therefore entitled to approach God boldly, drawing near to him through prayer and supplication.[36]

In his *Treatise on the New Testament* from 1520, Luther stresses these points by insisting that "faith alone is the true priestly office."[37] Faith is the means through which Christians appropriate the work of Christ and all its constituent benefits. In faith, the Christian offers up Christ to God, not doubting, as Luther explains, "that Christ in heaven is our priest, that he offers himself for us without ceasing, and presents us and our prayer

---

[33]LW 13:329. Luther also explains in this treatise how the Levitical priesthood is an anticipatory picture of Christ, the one *true* priest. See LW 13:321.

[34]By referring to this aspect in vertical terms, I do not mean to suggest that Luther denies the existence of divinely ordained, creaturely channels of mediation. See below.

[35]LW 13:294.

[36]This is an emphasis that emerges in *The Treatise on the Freedom of a Christian* (1520) in LW 31:355 (cf. LW 35:100).

[37]LW 35:101.

and praise, making all these acceptable."[38] Here we may observe very clearly the derivative status of the general priesthood. As priests, Christians truly are those qualified to offer themselves up to God, but they are capable of this self-offering only to the extent that they offer themselves up by offering up Christ, the one *true* priest, on their behalf. Faith makes one a priest because faith lays hold of Christ, and Christ reconciles sinners to God.

The general priesthood thus presupposes the wondrous exchange in relation to its implications for the Christian's status *coram Deo*. Through participation in Christ by faith, the Christian participates in all the benefits of Christ, and this principally includes access and standing before God. As a member of the spiritual estate, the Christian is entitled to intercessory prayer and is able to offer up his or her life in obedient service to God without need of some additional mediating agency.[39] It is this particular emphasis that pertains to Luther's polemical deployments of the general priesthood as a means of criticizing late medieval conceptions of the ministerial office in vicarious and sacerdotal terms.[40] The distinctiveness of the ordained ministry should be understood neither in terms of special access nor as denoting the possession of special qualities necessary for the performance of representative, expiatory works before God.[41] When it comes to vertical considerations of spiritual status (or "estate") and access, all Christians are priests.

Yet neither the wondrous exchange nor the general priesthood is exhaustively a vertical category for Luther. The great exchange must also be enacted, and this means that each theme carries with it a richly corporate set of entailments. With respect to the exchange motif, this

---

[38]LW 35:100.

[39]See LW 35:98-105.

[40]For a cursory overview of important tendencies in medieval understandings of church office, see Unche Anizor and Hank Voss, *Representing Christ: A Vision for the Priesthood of All Believers* (Downers Grove, IL: IVP Academic, 2016), 59-67. See also David V. N. Bagchi, *Luther's Earliest Opponents: Catholic Controversialists, 1518–1525* (Minneapolis: Fortress, 1991), 139-46.

[41]A representative example of this critique appears in Luther's treatise *The Babylonian Captivity of the Church* (1520) in LW 36:112-17.

corporate dimension becomes visible in Luther's frequent insistence that the dynamics of the wondrous exchange are to be enacted in the context of community life within the church. As Christ takes up our infirmities and imparts to us a share in his life-giving benefits, so likewise Christians ought to bear the burdens of their brethren and bestow on them various acts of Christian service. In *The Freedom of a Christian*, Luther alludes especially to Philippians 2 and explains the intrinsic relationship between vertical and horizontal in this way:

> Here we see clearly that the Apostle has prescribed this rule for the life of Christians, namely, that we should devote all our works to the welfare of others, since each has such abundant riches in his faith that all his other works and his whole life are a surplus with which he can by voluntary benevolence serve and do good to his neighbor.[42]

As Christ—who was rich, but became poor for our sake (2 Cor 8:9)—so also the Christian, having *become* rich, now turns to her brother, gladly bears all his burdens, and shares with him all of her own resources, be they spiritual or material in nature.[43] Or, as Luther himself summarizes the point, "A Christian lives not in himself, but in Christ and in his neighbor. Otherwise he is not a Christian. He lives in Christ through faith, in his neighbor through love. By faith he is caught up beyond himself into God. By love he descends beneath himself into his neighbor."[44]

Luther's doctrine of the general priesthood contains this same intrinsic movement toward service of neighbor. Having been made a priest before God, one is now to act as a priest in relation to one's neighbor. It functions rather frequently as an exhortation to the reciprocal service and admonition of Christian brothers and sisters within the church.

---

[42]LW 31:365.

[43]Another important example of this theme appears in Luther's exposition of the Lord's Supper in *The Blessed Sacrament of the Holy and True Body of Christ, and the Brotherhoods* (1519). Luther insists in this treatise that the sacrament signifies the sort of fellowship that ought to obtain among Christians within the church. In this sense, the enactment of the Lord's Supper in the Christian life would include exercises such as corporate collections for the poor. See LW 35:50-54.

[44]LW 31:371.

Luther often expresses this point in concrete terms by itemizing certain functions, which he presents as constitutive of the priestly office. These functions almost universally denote some obligation on the part of the Christian (as priest) to the service of his or her neighbor.[45] In his treatise *The Freedom of a Christian*, for instance, Luther stresses especially the responsibility for priests to instruct and support others through intercessory prayer.

> Not only are we the freest of kings, we are also priests forever, which is far more excellent than being kings, for as priests we are worthy to appear before God to pray for others and to teach one another divine things. These are the functions of priests, and they cannot be granted to any unbeliever.[46]

In each of these specific functions, Christians are obliged as priests not merely to appropriate but also to enact the singular priesthood of Christ through acts of mutual service. Through intercessory prayer, for instance, they are to present one another through Christ to God, and thus bear one another's burdens in imitation of the God who "has borne our griefs and carried our sorrows" (Is 53:4). Likewise, through proclamation, Christians present the Word one to another for purposes of mutual consolation, instruction, and admonition.[47] Even the offering up of spiritual sacrifices, a priestly function that might seem purely vertical in its orientation, is described by Luther as a means through which Christians may serve their neighbors by enkindling them to greater heights of devotion unto God.[48]

---

[45]In point of fact, Luther provides several distinct lists of priestly functions in various texts, and the lists do not always perfectly align. For a helpful overview, see Voss, *The Priesthood of All Believers*, 140-44.

[46]LW 31:355.

[47]LW 13:333.

[48]*Treatise on the New Testament* (1520) in LW 35:98. "What sacrifice, then, are we to offer? Ourselves, and all that we have, with constant prayer, as we say, 'Thy will be done, on earth as it is in heaven' [Mt 6:10]. With this we are to yield ourselves to the will of God, that he may make of us what he will, according to his own pleasure. In addition we are to offer him praise and thanksgiving with our whole heart, for his unspeakable, sweet grace and mercy, which he has promised and given us in this sacrament. And although such a sacrifice occurs apart from the mass, and should so occur—for it does not necessarily and essentially belong to the mass, as has been said—yet it is more precious, more appropriate, more mighty, and also more acceptable when it takes place with the multitude and in the assembly, where men encourage, move, and inflame one another to press close to God and thereby attain without any doubt what they desire."

This second layer of associations between the wondrous exchange and the general priesthood illustrates just how great of a mistake it would be to conclude that Luther dislocates Christian life from its native ecclesial setting. On the contrary, Luther's concept of the general priesthood presupposes and asserts the sheer inextricability of Christian existence from the context of Christian community. To be sure, Luther opposes the notion that Christians depend for their status before God upon the appropriation of meritorious works, performed by some specially consecrated sacerdotal priesthood. Yet the general priesthood simultaneously underscores the obligation laid on all Christians continually to enact the exchange of Christ's benefits in service to one another within the life of the church.[49] In both of these complementary respects, the priesthood of all believers presupposes a soteriology defined in terms of wondrous exchange. Christians *become* priests by participating in the wondrous exchange through faith and they *act* as priests by enacting the wondrous exchange through love.

Word mediation. The significance of the second theme—Luther's emphasis on the efficacy of the mediated Word—may be treated more briefly. Mediation is a category distinct from the reception of Christ's benefits, on the one hand (e.g., through faith), and the enactment of Christ's benefits, on the other (e.g., through love). By mediation, I refer to Luther's account of the *means* through which the benefits of Christ are dispensed and thus become operative in the lives of human beings. In this section, I will suggest that Luther identifies the general priesthood as one such means, that is, as a channel through which God communicates the benefits of Christ to Christians. It thus forms part of a larger pattern of mediation internal to Luther's theological vision.[50]

---

[49]For a similar approach to the general priesthood, which underscores its simultaneous stress on benefits and duties, see L. W. Spitz, "The Universal Priesthood of Believers with Luther's Comments," *Concordia Theological Monthly* 23 (1952): 1-15.

[50]I borrow loosely here from phraseology deployed by Kevin Vanhoozer, who speaks in parallel terms of a pattern of authority. See Kevin J. Vanhoozer, *Biblical Authority After Babel: Retrieving*

The previous section has already illustrated a few ways in which Christians operate as means of grace in relation to one another; for instance, through the ministry of bearing or through intercessory prayer.[51] Our focus in this section will rest upon the general priesthood as a conduit for the mutual administration of God's efficacious Word.

Luther's theology in general—and his doctrine of the church in particular—has a lot of space for divinely established channels of mediation. In his *Treatise on the Councils and the Church* (1539), for instance, Luther identifies seven marks of the true church, and he describes each of these marks (the Word, baptism, the Lord's Supper, the office of the keys, the ordained ministry, prayer/praise/thanksgiving, and the holy cross) as a "holy possession" through which God sanctifies his people. The "marks" of the church, for Luther, are durable means of grace through which God operates within, upon, and among Christians in order that they might be made holy.[52]

Luther's conception of normative mediation sprouts, to a large extent, from his efficacious understanding of the external Word of God. Luther describes this Word as the "chief holy possession" of the church.[53] As such, the proclamation of the Word is, for Luther, the principal mark of the church. It is the means of grace to which all other means of grace are subordinate. Indeed, Luther views the other marks of the church as

---

the Solas *in the Spirit of Mere Protestant Christianity* (Grand Rapids: Brazos, 2016).

[51]Dietrich Bonhoeffer provides a useful exploration of these mutual obligations in his classic text *Life Together*, which represents, in many respects, a faithful contemporary representation of Luther's understanding of Christian community. See especially chapter four in Dietrich Bonhoeffer, Geffrey B. Kelly, Daniel W. Bloesch, and James H. Burtness, *Life Together; Prayerbook of the Bible* (Minneapolis: Fortress, 2005). Limitations of space preclude an in-depth comparison between Luther and Bonhoeffer, but the parallels are profound and worthy of closer examination.

[52]LW 41:143-78. This emphasis on sanctifying mediation reinforces Luther's insistence on the utter inextricability of Christian existence from the life of the church. The benefits of the wondrous exchange are not appropriated and enacted just anywhere. They are mediated rather through a particular set of divinely appointed channels, through the ecclesiastically moored ministrations of Word and sacrament. For more on Luther's concept of mediation in relation to the sacrament of baptism, see Jonathan D. Trigg, *Baptism in the Theology of Martin Luther* (Leiden: Brill, 1994).

[53]LW 41:151.

themselves nothing other than diverse forms and manifestations of the efficacious Word.[54] So Luther will argue in a text from 1523, for instance, that it would be better for the church to forgo the office of the ordained ministry altogether rather than to retain a form of ministerial office in which the proclamation of the external Word is neglected or marginalized.[55] Luther's point in saying this is not to denigrate the office of the ministry. Indeed, he assures his readers that situations of this sort are to be regarded as highly undesirable and exceptional to the extreme.[56] His purpose is rather to stress the utter centrality of the Word within the life of the church. As Cheryl Peterson and others have noted, Luther's doctrine of the church is essentially a Word ecclesiology.[57] "For since the church owes its birth to the Word, is nourished, aided and strengthened by it, it is obvious that it cannot be without the Word. If it is without the Word it ceases to be a church."[58] The proclamation of the Word creates the church, and the church is also a spiritual community governed and structured by the mediation of Christ's benefits through the Word in a variety of forms.

In each of these various ways, Luther treats the Word as an efficacious conduit of communicative exchange. Again, in his treatise on *The Freedom of a Christian*, Luther stresses that it is through the Word that God bestows his riches on the believer. "If [the soul] has the Word of God it is rich and lacks nothing since it is the Word of life, truth, light, peace, righteousness, salvation, joy, liberty, wisdom, power, grace, glory and of every incalculable blessing."[59] The Word possesses these

---

[54]Luther's understanding of the sacraments, for instance, is shaped by Augustine's influential statement that a sacrament is essentially the Word added to a tangible sign. See, for instance his discussion of baptism in the Large Catechism in *The Book of Concord: The Confessions of the Evangelical Lutheran Church*, ed. Robert Kolb and Timothy Wengert (Minneapolis: Fortress, 2000), 458-59.

[55]Martin Luther, *Concerning the Ministry* (1523) in LW 40:9.

[56]LW 40:10.

[57]Cheryl M. Peterson, "Martin Luther on the Church and Its Ministry," *Oxford Research Encyclopedia of Religion*, article published March, 2017, accessed April 10, 2017, religion.oxfordre.com /view/10.1093/acrefore/9780199340378.001.0001/acrefore-9780199340378-e-362.

[58]LW 40:37.

[59]LW 31:345.

life-bestowing properties because the Word communicates Christ. Luther explains, "The Word is the gospel of God concerning his Son, who was made flesh, suffered, rose from the dead, and was glorified through the Spirit who sanctifies. To preach Christ means to feed the soul, make it righteous, set it free, and save it, provided it believes the preaching."[60] The Word is thus a conduit of wondrous exchange, and this explains why Luther describes the proclamation of the Word in efficacious, even mystical terms.[61] "Just as heated iron flows like fire because of the union of fire with it, so the Word imparts its qualities to the soul."[62] These quotes show that the Word is a means through which communicative exchange and all its sanctifying effects become operative in the lives of human beings.

This framework is significant for our topic because Luther insists that the general priesthood has an important role to play in the reciprocal mediation of the Word among Christians. The previous section has already alluded to this fact by noting that proclamation and mutual instruction are the principal functions Luther associates with priests.[63] In his treatise *Concerning the Ministry* from 1523, Luther elaborates on this point by insisting that the proclamation of the Word is a priestly office pertaining to all believers.

> The first office, that of the ministry of the Word, therefore, is common to all Christians. This is clear . . . from 1 Pet. 2[:9], "You are a royal priesthood that you may declare the wonderful deeds of him who called you out of darkness into his marvelous light." I ask, who are these who are called out of darkness into marvelous light? Is it only the shorn and anointed masks? Is it not all Christians? And Peter not only gives them the right, but the command, to declare the wonderful deeds of God, which certainly is nothing else than to preach the Word of God.[64]

---

[60]LW 31:346.
[61]The wondrous exchange is itself a benefit of faith in the Word. See LW 31:351. See Ron Rittgers's chapter four above, which touches on these same topics.
[62]LW 31:349.
[63]See, for instance, LW 31:354-55.
[64]LW 40:21-22; LW 39:235-36.

This consistent refrain may seem to displace the ordained ministry, but this is not so.[65] On the contrary, the general priesthood is part of a pattern of Word-mediation composed of several constituent layers. In his Smalcald Articles of 1537, for instance, Luther lists four distinct ways in which the gospel is communicated by God's grace. The list includes familiar points of emphasis (preaching, the sacraments, and so on) but concludes by making special mention of "the mutual conversation and consolation of brothers and sisters."[66] What becomes clear in this text and a number of others is that Luther conceives of the general priesthood and the ordained ministry as distinct but inseparable modes of Word-mediation, each with its own particular set of responsibilities, duties, and privileges, and each with its own distinctive sort of authoritative weight. As Robert Fischer helpfully summarizes, "The foremost function of the spiritual priesthood is the ministry of the Word, which is to proclaim God's wonderful deeds. This office, common to all Christians . . . is fulfilled privately and publicly in due order: privately under certain circumstances by any lay[person], e.g., 'mutual consolation,' but in a special sense, with public responsibility, by the ordained clergy."[67]

These distinctions according to mode explain how Luther can insist on the special uniqueness of the ministerial office in his commentary on Psalm 110 while simultaneously enjoining all Christians in the very same passage to administer the efficacious Word of God one to another.

> Even though not everybody has the public office and calling, every Christian has the right and the duty to teach, instruct, admonish, comfort, and rebuke his neighbor with the Word of God at every opportunity and whenever necessary. For example, father and mother should do this for their children and household; a brother, neighbor, citizen, or peasant for the other. Certainly one Christian may instruct and admonish another ignorant or weak Christian

---

[65]See, for instance, Gerhard Müller, "Allgemeines Priestertum aller Getauften und kirchliches Amt in der Reformationszeit," *Kerygma und Dogma* 52, no. 1 (2006): 98-104.

[66]The Smalcald Articles, in *The Book of Concord*, 319.

[67]Robert H. Fischer, "Another Look at Luther's Doctrine of the Ministry," *Lutheran Quarterly* 18, no. 3 (1966): 270, as quoted in Cheryl M. Peterson, "Martin Luther on the Church." See also Gerrish, "Priesthood and Ministry," 416-19.

concerning the Ten Commandments, the Creed, or the Lord's Prayer. And he who receives such instruction is also under obligation to accept it as God's Word and publicly to confess it.[68]

By the same token, Luther can still extol and promote unofficial mediations of the Word, even during a period of time (the mid-1530s) when he is especially motivated to oppose the infiltration of self-appointed preachers lacking proper ordination.[69] Contrary to first appearances, these are not antithetical impulses, because Luther conceives of the general priesthood and the ordained ministry as distinct channels through which God's efficacious Word is mediated.

CONCLUSION

Our task in this paper has been to provide an embedded account of Luther's doctrine of the general priesthood. By situating this doctrine in relation to two major themes from Luther's theology, it has become clear that the priesthood of all believers does not function for Luther as an anti-ecclesiological principle. On the contrary, it conveys and presupposes a genuinely constructive account of the church as an indispensable locus of God's sanctifying action in the world. To be a priest, on Luther's account, is to be a beneficiary and a conduit of the wondrous exchange through which Christ bestows his life-giving benefits on his church. As beneficiary, the Christian enjoys a privileged spiritual status, which liberates him or her from the project of self-justification by the accrual of merit. As a conduit, the Christian is simultaneously obliged to the service of one's neighbor through priestly functions of various kinds.[70] Above all, these relations of mutual dependency among Christians center on the

---

[68]LW 13:333.

[69]See, for instance, *Infiltrating and Clandestine Preachers* (1532) in LW 40:383-94. In a lecture on Psalm 90 from 1534, Luther writes: "I am indeed a Doctor of Theology and many tell me that they were signally advanced in their knowledge of Scripture through my help. But I have also experienced that I was helped and cheered through a single word of a brother who believed himself to be in no sense my equal." LW 13:111.

[70]For more on this emphasis on mutual service, see Kolb, "Ministry in Martin Luther and the Lutheran Confessions," 52.

mediation of the Word, which Luther regards to be the very communication of Christ. And so, to repeat my initial thesis—here by way of conclusion—the doctrine of the priesthood of all believers conveys Luther's conception of the church as a spiritual community within which Christians mediate Christ one to another through the corporate sharing of benefits and burdens, especially through the mutual administration of God's efficacious Word.

WHAT EVANGELICALS CAN LEARN
from the REFORMATION

TIMOTHY GEORGE

I WANT TO BEGIN WITH A PERSONAL reminiscence of the first time I visited Trinity Evangelical Divinity School. It was May of 1989, and the world looked quite different than it does today. Ronald Reagan had just departed the White House. The Berlin Wall was still standing, though it would come down later that year. A devout Sunni Muslim from Saudi Arabia, thirty-two-year-old Osama Bin Laden, had just founded al-Qaeda the previous year. Down in Louisiana, Britney Spears was a Southern Baptist sunbeam getting ready for Vacation Bible School that summer, while over in Birmingham, Alabama, I had just been installed as the dean of a new divinity school. The speaker at my installation was Dr. Carl F. H. Henry, whom I had come to know several years before at the Southern Baptist Theological Seminary, where I had taught before moving to Samford University to organize the work of Beeson Divinity School. He told me about an important conference he would be co-chairing with Dr. Kenneth Kantzer on the campus of Trinity Evangelical Divinity School, and he invited me to come and be a part of it.

It was a Consultation on Evangelical Affirmations, which brought together the leading lights of North American evangelicalism for four days of reflection, discussion, and debate, with the purpose of clarifying "the character of the evangelical movement" and affirming "certain truths critical to the advancement of the church of Christ." The framers of the conference realized, as they put it, "that our own house is not entirely in order."[1] The sharpest exchange I remember from the proceedings was a debate over whether John Stott could rightly be called an evangelical. Dr. Stott was not with us on that occasion, but Dr. J. I. Packer was. He rose to say that if Stott were not an evangelical, then neither was he—this despite his strong disagreement with Stott over certain views he had set forth in his exchange with liberal Anglican David L. Edwards.

Much has changed even in the evangelical world since 1989. First, many of the issues that would preoccupy evangelicals and other Christians since 1989 were hardly on the radar back then. We were hardly worried about questions of race, gender (much less transgenderism or transhumanism), the rise of Islam, radical pluralism more generally, ecumenism, the evacuation of religious freedom, the rise of militant atheism, the phenomenon of the "nones," semi-process views of God, and so on—all of these things that have occupied our attention for the last thirty years. Such matters were hardly visible in our discussions in 1989. Reading back through the major presentations at the conference and the nine evangelical affirmations that it produced, I am surprised that almost nothing was said about the Reformation. Only one speaker, Dr. David Wells, who addressed the question of religious authority, devoted a few paragraphs to the Reformation tradition. And yes, there was dear Chuck Colson, who gave the opening keynote address and concluded his remarks by quoting the final verse of "Ein feste Burg": "That word above all earthly powers, no thanks to them abideth." Otherwise, it was as though the

---

[1]Kenneth Kantzer and Carl F. H. Henry, eds., *Evangelical Affirmations* (Grand Rapids: Zondervan, 1990), 29.

Reformation had not happened, or had been forgotten, or meant nothing to the question of evangelical identity in 1989.

Admittedly, this was not a conference on church history, much less one on the Reformation. But I am still struck by the fact that the Reformation was so noticeable by its absence. But why was this the case? Surely it was not because the leaders of the conference were ignorant of Reformation history or theology. After all, Ken Kantzer had written his Harvard dissertation on the theology of John Calvin. So too, J. I. Packer had done probably more than any other person alive to revive a lively interest in the Puritans and, as a young scholar, had helped to translate from Latin into felicitous English Martin Luther's greatest theological work, *On the Bondage of the Will.* In order to probe more deeply into why the focus on the Reformation was so muted within the wider evangelical community as represented at that conference, I call to the witness stand an earlier visitor to America from the Land of Luther, Dietrich Bonhoeffer.

PROTESTANTISM WITHOUT REFORMATION

I want to go from 1989 back to 1939. We should say right up front that Bonhoeffer was not an evangelical, at least not of the North American card-carrying variety—this despite the warm enthusiasm given to Bonhoeffer by evangelicals in recent years as seen, for example, in Eric Metaxas's bestselling biography *Bonhoeffer: Pastor, Prophet, Martyr, Spy.*[2] Now, Bonhoeffer was certainly *evangelisch* in the ordinary German sense of Protestant, but he was not *evangelikale.* That's a new word in German invented to talk about people like us: North American, British evangelical types.

Bonhoeffer spent two periods of time in America: ten months in 1930–1931 and a brief three and a half weeks in the summer of 1939. On both visits, he was based at Union Theological Seminary in New York City. There he developed a keen friendship with Reinhold Niebuhr and

---

[2]Eric Metaxas, *Bonhoeffer: Pastor, Prophet, Martyr, Spy* (Nashville: Thomas Nelson, 2011).

spoke appreciatively of other friends and teachers at Union. At the University of Berlin, Bonhoeffer had studied with Reinhold Seeberg and Adolf von Harnack, at whose funeral he offered a eulogy. During that time, he had also come to appreciate the neo-Reformational theology of Karl Barth, though he never became a Barthian with a capital "B." What he missed most, he said, in that yearlong study at Union in 1930–1931, both in his seminars and in conversations with his fellow students, was the kind of theological rigor he had known in Germany, together with the noticeable absence of the Christian kerygma. The Union students, he said, "talk a blue streak without the slightest substantive foundation and with no evidence of any criteria . . . they are unfamiliar with even the most basic questions, they become intoxicated with liberal and humanistic phrases, they laugh at the fundamentalists, and yet basically are not even up to their level." And he found the same kind of milieu in many of the churches that he visited. "In New York," he wrote, "they preach about virtually everything, only one thing is not addressed, or is addressed so rarely that I have as yet been unable to hear it, namely, the gospel of Jesus Christ, the cross, sin and forgiveness, death and life."[3]

On his abortive return to New York in the summer of 1939, Bonhoeffer found that the situation had not changed that much. On Sunday June 18, he visited Riverside Church. The pastor, the famous Harry Emerson Fosdick, was not there that day, but there was a visiting preacher, a scholar very well known in the academy, Halford E. Luccock, who was professor of homiletics at Yale. That Sunday, he spoke on the American philosopher of pragmatism, William James. "Quite unbearable," Bonhoeffer wrote in his diary. Do people not know that one could get along as well, even better, without "religion" of this sort? "Such sermons make for libertinism, egotism, indifference."[4] It was in this context that Bonhoeffer wrote an essay titled "Protestantismus ohne Reformation"

---

[3]Metaxas, *Bonhoeffer*, 99.
[4]Metaxas, *Bonhoeffer*, 333.

(Protestantism without Reformation). He began to write this essay while still in New York in the library of Union Seminary, his biographer Eberhard Bethge tells us, and completed it when he had gone back to Germany. It was begun just prior to that fateful return to Germany on one of the last ships to cross the Atlantic before the outbreak of hostilities on September 1, 1939.

His essay is a withering analysis of American Christianity as he had come to know it mainly through his encounter with mainline Protestant theology and church life in New York City. Bonhoeffer made a number of points in this essay that are still relevant today to American Christianity more broadly, but my focus is especially on the evangelical church of the twenty-first century, which in some ways has come to represent the kind of social space occupied by mainline Protestants in the 1930s. We dare not sit too smugly when we hear Bonhoeffer criticize the kind of religion he encountered then, because it may be our kind of religion today. Here are five points from Bonhoeffer's essay that still resonate:

1. Bonhoeffer criticized the rampant denominationalism in American Christianity, with its roots in pre-Reformation dissent (he mentions the Wycliffites); aspects of the Radical Reformation that he, following Luther, dubs "enthusiasm" (*Schwärmertum*); and the extreme separation of church and state, which issues in the divorce of faith and public life.

2. He observed that the quest for Christian unity had been problematic in American Christianity. This is the result, in part, of the failure to recognize that "the division of the church that came about in the Reformation can only be understood as a struggle for the true unity of the church."[5] This runs counter to the myth still common today that the Reformation divided the church. No, the Reformation did not divide the church. Rather, division was its point of origin. Schism was its point of beginning, going back at least to 1054 and the many other divisions leading to the sixteenth century. The Reformation was an attempt to

---

[5]Dietrich Bonhoeffer, *Dietrich Bonhoeffer Works English Edition*, ed. Victoria Barnett (Minneapolis: Fortress, 2011), 15:442. Hereafter abbreviated as DBWE.

recover, as Bonhoeffer said, the true unity of the church on the basis of the Word of God.

3. Religious toleration as a result of political accommodation undermines the Reformation meaning of freedom as the gift of the gospel. "The essential freedom of the church is not a gift of the world to the church but the freedom of the Word of God to make itself heard." Thus, "the American praise of freedom is more a tribute to the world, the state, and society than it is a statement concerning the church."[6] Now while this may result in a kind of concessive toleration, it is always fragile and evanescent. For what the state grants, the state can also take away. We are witnessing in our own culture and country today what Bonhoeffer predicted in 1939.

4. Bonhoeffer recognized the contradiction between racism and faithful Christian witness, an experience which informed his advocacy for Jewish people in Germany. Bonhoeffer was arrested not for attempting to assassinate Hitler (that came later) but rather for helping Jews to escape from Germany. While in America, he was active as a Sunday school teacher in an African American church, Abyssinian Baptist Church in Harlem. He also took an extensive road trip through a great swath of the American continent, including the Deep South. On this trip, he visited African American churches in Mississippi and drove through Birmingham, Alabama, where his friend and classmate Frank Fisher had grown up as the son of the pastor of the Sixteenth Street Baptist Church. On this same trip, Bonhoeffer made a detour to visit Scottsboro, Alabama, where the Scottsboro Boys were then on trial. He continued to follow this judicial proceeding even after he had returned to Germany.[7]

"Protestantism without Reformation" contains a section titled "The Negro Church." Bonhoeffer recognized what he called "a destructive rift within the church of Jesus Christ," exemplified by the positing of the

---

[6]DBWE 15:449.
[7]Charles Marsh outlines this trip in vivid detail in his biography of Bonhoeffer, *Strange Glory* (New York: Vintage, 2014), 101-35.

"black Christ" against the "white Christ," a division evident in the racial fragmentation of American Protestantism. A full quarter century before Martin Luther King Jr. described eleven o'clock on Sunday morning as "the most segregated hour of the week," Bonhoeffer recognized the enervating effect of the racial divide within the church. "Blacks and whites come separately to word and sacrament. They have no common worship."[8] At the same time, Bonhoeffer recognized the spiritual vitality of African American Christianity, especially the theological substance of the "Negro spirituals" and the power of black preaching. The vibrant Christianity he witnessed at Abyssinian Baptist Church and in other black congregations he visited prompted him to declare, "Here the Gospel of Jesus Christ, the Savior of sinners, is truly preached and received with great welcome and visible emotion."[9]

5. Through his knowledge of his teachers at Union and his reading of mainline liberal theology, Bonhoeffer came to recognize that American Christianity was not only ecclesiologically challenged (that was his first point in this essay) but also christologically deficient. This applied even to his friend Reinhold Niebuhr, whose work he admired. Niebuhr tried to combine neo-orthodoxy on the one hand and true liberalism on the other. "But even here [in Niebuhr's theological work]," Bonhoeffer wrote, "a doctrine on the person and the work of salvation in Jesus Christ is missing."[10]

From this analysis, Bonhoeffer drew a grim conclusion: "God did not grant a Reformation to American Christendom. He gave strong revivalist preachers, but no reformation of the church of Jesus Christ from the Word of God."[11] Bonhoeffer did not equate American Protestantism with the *Deutsche Christen*, the Nazified church in Germany that said "Heil Hitler." He did not make that easy analogy, but his analysis does show what can happen to a group of churches that have lost touch with the

---

[8]DBWE 15:457.
[9]DBWE 15:458.
[10]DBWE 15:460.
[11]DBWE 15:461.

Reformation roots by which they once lived. That was a danger in American Protestantism in the 1930s, and it is a danger in American evangelicalism today. The name for this phenomenon in German is *Kulturprotestantismus*, an accommodated, acculturated form of Protestant church life. It is a phenomenon in which many things work very well, things are done nicely and properly, with a great deal of sophistication and cultural élan, but which at its heart conveys a betrayal of the gospel. With Bonhoeffer's warning ringing in our ears, dare we ask the question: Is the evangelical church in America losing the Reformation foundations on which it once stood? Has God given no Reformation to the evangelical church? Do we have *Evangelikalismus ohne Reformation*?

WHAT CAN EVANGELICALS LEARN FROM THE REFORMATION?

I will not engage anymore in the ongoing debate on what is evangelicalism, though I have made a few modest contributions to that discussion over the years. In his book *Deconstructing Evangelicalism*, D. G. Hart has noted that between 1980 and 2000, a tsunami of studies on evangelicalism in the United States deluged the field of American religious history.[12] Now the torrent of such studies may have subsided a bit since the turn of the millennium, but they are still at monsoon level, judging by the recent symposia, conferences, and publications on the subject. Much of this discussion centers on the by now classic construal that David Bebbington first set forth in his book *Evangelicalism in Modern Britain*, published in 1989—the same year as the Trinity Consultation on Evangelical Affirmations.[13] Bebbington's quadrilateral describes evangelicalism as a movement of spiritual vitality within the Protestant tradition characterized by four distinguishing traits: *conversion*—evangelicals recognize the need for a definite turning away from self and sin in order to find God in Jesus Christ; the *Bible*—evangelicals accept Holy Scripture

---

[12]D. G. Hart, *Deconstructing Evangelicalism: Conservative Protestantism in the Age of Billy Graham* (Grand Rapids: Baker Academic, 2005).

[13]David Bebbington, *Evangelicalism in Modern Britain: A History from the 1730s to the 1980s* (1988; repr., Grand Rapids: Baker, 1992).

as the normative authority for all matters of faith and religious practice; the *cross*—evangelicals believe that the death of Christ on the cross followed by his resurrection on Easter Sunday is at the heart of Christian faith; and *activism*—understood not simply as frenetic activity but rather as the call of the Lord to serve the church in the world through evangelism, mission, and good works. Bebbington's model has been criticized by some for being too phenomenological or not propositional enough, and by others for being too theological and not focused enough on "lived religion." Mark Noll, a friendly critic, declares that there is no such thing as evangelicalism and that David Bebbington has described it better than anyone else![14] I stand by my own assessment, written in 2008: no one to date has yet given a more compelling or enduring model of evangelicals in the modern era than David Bebbington, though I myself would prefer a more diachronic than synthetic model—evangelicalism understood as a renewal movement within the one holy, catholic, and apostolic church.[15] Bebbington's historical work focuses more on the eighteenth century rather than the sixteenth or seventeenth centuries, but it poses a question as important for the world of Martin Luther and John Calvin as for the world of John Wesley and George Whitefield— namely, the question of continuity and discontinuity with the preceding Christian story.

For its entire history, the Christian church has been pulled toward one of two poles: *identity* or *adaptability*. As I have argued, these two poles create a tension that

> arises from the most central theological affirmation of the New Testament: the Word became flesh (Jn 1:14). The need to communicate the gospel in such a way that it speaks to the total context of the people to whom it is addressed courses through every age of church history and shapes the various disputes and controversies that have marked the development of Christian doctrine

---

[14]Mark Noll, "Noun or Adjective? The Ravings of a Fanatical Nominalist," *Fides et Historia* 47, no. 1 (2015): 73-83.

[15]See Timothy George, foreword to *The Advent of Evangelicalism: Exploring Historical Continuities*, ed. Michael A. G. Haykin and Kenneth J. Stewart (Nashville: B & H, 2008), 17-18.

and spirituality: rigorism and laxism, orthodoxy and heresy, ecumenism and schism, reformation and retrenchment, to name only a few. Speaking of the Middle Ages, Roland Bainton once said that Christianity is wont either to conquer the world or to flee from it and sometimes it seeks to do both at once—think of both monasticism and the Crusades. This very tension was certainly present in the eighteenth century as the evangelical awakening swept through many of the Protestant churches of Great Britain and North America.[16]

But it was no less present, I say, in the program of renewal within the churches of Western Christendom in the sixteenth century. Luther, Calvin, Melanchthon, Zwingli, Bullinger, Bucer, Cranmer, Tyndale, and many of the Continental Anabaptists understood themselves as engaged in a project of retrieval for the sake of renewal. They understood the movement of which they were a part as standing in fundamental continuity with the great tradition of Christian believing, confessing, worshiping, and acting across the centuries. It was not their intention to start a new church but rather to be faithful ministers of the gospel within the one, holy, catholic, and apostolic church—another quadrilateral, one confessed by all Nicene Christians. But how did this agenda apply to the four defining markers of the evangelical movement as Bebbington described it? We can make a few brief comments about each of the four tiles in the Bebbington mosaic.

Conversion. The Protestant Reformation was born in a struggle over conversion. In 1516, Erasmus published at Basel the first-ever critical edition of the Greek New Testament, and a copy soon came into Martin Luther's hands in Wittenberg, where he was then lecturing on Paul's letter to the Romans. We know exactly where he was in the text of Romans when he began to use Erasmus's Greek New Testament. He was midway through chapter nine. This same Greek New Testament was also at hand a little over one year later when he sat down to compose his Ninety-Five Theses, or, to use the actual title, "Disputation for Clarifying the Power

---

[16]George, foreword to *The Advent of Evangelicalism*, 14.

of Indulgences." The first of these declares, "Our Lord and Master Jesus Christ, in saying 'Do penance . . . ,' (*poenitentiam agite* in the Vulgate Latin) wanted the entire life of the faithful to be one of penitence." As Luther learned from Erasmus's Greek New Testament, the operative word was *metanoeite*, which did not mean "do penance" but rather "come to one's senses," undergo a change of mind and heart, turn around, be converted. Thesis two of the ninety-five denies that the medieval sacrament of penance, with its fourfold structure of contrition, confession, satisfaction, and absolution (another quadrilateral!), corresponds to the true meaning of the change of direction called for by Jesus in the Gospel of Matthew.

What was really at stake was an intensified understanding of the first step, *contritio cordis*, "contrition of the heart," the kind of godly sorrow the New Testament says leads to repentance, to a complete change of direction in one's life. At the headwaters of the Reformation, there was not only a new understanding of *iustitia*, "righteousness," but also a new understanding of *poenitentia*, "repentance" and conversion. To arrive at this point, Luther had already experienced several theological breakthroughs, including his abandonment of the scholastic view of the necessity of preparation for the reception of grace and his letting go of a kind of Dionysian mysticism with its belief in an inner spark of divinity as the basis of union with God—though other insights from the mystical tradition continued to shape his spirituality. In his comments on 2 Corinthians 4:6, "For God, who said 'Let light shine out of darkness,' has shone in our hearts to give the light of the knowledge of the glory of God in the face of Jesus Christ," Luther noted two things about the conversion Paul describes: (1) it is effected by the Word and (2) it is "a new work of creation."[17] Luther added, "This conversion consists in that through the Word of grace, the hearts are enlightened toward God so that we cease from our righteousness, our confidence, our endeavors which turn us

---

[17]LW 1:17.

away from God and are the supreme idolatries." It is "the gospel truly that converts us to God."[18]

Thus the meaning of conversion was basic to Protestantism from the outset. As David Steinmetz once put it, "From the early and formative decades of the Protestant Reformation through the Evangelical Awakening of the eighteenth century to the Bangkok Assembly in 1973 and the Lausanne Covenant in 1974, Protestants have returned again and again to the theme of penitence and conversion."[19] Now, Calvin was more cryptic than Luther when he referred to his own decisive turning to God as "a sudden conversion" (*subita conversio*). But what was key for him as for Luther is that this conversion was entirely the work of God, "beyond all expectation" (*praeter spem*), beyond all hope. When Calvin does give just a brief word of explanation about the content of his conversion, he describes it as God "changing my heart and making it teachable."[20]

Teachableness (*docilitas*), becomes a major theme in the Reformed tradition. This means that conversion to Jesus Christ, for Calvin, is more like enrolling in school for a long course of study than riding the Ferris wheel at the county fair. In Calvin's school, there are two courses in the curriculum: the mortification of the flesh and the vivification of the spirit, as he describes it in book three of the *Institutes*. Sometimes evangelicals have focused more on the drama of the beginning of conversion rather than on the divine agency of the Holy Spirit who brought it about in the first place and on the twists and turns, the starts and stops, that lead from the City of Destruction to the gates of the Celestial City. For, as Bunyan's Christian found out as he neared his destination, there is "a road to hell, that leads from the gates of heaven."[21]

---

[18]LW 17:174.

[19]David Steinmetz, *Taking the Long View: Christian Theology in Historical Perspective* (New York: Oxford University Press, 2011), 70.

[20]John Calvin, "Preface to the Commentary on the Psalms," in *John Calvin: Writings on Pastoral Piety*, ed. Elsie Anne McKee (New York: Paulist, 2001), 59.

[21]John Bunyan, *The Pilgrim's Progress* (London: Oxford University Press, 1956), 195.

The Bible. In the most succinct and best definition of evangelicals I have ever come across, John Stott wrote that evangelicals are gospel people and Bible people. Here we have both the material and the formal principles of the Reformation. I am glad that Stott put the material principle first because that was the order in which it came in the course of the Reformation. Luther said that it was in the course of his studying the Bible and finding therein the message of God's forgiveness and grace that the papacy simply slipped away from him. The key moment came in 1519 in his famous debate with John Eck at Leipzig, halfway between the Indulgence Controversy two years earlier and his appearance at the Diet of Worms two years later. The formal principle was expressed in classic form ten years after Leipzig at the Second Diet of Speyer, which gave us the word *Protestant*, understood not merely as "protest against" something but rather "witness on behalf of" (*pro-testantes*).

We are determined by God's grace and aid to abide by God's Word alone, the holy gospel contained in the biblical books of the Old and New Testaments. This Word alone should be preached, and nothing that is contrary to it. It is the only truth. It is the sure rule of all Christian doctrine and conduct. It can never fail us or deceive us. Whoso builds and abides on this foundation shall stand against all the gates of hell, where all merely human additions and vanities set up against it must fall before the presence of God.[22]

What can evangelicals today learn from the Reformation about the Bible? Three things, I suggest:

1. *The People's Book.* That is the title of a fine collection of essays edited by Jennifer Powell McNutt and David Lauber and published recently by InterVarsity Press. It is not coincidental that the Scripture principle in Protestant theology emerged historically at the same time as the biblical text was being restored, historical-critical studies were being advanced by humanist scholars, and the technology of printing was providing the

---

[22]See E. G. Leonard, *A History of Protestantism* (Indianapolis: Bobbs-Merrill, 1968), 122-28.

basis for a popular literate culture. Erasmus famously called for the translation of the Bible into the vernacular languages so that the mysteries of
Christ could be accessible to all:

> I would that even the lowliest women read the Gospels, and the Pauline
> Epistles. And I would that they were translated into all languages so that they
> could be read and understood not only by Scots and Irish, but also by Turks
> and Saracens. . . . Would that, as a result, the farmers sing some portion of
> them at the plow, the weaver hums some parts of them to the movement of his
> shuttle, the traveler lighten the weariness of the journey with stories of
> this kind.[23]

Now, Erasmus said that, but he never translated anything into Dutch. Not
one single page of the New Testament. He spent his time bringing out
new editions of his Greek New Testament and polishing his Latin translation. But others took up the task of giving the Word of God to the
people in the language they could hear and understand, and that is a
work that has characterized evangelicalism to this very day through the
work of the Wycliffe Bible Translators and many others.

2. *We read the Bible in the context of prayer.* Luther was released from
his monastic vow in November 1521, but he continued to wear the cowl
of the Augustinian Order until 1524, the year before he married Katarina
von Bora. His monastic formation continued to shape his work as an
exegete and an interpreter of Holy Scripture. Let me point out one
important innovation he made in this regard. The traditional monastic
triad of *lectio, meditatio, contemplatio* was altered when he substituted
for the word *contemplatio* the Latin word *tentatio,* or in German *Anfechtung. Anfechtung* is a hard word to translate into English, and "temptation" hardly does it justice. It has to do with conflict, with struggle, bouts
of dread and despair. Right in the middle of the word *Anfechtung* is the
word *Fechter.* A *Fechter* is a fencer or gladiator, someone attacking you,
coming at you with a sword. This is how we read the Bible. This is how
we pray. It involves struggle and confrontation, which means always that

---

[23]Timothy George, *Reading Scripture with the Reformers* (Downers Grove, IL: IVP Academic, 2011), 91.

Bible study is a spiritual discipline. This does not contradict the Protestant principle of the perspicuity of Scripture, but it does contradict the assumption that the Bible is always easy to understand. Clear does not mean easy.

In retelling his encounter with Romans 1:17, which led to his famous breakthrough on the doctrine of justification, Luther described the process of not only meditating day and night but also of "beating importunately upon Paul at that place" (*pulsabam importunus eo loco Paulum*).[24] This note of struggle and temptation is often missing in evangelical programs of Bible study today. But the Scripture principle becomes Scripture practice only in such a process of prayer, meditation, and temptation.

3. *The coinherence of Scripture and tradition.* In the Reformation Commentary on Scripture project, launched by InterVarsity Press in 2011, we have been learning to read the Bible in the company of the Reformers of the sixteenth century. Each volume is filled with surprises and new insights. Often enough, these insights represent a rediscovery from one or other of the church fathers who lived long before the Reformation. In nineteenth-century America, Alexander Campbell advised his followers to "open the New Testament as if mortal man had never seen it before."[25] Thankfully the Reformers of the sixteenth century did not follow that strategy! Their work reveals an intimate familiarity with the preceding exegetical tradition, which they used respectfully as well as critically in their own expositions of the sacred text. The Reformers practiced an ecclesial hermeneutics, for they saw the Scriptures as the book given to the church, gathered and guided by the Holy Spirit. In his debate with Sadoleto, Calvin restated the Vincentian canon in this way:

> [The church is] a society of all the saints, a society which, spread over the whole world, and existing in all ages, and bound together by one doctrine and one spirit of Christ, cultivates and observes unity of faith and

---

[24]WA 54:185-86; LW 34:337.
[25]Cited in Nathan O. Hatch and Mark Noll, eds., *The Bible in America* (New York: Oxford University Press, 1982), 72.

brotherly concord. With this church we deny that we have any dis-agreement. Nay, rather, as we revere her as our mother, so we desire to remain in her bosom.[26]

Defined thus, the church has a real, albeit relative and circumscribed, authority since, as Calvin admits, "We cannot fly without wings." It was this instrumental authority of the church that Augustine had in mind when he remarked that he would not have believed the Bible unless he had been moved thereto by the church, a statement quoted with favor by Calvin. He certainly did not mean that the Bible would have no credibility unless it had been approved by a committee of bishops or a panel of theologians. Rather, he meant that the church is the place where the Bible is received, believed, loved, translated, preached, and passed on. In this construal, the creeds and confessions of the church serve as guardrails to keep us on the road.

The cross. Bebbington correctly identified cross-centeredness as one of the four defining traits of evangelicalism. While in a sense the cross is central to every tradition of orthodox Christianity, East and West, Catholic and Protestant alike, evangelicals have developed a cross-shaped spirituality that harks back to a central emphasis of the Reformation. In this regard, John Stott's *The Cross of Christ* is one of the most important books of the past one hundred years.[27]

Luther and the other Reformers did not expand on the classical arguments for the existence of God, such as the "five ways" found in Thomas Aquinas, nor were they concerned with the various theories of atonement set forth by medieval theologians. In particular, Luther reacted negatively to the word *satisfaction* when applied to the work of Christ, as Anselm had used it in his treatise *Why God Became Man*. Luther objected to this word primarily because he rejected its association with the sacrament of penance.

---

[26]John C. Olin, ed., *John Calvin and Jacopo Sadoleto: A Reformation Debate* (Grand Rapids: Baker, 1976), 61-62.

[27]John Stott, *The Cross of Christ* (1988; repr., Downers Grove, IL: InterVarsity Press, 2006).

Luther's way of theologizing about the atonement also differs from that of scholastic theology in another way. He did not believe that one could prove the necessity of the incarnation by reason alone, apart from the data of revelation, that is to say, without any prior knowledge of the cross and its consequences. "The proper subject of theology is man accursed for his sin and lost, and the God who justifies and saves the sinner," Luther once wrote. "In theology, whatever outside of this subject is researched or disputed is error and poison."[28] The suffering of the Son of God on the cross—his being made a curse for us (see Gal 3:13)—makes no sense by the canons of human logic. But, from the standpoint of biblical faith, it is a window into the heart of God and the only means by which we see God's eternal purpose fulfilled in history.

In *The Kingdom of God in America* (1934), H. Richard Niebuhr famously described the creed of liberal Protestant theology: "A God without wrath brought man without sin into a kingdom without judgment through the ministrations of a Christ without a cross."[29] Evangelicals today are not exempt from the temptation to proclaim "a God without wrath." The wrath of God became a point of controversy within the Presbyterian (PCUSA) Committee on Congregational Song. In putting together a new hymnal, this committee debated the theological suitability of including the much-loved song "In Christ Alone" by Keith Getty and Stuart Townend. Because of its popularity, the committee wanted to include this song, but they could not abide the line: "Till on that cross as Jesus died/the wrath of God was satisfied." For this they wanted to substitute "as Jesus died/the love of God was magnified."[30]

Why do so many Christians shrink from any thought of the wrath of God? R. P. C. Hanson has said that many preachers today deal with God's wrath the way the Victorians handled sex, treating it as something a bit shameful, embarrassing, and best left in the closet. The result is a less

---

[28]WA 40/2:328; LW 12:311.

[29]H. Richard Niebuhr, *The Kingdom of God in America* (New York: Harper & Row, 1959), 193.

[30]Timothy George, "No Squishy Love," *First Things*, July 29, 2013, https://firstthings.com/web-exclusives/2013/07/no-squishy-love.

than fully biblical construal of who God is and what he has done, especially in the redemptive mission of Jesus Christ. But whenever we proclaim less than the full biblical message of Christ's absorption of God's wrath in our stead at the cross, we trivialize the mystery of evil and cheapen the grace of God. We cannot accept the gentleness and love of God by quietly setting aside the word of divine judgment.

However we account for the work of Christ on the cross—and, as Luther knew, none of our atonement theories is adequate to explain fully so profound a reality—it surely means this: that God was in Christ reconciling the world to himself, and that this event involved his purposeful "handing over" and "delivering up" of his Son to a cursed-filled death at the Skull Place outside the gates of Jerusalem (2 Cor 5:19; Rom 8:32; Acts 2:23). As the early Christians understood Isaiah 53:4-5, Christ was pierced there for our transgressions, smitten by God and afflicted. But far from being a tragic bystander, Christ made there what the Book of Common Prayer calls "a full, perfect, and sufficient sacrifice, oblation, and satisfaction, for the sins of the whole world."[31] As a great evangelical hymn puts it, "Bearing shame and scoffing rude—in my place condemned he stood."[32] The full New Testament teaching about the cross involves both expiation, which means providing a covering for sin, and propitiation, which means averting divine judgment. That is why the wrath of God cannot be brushed out of the story of the cross without remainder.

Activism. It is often said that the activists in the sixteenth century were not the Protestant reformers but the Catholic reformers. They were the ones who went out into the world, the Jesuits to Japan and China, and that is certainly true. But from the very beginning, this idea of mission, outreach, and evangelism was endemic to the Protestant vision—all of

---

[31] *Book of Common Prayer and Administration of the Sacraments and Other Rites and Ceremonies of the Church: According to the Use of the Protestant Episcopal Church in the United States of America: Together with the Psalter, or, Psalms of David* (New York: Oxford University Press, 2007), 80.

[32] For the full text of the hymn "Hallelujah, What A Savior!" see www.traditionalhymns.org/Praise/lyrics/HallelujahWhataSavior.php.

the Reformers were concerned with confronting individuals with the claims of Christ and with calling them to repent and believe the gospel.

An example of the depth of this concern is the way in which the church in Geneva became a base for an aggressive evangelistic mission to France. Between 1555 and 1562 the Genevan Company of Pastors commissioned eighty-eight men who were sent forth as bearers of the gospel into nearly every corner of Calvin's native country.[33] Also, in 1556 Calvin and his colleagues in Geneva sponsored an ill-fated attempt to plant an evangelical church in Brazil.[34] This mission strategy was in keeping with Calvin's interpretation of the Great Commission. In commenting on the word "go" in Matthew 28:19, Calvin wrote, "This is the point of the word go (*exeundi*): the boundaries of Judea were prescribed to the prophets under the law, but now the wall is pulled down and the Lord orders the ministers of the gospel to go far out to scatter the teaching of salvation throughout all the regions of the earth."[35]

This missionary impulse also included figures such as Guillaume Farel and Pierre Viret, who came into the mountains and valleys of Switzerland preaching the gospel and converting people. There was also that remarkable German noblewoman, Argula von Grumbach, who dared to stand against the learned doctors of theology at the University of Ingolstadt, among whose number was none other than John Eck, and correct them on the basis of the Word of God.[36]

While many descendants of the magisterial Reformers eventually adopted the position that the missionary mandate was restricted to the original apostles only, it was the radicals of the sixteenth century, notably the Anabaptists, who were most active in evangelizing the far corners of

---

[33]See Robert M. Kingdon, *Geneva and the Coming of the Wars of Religion in France, 1555–1563* (Geneva: Librairie Droz, 1956).

[34]See R. Pierce Beaver, "The Genevan Mission to Brazil," in *The Heritage of John Calvin*, ed. John H. Bratt (Grand Rapids: Eerdmans, 1973), 55-73.

[35]John Calvin, *New Testament Commentaries*, ed. D. W. Torrance and T. F. Torrance (Grand Rapids: Eerdmans, 1971), 251.

[36]For more on this remarkable woman, see the preface to this volume and Peter Matheson, ed., *Argula von Grumbach: A Woman's Voice in the Reformation* (Edinburgh: T&T Clark, 1995).

Europe. As Franklin Littell has pointed out, the Anabaptists desired not merely to reform the church but rather to restore it to its primitive, New Testament condition.[37] This goal set them at odds with the Church of Rome and the established Protestant reformers. By insisting on the necessity of preaching the gospel outside the boundaries imposed by the political authorities, the Anabaptists recovered an important dimension of the evangelistic witness of the early Christians, even as the magisterial Reformers re-established the foundational doctrines of biblical faith. Though they were often at odds with each other in their own times, both traditions have something crucial to contribute to a proper theology of evangelism: the gospel of free grace proclaimed by a free church in the power of the Holy Spirit.

What do you call this? There is a word in the Greek New Testament that captures the spirit of activism of the early Protestant reformers. It is the word *parresia*, boldness, a willingness to step forward and stand out at great peril, a willingness to risk one's life for the sake of the gospel of Jesus Christ. Soon enough, the Protestants were indeed going into all the world. When William Carey went to India in the eighteenth century, he went there to continue the work of the Protestant Reformation, which he did in translating the Scripture into dozens and dozens of the languages of India and the Far East, including Chinese, establishing schools, protesting against the abuse of women, becoming involved in the struggle of the people who were oppressed in that part of India. This is a part of the evangelical vision that we get from the Reformation.

CONCLUSION

If we have an evangelicalism without Reformation, it is too thin, it will not endure, it will not last. On each of these four points and many others we could identify, we need to dig more deeply back into the heart of the Reformation faith. We need to develop an evangelicalism that is not only

---

[37]Franklin H. Littell, *The Origins of Sectarian Protestantism* (New York: Macmillan, 1964).

aware of the Reformation and in dialogue with it but also one that is deeply rooted in the vision of a full-sized God, in the vision of salvation through Jesus Christ alone, and in the vision of a church, the pilgrim people of God, renewed in the power of the Holy Spirit.

BIBLIOGRAPHY

Abelard, Peter. *Commentary on the Epistle to the Romans*. Translated by Steven R. Cartwright. The Fathers of the Church: Mediaeval Continuation 12. Washington, DC: Catholic University of America Press, 2011.

Aldridge, J. W. *The Hermeneutics of Erasmus*. Richmond: John Knox, 1966.

Allen, Henry. "The Historical Legacy of Luther." In *Reformation 500: How the Greatest Revival Since Pentecost Continues to Shape the World Today*, edited by Ray Van Neste and J. Michael Garrett, 173-87. Nashville: B & H, 2016.

Allen, Michael. *Justification and the Gospel: Contexts and Controversies*. Grand Rapids: Baker Academic, 2013.

———. "Sanctification, Perseverance, and Assurance." In *Reformation Theology: A Systematic Summary*, edited by Matthew Barrett, 549–76. Wheaton, IL: Crossway, 2017.

Allgaier, Walter. "Der 'froehliche Wechsel' bei Martin Luther; eine Untersuchung zu Christologie und Soteriologie bei Luther unter besonderer Beruecksichtigung der Schriften bis 1521." PhD diss., University of Erlangen-Nürnberg, 1966.

Althaus, Paul. *The Theology of Martin Luther*. Translated by Robert C. Schultz. Philadelphia: Fortress, 1966.

Anderson, Marvin. "Reformation Interpretation." In *Hermeneutics*, edited by Bernard Ramm, 81-93. Grand Rapids: Baker, 1971.

Anizor, Unche, and Hank Voss. *Representing Christ: A Vision for the Priesthood of All Believers*. Downers Grove, IL: IVP Academic, 2016.

Atherstone, Andrew. *The Martyrs of Mary Tudor*. Leominster, England: Day One, 2005.

Avis, Paul D. L. *The Church in the Theology of the Reformers*. Atlanta: John Knox, 1981.

Bagchi, David V. N. *Luther's Earliest Opponents: Catholic Controversialists, 1518–1525*. Minneapolis: Fortress, 1991.

Baier, John. *Compendium Theologiae Positivae.* 1695.

Bainton, Roland H. *Here I Stand: A Life of Martin Luther.* 1950. Reprint, Nashville: Abingdon, 1978.

Barnes, Robin Bruce. *Prophecy and Gnosis: Apocalypticism in the Wake of the Lutheran Reformation.* Stanford, CA: Stanford University Press, 1988.

Barrett, Matthew. *God's Word Alone—The Authority of Scripture: What the Reformers Taught . . . and Why It Still Matters.* Grand Rapids: Zondervan, 2016.

———, ed. *Reformation Theology. A Systematic Summary.* Wheaton, IL: Crossway, 2017.

Barth, Hans-Martin. *Einander Priester sein: Allgemeines Priestertum in ökumenischer Perspektive.* Göttingen: Vandenhoeck & Ruprecht, 1990.

Bayer, Oswald. "Martin Luther." In *The Reformation Theologians,* edited by Carter Lindberg, 51-66. Oxford: Blackwell, 2002.

———. *Martin Luther's Theology: A Contemporary Interpretation.* Translated by Thomas H. Trapp. Grand Rapids: Eerdmans, 2008.

Beaver, R. Pierce. "The Genevan Mission to Brazil." In *The Heritage of John Calvin,* edited by John H. Bratt. Grand Rapids: Eerdmans, 1973.

Bebbington, David. *Evangelicalism in Modern Britain: A History from the 1730s to the 1980s.* Grand Rapids: Baker Academic, 1992.

Becon, Thomas. *Sick Mans Salve.* London: John Daye, 1572.

Beer, Theobald. *Der fröhliche Wechsel und Streit: Grundzüge der Theologie Luthers.* Leipzig: St. Benno-Verlag, 1974.

Berger, Peter L. *The Desecularization of the World: Resurgent Religion and World Politics.* Grand Rapids: Eerdmans, 1999.

———. *The Sacred Canopy: Elements of a Sociological Theory of Religion.* New York: Anchor, 1967.

Berkhof, L. *Principles of Biblical Interpretation.* Grand Rapids: Baker, 1950.

Biel, Pamela. *Doorkeepers at the House of Righteousness: Heinrich Bullinger and the Zurich Clergy, 1535–1575.* Bern, Switzerland: Verlag Peter Lang, 1991.

Billings, J. Todd. *Calvin, Participation, and the Gift: The Activity of Believers in Union with Christ.* Oxford: Oxford University Press, 2007.

Black, M. H. "The Printed Bible." In *Cambridge History of the Bible.* Vol. 3. Cambridge: Cambridge University Press, 1970.

Bonhoeffer, Dietrich. *Theological Education Underground: 1937–1940.* Edited by Victoria J. Barnett. Translated by Dirk Schulz. Vol. 15. Dietrich Bonhoeffer Works. Minneapolis: Fortress, 2011.

Bonhoeffer, Dietrich, Geffrey B. Kelly, Daniel W. Bloesch, and James H. Burtness. *Life Together; Prayerbook of the Bible*. Minneapolis: Fortress, 2005.

Bornkamm, Heinrich. *Luther and the Old Testament*. Edited by V. I. Gruhn. Philadelphia: Fortress, 1966.

Bozeman, Theodore Dwight. *The Precisianist Strain: Disciplinary Religion and Antinomian Backlash in Puritanism to 1638*. Chapel Hill: University of North Carolina Press, 2004.

Bray, Gerald. *Biblical Interpretation: Past and Present*. Downers Grove, IL: Inter-Varsity Press, 1996.

Brecht, Martin. *Martin Luther: His Road to Reformation, 1483–1521*. Translated by James L. Schaaf. Minneapolis: Fortress, 1993.

Briesmann, Johann. *Etliche Trostspru[e]che Fur Die Blo[e]den/ Schwachen Gewissen. Von Anfechtung Des Glaubens Vnd Der Hoffnung*. Wittenberg, 1525.

Brooks, Peter Newman. *Cranmer in Context: Documents from the English Reformation*. Minneapolis: Fortress, 1989.

Brown, Christopher Boyd. *Singing the Gospel: Lutheran Hymns and the Success of the Reformation*. Cambridge, MA: Harvard University Press, 2005.

Bruce, F. F. *The English Bible: A History of Translations*. Oxford: Oxford University Press, 1961.

Bruce, Steve, ed. *Religion and Modernization: Sociologists and Historians Debate the Secularization Thesis*. Oxford: Oxford University Press, 1992.

———. *Religion in the Modern World: From Cathedrals to Cults*. Oxford: Oxford University Press, 1996.

Brunotte, Wilhelm. *Das geistliche Amt bei Luther*. Berlin: Lutherisches Verlagshaus, 1959.

Bullinger, Heinrich. *Bericht der krancken*. Zurich: Froshauer, 1544.

Bunyan, John. *The Pilgrim's Progress*. London: Oxford University Press, 1956.

Burnaby, John. *Amor Dei*. London: Hodder & Stoughton, 1938.

Burnett, Stephen. *Christian Hebraism in the Reformation Era (1500–1660)*. Leiden: Brill, 2012.

Buringh, Eltjo, and Jan Luiten Van Zanden. "Charting the 'Rise of the West': Manuscripts and Printed Books in Europe, a Long-Term Perspective from the Sixth Through Eighteenth Centuries." *The Journal of Economic History* 69, no. 2 (2009): 409-45.

Calvin, John. *Acts and Antidote*, in Vol. 3, *Selected Works of John Calvin: Tracts and Letters*. Edited by Henry Beveridge and Jules Bonnet. Translated by Henry Beveridge. Grand Rapids: Baker Book House, 1983.

————. *Commentary on the Epistles of Paul the Apostle to the Corinthians,* in Vol. 40, *Calvin's Commentaries.* Edited by John Pringle. Edinburgh: Calvin Translation Society, 1849.

————. *Institutes of the Christian Religion.* Edited by John T. McNeill. Translated by Ford Lewis Battles. 2 vols. Library of Christian Classics. Louisville: Westminster John Knox, 1960.

————. *New Testament Commentaries.* Edited by D. W. Torrance and T. F. Torrance. Grand Rapids: Eerdmans, 1971.

————. "Preface to the Commentary on the Psalms." In *John Calvin. Writings on Pastoral Piety,* edited by Elsie Anne McKee. New York: Paulist, 2001.

————. *Supplementa Calviniana Sermon Inédit.* Edited by Erwin Mülhaupt, James Iley MacCord, and Georges Augustin Barrois. Neukirchen: Neukirchener, 1936.

Cameron, Euan. *The European Reformation.* 2nd ed. Oxford: Oxford University Press, 2012.

Campbell, Douglas A. "'The Priesthood of All Believers': A Pauline Perspective." *The Journal of the Christian Brethren Research Fellowship* 129 (1992): 14-24.

Chambers, Bettye Thomas. *Bibliography of French Bibles: Fifteenth- and Sixteenth-Century French Language Editions.* Geneva: Librairie Droz, 1983.

Chan, Sam. *Preaching as the Word of God: Answering an Old Question with Speech-Act Theory.* Eugene, OR: Pickwick, 2016.

Charlesworth, James H., trans. *The Earliest Christian Hymnbook: The Odes of Solomon.* Eugene, OR: Wipf & Stock, 2009.

Chester, Allan Griffith. *Hugh Latimer, Apostle to the English.* Philadelphia: University of Pennsylvania Press, 1954.

————. *Selected Sermons of Hugh Latimer.* Charlottesville, VA: The University Press of Virginia for The Folger Shakespeare Library, 1968.

Chrysostom. *Commentary on Galatians.* In *Saint Chrysostom,* edited by Philip Schaff. Vol. 12. A Select Library of the Nicene and Post-Nicene Fathers of the Christian Church. Edinburgh: T&T Clark, 1988.

————. *The Epistle to the Romans.* In *Saint Chrysostom,* edited by Philip Schaff. Vol. 11. A Select Library of the Nicene and Post-Nicene Fathers of the Christian Church. Edinburgh: T&T Clark, 1989.

————. *Homilies on Colossians.* In *Saint Chrysostom,* edited by Philip Schaff. Vol. 12. A Select Library of the Nicene and Post-Nicene Fathers of the Christian Church. Edinburgh: T&T Clark, 1988.

———. *Homilies on Philippians*. In *Saint Chrysostom*, edited by Philip Schaff. Vol. 12. A Select Library of the Nicene and Post-Nicene Fathers of the Christian Church. Edinburgh: T&T Clark, 1988.

Clare College 1326–1926. 2 vols. Cambridge: Cambridge University Press, 1928.

Cole, Graham A. "The Holy Spirit." In *Reformation Theology: A Systematic Summary*, edited by Matthew Barrett, 393-421. Wheaton, IL: Crossway, 2017.

Collett, Barry. *Italian Benedictine Scholars and the Reformation: The Congregation of Santa Guistinia of Padua*. Oxford Historical Monographs. Oxford: Clarendon Press, 1985.

Collinson, Patrick. *Archbishop Grindal, 1519–1583: The Struggle for a Reformed Church*. London: Jonathan Cape, 1979.

Cranfield, C. E. B. *A Critical and Exegetical Commentary on the Epistle to the Romans*. Edinburgh: T&T Clark, 1975.

Cranmer, Thomas. "Homily of Salvation." In *The Works of Thomas Cranmer*. Cambridge: Cambridge University Press, 1846.

———. "A Short Declaration of the True, Lively, and Christian Faith." In *The Works of Thomas Cranmer*. Cambridge: Cambridge University Press, 1846.

Crespin, Jean. *Histoire de vrai Tesmoins de la verité de l'Evangile, Qui de leur sang l'on signée depuis Jean Hus; jusques autemps present*. Geneva: Ancre de J. Crespin, 1570.

———. *Histoire des Martyrs, Édition Nouvelle Précédée de Notes*. Edited by Daniel Benoit and Matthieu Lelièvre. 3 vols. Toulouse: Société des livres religieux, 1885.

Cressy, David. "Literacy in Context: Meaning and Measurement in Early Modern England." In *Consumption and the World of Goods*, edited by John Brewer and Ray Porter, 305-19. London: Routledge, 1993.

Cyprian. "Epistle 7.2." In *Apostolic Fathers, Justin Martyr, Irenaeus*, edited by Alexander Roberts, James Donaldson, and A. Cleveland Cox. Vol. 1. Ante-Nicene Fathers. Edinburgh: T&T Clark, 1989.

Da Mantova, Benedetto. *Il Beneficio di Christo: con le version del secolo xvi, documenti e testimonianze*, edited by S. Caponetto. Corpus Reformatorum Italicorum. Dekalb, IL: Northern Illinois University Press and The Newberry Library, 1972.

Darby, Harold S. *Hugh Latimer*. London: Epworth, 1953.

Davenant, John. *A Treatise on Justification*. Translated by Josiah Allport. London, 1844.

Demaus, Robert. *Hugh Latimer: A Biography*. London: Religious Tract Society, 1904.

DeVries, Dawn. "Calvin's Preaching." In *The Cambridge Companion to John Calvin*, edited by Donald K. McKim. Cambridge: Cambridge University Press, 2004.

Dockery, David S. *Biblical Interpretation Then and Now*. Grand Rapids: Baker, 1992.

———. *Christian Scripture: An Evangelical Perspective on Inspiration, Authority, and Interpretation*. Nashville: B & H, 1995.

———. "The Foundation of Reformation Hermeneutics: A Fresh Look at Erasmus." In *Evangelical Hermeneutics*, edited by Michael Bauman and David Hall, 53-75. Camp Hill, PA: Christian Publications, 1995.

———. "A Historical Model." In *Hermeneutics for Preaching: Approaches to Contemporary Interpretations of Scripture*, edited by Raymond Bailey, 27-52. Nashville: Broadman, 1992.

———. "Martin Luther's Christological Hermeneutics." *Grace Theological Journal* 4, no. 2 (1983): 189-203.

———. "New Testament Interpretation: A Historical Survey." In *New Testament Criticism and Interpretation*, edited by David Alan Black and David S. Dockery, 41-69. Grand Rapids: Zondervan, 1991.

———. "A Reformation Day Sermon (Romans 3:21-26)." *Preaching Magazine*, October 1989.

———. "Romans 1:16-17." *Review and Expositor* 86 (1989): 87–91.

———. "The Study and Interpretation of the Bible." In *Foundations for Biblical Interpretation*, 36-54. Nashville: B & H, 1994.

———. "Theological Education: An Introduction." In *Theology, Church, and Ministry: A Handbook for Theological Education*, 8-12. Nashville: B & H, 2017.

———. "The Use of Hab. 2:4 in Rom. 1:17: Some Hermeneutical and Theological Considerations," *Wesleyan Theological Journal* 22, no. 2 (1987): 24-36.

———. "The Value of Typological Exegesis." In *Restoring the Prophetic Mantle: Preaching the Old Testament*, edited by G. Klein, 161-78. Nashville: Broadman, 1992.

Dockery, David S., and George H. Guthrie. *The Holman Guide to Interpreting the Bible*. Nashville: B & H, 2004.

Dodd, C. H. *There and Back Again*. London: Hodder, 1932.

Dunn, James D. G. "The New Perspective on Paul: Whence, What, and Whither?" In *The New Perspective on Paul: Collected Essays*, edited by James D. G. Dunn. Grand Rapids: Eerdmans, 2005.

Dyck, Cornelius J. "The Role of Preaching in Anabaptist Tradition." *Mennonite Life* 17, no. 1 (1962): 21-26.

Ebeling, Gerhard. "The New Hermeneutics and the Early Luther." *Theology Today* 21 (1964): 34-46.

Edwards, Mark U., Jr. *Printing, Propaganda, and Martin Luther*. Berkeley: University of California Press, 1994.

Edwards, O. C., Jr. *History of Preaching*. Nashville: Abingdon, 2004.

Eire, Carlos. *The War Against the Idols: The Reformation of Worship from Erasmus to Calvin*. Cambridge: University of Cambridge Press, 1986.

Elton, G. R. *Reformation Europe, 1517–1559*. New York: Harper & Row, 1963.

Engles, W. M. *Select Sermons and Letters of Dr. Hugh Latimer*. London: The Religious Tract Society, 1923.

Fischer, Robert H. "Another Look at Luther's Doctrine of the Ministry." *Lutheran Quarterly* 18, no. 3 (1966): 260–71.

Forde, Gerhard. "The Christian Life: Introduction." In vol. 2 of *Christian Dogmatics*, edited by Carl Braaten and Robert W. Jenson. Minneapolis: Fortress, 1984.

———. "The Christian Life: Justification." In vol. 2 of *Christian Dogmatics*, edited by Carl Braaten and Robert W. Jenson. Minneapolis: Fortress, 1984.

———. "The Christian Life: Justification and Sanctification." In vol. 2 of *Christian Dogmatics*, edited by Carl Braaten and Robert W. Jenson. Minneapolis: Fortress, 1984.

———. "The Lutheran View." In *Christian Spirituality: Five Views*, edited by Donald L. Alexander. Downers Grove, IL: InterVarsity Press, 1988.

Foxe, John. *The Acts and Monuments of the Church*, 1570. Accessed April 19, 2017. www.johnfoxe.org/index.php?realm=text&gototype=&edition=1570&page id=1976.

Franz, Gunter, ed. *Huberinus—Rhegius—Holbein. Bibliographische und druck-geschichtliche Untersuchung der verbreitesten Trost- und Erbauungschriften des 16. Jahrhunderts*. Nieuwkoop: B. De Graaf, 1973.

Frymire, John. *The Primacy of the Postils: Catholics, Protestants, and the Dissemination of Ideas in Early Modern Germany*. Leiden: Brill, 2010.

Gay, Craig M. *The Way of the (Modern) World, Or, Why It's Tempting to Live as if God Doesn't Exist*. Grand Rapids: Eerdmans, 1998.

George, Timothy. Foreword to *The Advent of Evangelicalism: Exploring Historical Continuities*, edited by Michael A. G. Haykin and Kenneth J. Stewart. Nashville: B & H, 2008.

———. "No Squishy Love." *First Things* (July 29, 2013). https://firstthings.com
/web-exclusives/2013/07/no-squishy-love.

———. "The Priesthood of All Believers and the Quest for Theological Integrity."
Criswell Theological Review 3 (1983): 283-94.

———. *Reading Scripture with the Reformers*. Downers Grove, IL: InterVarsity
Press, 2011.

———. *Theology of the Reformers*. 2nd ed. Nashville: Broadman & Holman, 2013.

Gerrish, Brian A. *Grace and Gratitude: The Eucharistic Theology of John Calvin*.
Minneapolis: Fortress, 1993.

———. "Luther on Priesthood and Ministry." *Church History* 34, no. 4 (1965):
404-22.

Gilmont, Jean-François. *Jean Crespin. Un éditeur réformé du XVIe siècle*. Geneva:
Librairie Droz, 1981.

Gordon, Bruce. "Bullinger's Vernacular Writings: Spirituality and the Christian
Life." In *Architect of the Reformation: An Introduction to Heinrich Bullinger,
1504–1575*, edited by Bruce Gordon and Emidio Campi. Grand Rapids: Baker
Academic, 2004.

Green, Ian. "Varieties of Domestic Devotion in Early Modern English Protestantism." In *Private and Domestic Devotion in Early Modern Britain*,
edited by Alec Ryrie and Jessica Martin. Farnham, Surrey, England:
Ashgate, 2012.

Greer, Rowan A. *Theodore of Mopsuestia: Exegete and Theologian*. London: Faith,
1961.

Greggs, Tom. "The Priesthood of No Believer: On the Priesthood of Christ and
His Church." *International Journal of Systematic Theology* 17 (2015): 386-90.

Gregory, Brad. *Salvation at Stake, Christian Martyrdom in Early Modern Europe*.
Cambridge, MA: Harvard University Press, 1999.

Grundler, Otto. "John Calvin: Ingrafting in Christ." In *The Spirituality of Western
Christendom*, edited by E. Rozanne Elder. Kalamazoo, MI: Cistercian, 1976.

Habermann, Johannes. *Postilla*. Wittenberg, 1583.

Hagen, Kenneth. "The History of Scripture in the Church." In *The Bible in the
Churches: How Various Christians Interpret the Scriptures*, edited by Kenneth
Hagen. Milwaukee, WI: Marquette University Press, 1994.

———. *Luther's Approach to Scripture as Seen in His "Commentaries" on Galatians,
1519–1538*. Tübingen: Mohr Siebeck, 1993.

———. "What Did the Term *Commentarius* Mean to Sixteenth-Century Theologians?" In *Théorie et pratique de l'exégèse. Actes du troisième colloque*

international sur l'histoire de l'exégèse biblique du XVIe siècle, edited by Irena Backus and Francis Higman. Geneva: Droz, 1990.

Halverson, James L. *Peter Aureol on Predestination: A Challenge to Late Medieval Thought*. Leiden: Brill, 1998.

Hart, D. G. *Deconstructing Evangelicalism: Conservative Protestantism in the Age of Billy Graham*. Grand Rapids: Baker Academic, 2005.

Hastings, Elizabeth T. "A Sixteenth Century Manuscript Translation of Latimer's *First Sermon Before Edward*." *Publications of the Modern Language Association* 60 (1945): 959-1002.

Hatch, Nathan O., and Mark Noll, eds. *The Bible in America*. New York: Oxford University Press, 1982.

Heen, Erik M. "Scripture." In *Dictionary of Luther and the Lutheran Tradition*, edited by Timothy J. Wengert, 673-76. Grand Rapids: Baker, 2017.

Heidegger, Johannes. *Corpus Theologiae Christianae*. Zurich, 1700.

Heming, Carol Piper. *Protestants and the Cult of the Saints in German-Speaking Europe, 1517–1531*. Kirksville, MO: Truman State University Press, 2003.

Hendrix, Scott H. "The Authority of Scripture at Work: Luther's Exegesis of the Psalms." In *Encounters with Luther*, edited by Eric W. Gritsch, 144-59. Gettysburg, PA: Institute for Luther Studies, 1982.

——. "Luther Against the Background of the History of Biblical Interpretation." *Interpretation* 37 (1983): 229-39.

Heppe, Heinrich. *Reformed Dogmatics: Set Out and Illustrated from the Sources*. London: George Allen and Unwin, 1950.

Hillerbrand, Hans J., ed. *The Reformation*. Reprint, Grand Rapids: Baker, 1978.

Hodge, Charles. *An Exposition of the Second Epistle to the Corinthians*. New York: Robert Carter and Brothers, 1876.

Hollatz, David. *Examen Theologicum Acromaticum*. 1763. Reprint, Darmstadt: Wissenschaftliche Buchgesellschaft, 1971.

Holloway, Stewart. "Past Masters: Hugh Latimer." Accessed September 9, 2017. www.preaching.com/articles/past-masters/past-masters-hugh-latimer.

Hooker, Richard. *Golden Words: The Rich and Precious Jewel of God's Holy Word*. Oxford and London, 1863.

Horan, David. *Oxford: A Cultural and Literary Companion*. New York: Interlink Books, 2000.

Horton, Michael. "Atonement and Ascension." In *Locating Atonement: Explorations in Constructive Dogmatics*, edited by Oliver Crisp and Fred Sanders, 226-50. Grand Rapids: Zondervan Academic, 2015.

——. *The Christian Faith: A Systematic Theology for Pilgrims on the Way*. Grand Rapids: Zondervan, 2011.

——. *Justification*. 2 vols. New Studies in Dogmatics. Grand Rapids: Zondervan Academic, 2018.

Hsia, R. Po-Chia. *Social Discipline in the Reformation: Central Europe, 1550–1750*. London: Routledge, 1992.

Huberinus, Caspar. *Caspar Huberinus, Works*. Zug, Switzerland: Interdocumentation Publications, 1983.

——. *Eyn kurtzer außzug der heyligen schrift*. Erfurt, 1525.

——. *Vom Zornn Vnd Der Gu[e]tte Gottes*. Augsburg, 1529.

Irenaeus. "Against Heresies." In *Apostolic Fathers, Justin Martyr, Irenaeus*, edited by Alexander Roberts, James Donaldson, and A. Cleveland Cox. Vol. 1. Ante-Nicene Fathers. Edinburgh: T&T Clark, 1989.

Iserloh, Erwin. "Luther's Christ-Mysticism." In *Catholic Scholars Dialogue with Luther*, 37-58. Chicago: Loyola University Press, 1970.

Jensen, Phebe. "'Mirth in Heaven': Religion and Festivity in *As You Like It*." In *Shakespeare and Religious Change*, edited by Kenneth J. E. Graham and Philip D. Collington. New York: Palgrave-Macmillan, 2009.

Jenson, Robert W. *A Theology in Outline*. Oxford: Oxford University Press, 2016.

Kantz, Caspar. *Wie man dem krancken vnd sterbenden menschen/ ermanen/ tro[e]sten/ vnnd Gott befelhen soll*. Augsburg, 1539.

Kantzer, Kenneth, and Carl F. H. Henry, eds. *Evangelical Affirmations*. Grand Rapids: Zondervan, 1990.

Karant-Nunn, Susan C. *The Reformation of Ritual: An Interpretation of Early Modern Germany*. New York: Routledge, 1997.

King, John N. *Foxe's* Book of Martyrs *and Early Modern Print Culture*. Cambridge: Cambridge University Press, 2006.

Kingdon, Robert M. *Geneva and the Coming of the Wars of Religion in France, 1555–1563*. Geneva: Librairie Droz, 1956.

Klug, E. F. *From Luther to Chemnitz*. Grand Rapids: Eerdmans, 1971.

Kolb. Robert. "The Bible in the Reformation and Protestant Orthodoxy." In *The Enduring Authority of the Christian Scriptures*, edited by D. A. Carson, 89-114. Grand Rapids: Eerdmans, 2016.

——. *Martin Luther and the Enduring Word of God*. Grand Rapids: Baker Academic, 2016.

————. "Ministry in Martin Luther and the Lutheran Confessions." In *Called and Ordained: Lutheran Perspectives of the Office of the Ministry*, edited by Todd Nichol and Mark Kolden, 49-66. Minneapolis: Fortress, 1990.

Kolb, Robert, and Timothy Wengert, eds. *The Book of Concord: The Confessions of the Evangelical Lutheran Church*. Minneapolis: Fortress, 2000.

Kooiman, W. J. *Luther and the Bible*. Philadelphia: Mulenberg, 1961.

Kreitzer, Beth. "The Lutheran Sermon." In *Preachers and People in the Reformation and Early Modern Period*, edited by Larissa Taylor. Leiden: Brill, 2003.

Kymaeus, Johannes. *Passional*. Wittemberg, 1539.

Latimer, Hugh. "First Sermon on the Lord's Prayer." In *The Works of Hugh Latimer*, edited by George Elwes Corrie. Vol. 1. Cambridge: Cambridge University Press, 1844.

————. "The Fourth Sermon Preached Before King Edward, March 29, 1549." In *The Works of Hugh Latimer*, edited by George Elwes Corrie. Vol. 1. Cambridge: Cambridge University Press, 1844.

————. "Letter LI." In *The Works of Hugh Latimer*, edited by George Elwes Corrie. Vol. 2. Cambridge: Cambridge University Press, 1845.

————. "Letter to Edward Baynton." In *The Works of Hugh Latimer*, edited by George Elwes Corrie. Vol. 2. Cambridge: Cambridge University Press, 1845.

————. "A Most Faithful Sermon Preached Before King's Most Excellent Majesty and His Most Honourable Council." In *The Works of Hugh Latimer*, edited by George Elwes Corrie. Vol. 1. Cambridge: Cambridge University Press, 1844.

————. "Residue of the Same Gospel Declared in the Afternoon [at Stamford, November 9, 1550]." In *The Works of Hugh Latimer*, edited by George Elwes Corrie. Vol. 1. Cambridge: Cambridge University Press, 1844.

————. "Second Sermon on the Gospel of All Saints." In *The Works of Hugh Latimer*, edited by George Elwes Corrie. Vol. 1. Cambridge: Cambridge University Press, 1844.

————. "The Second Sunday in Advent." In *The Works of Hugh Latimer*, edited by George Elwes Corrie. Vol. 2. Cambridge: Cambridge University Press, 1845.

————. "A Sermon on the Parable of a King That Married His Son." In *The Works of Hugh Latimer*, edited by George Elwes Corrie. Vol. 1. Cambridge: Cambridge University Press, 1844.

————. "The Sermon on the Plough." In *The Works of Hugh Latimer*, edited by George Elwes Corrie. Vol. 1. Cambridge: Cambridge University Press, 1844.

————. "Sermon Preached at Grimsthorpe on Twelfth Day, 1553." In *The Works of Hugh Latimer*, edited by George Elwes Corrie. Vol. 2. Cambridge: Cambridge University Press, 1845.

————. "A Sermon Preached at Stamford, November 9, 1550." In *The Works of Hugh Latimer*, edited by George Elwes Corrie. Vol. 1. Cambridge: Cambridge University Press, 1844.

————. "Sermon Preached on the First Sunday After Epiphany." In *The Works of Hugh Latimer*, edited by George Elwes Corrie. Vol. 2. Cambridge: Cambridge University Press, 1845.

————. "Sermons on the Card." In *The Works of Hugh Latimer*, edited by George Elwes Corrie. Vol. 1. Cambridge: Cambridge University Press, 1844.

————. "The Sixth Sermon Preached Before King Edward, April 12, [1549]." In *The Works of Hugh Latimer*, edited by George Elwes Corrie. Vol. 1. Cambridge: Cambridge University Press, 1844.

————. "The Third Sermon upon the Lord's Prayer." In *The Works of Hugh Latimer*, edited by George Elwes Corrie. Vol. 1. Cambridge: Cambridge University Press, 1844.

Latimer, Hugh, and Edward Arber. *Sermon on the Ploughers*. London: Alex Murray & Son, 1868.

Leonard, E. G. *A History of Protestantism*. Indianapolis: Bobbs-Merrill, 1968.

Letham, Robert. "Amandus Polanus: A Neglected Theologian?" *Sixteenth Century Studies* (1990): 463-76.

Lieberg, Hellmut. *Amt und Ordination bei Luther und Melanchthon*. Göttingen: Vandenhoeck & Ruprecht, 1962.

Lim, P. C.-H. "Latimer, Hugh." In *Biographical Dictionary of Evangelicals*, edited by Timothy Larsen. Leicester, England: InterVarsity Press, 2003.

Lindberg, Carter. *The European Reformations*. Cambridge, MA: Blackwell, 1996.

Littell, Franklin H. *The Origins of Sectarian Protestantism*. New York: Macmillan, 1964.

Loane, Marcus L. *Masters of the English Reformation*. London: Church Book Room Press, 1954.

Lohse, Bernhard. *Martin Luther's Theology: Its Historical and Systematic Development*. Translated by Roy A. Harrisville. Minneapolis: Fortress, 2006.

Longenecker, Richard N. *The Epistle to the Romans*. Grand Rapids: Eerdmans, 2016.

Loofs, Friedrich. *Leitfaden zum Studium der Dogmengeschichte*. 4th ed. Halle, 1906.

Lotz, David W. "Sola Scriptura: Luther on Biblical Authority." *Interpretation* 35 (1981): 258-73

Lull, Timothy, ed. *Martin Luther's Basic Theological Writings.* Minneapolis: Fortress, 1989.

Luther, Martin. *The Babylonian Captivity of the Church.* In *Word and Sacrament II.* Vol. 36 of Luther's Works, edited by Abdel Ross Wentz, translated by A. T. W. Steinhäuser, 3-126. Philadelphia: Muhlenberg, 1959.

———. *The Christian in Society II*, edited by Helmut T. Lehmann and Walther I. Brandt. Vol. 45. Luther's Works. Philadelphia: Muhlenberg, 1962.

———. *The Second Invocavit Sermon.* In *Karlstadt's Battle with Luther: Documents in a Liberal-Radical Debate*, edited by Ronald J. Sider. Philadelphia: Fortress, 1978.

———. *Career of the Reformer I*, edited by Harold J. Grimm. Vol. 31. Luther's Works. Philadelphia: Fortress, 1957.

———. *Career of the Reformer II*, edited by George W. Forell. Vol. 32. Luther's Works. St. Louis: Concordia, 1968.

———. *Church and Ministry I*, edited by Eric W. Gritsch. Vol. 39. Luther's Works. Philadelphia: Fortress, 1970.

———. *Church and Ministry II*, edited by Conrad Bergendoff. Vol. 40. Luther's Works. Philadelphia: Muhlenberg, 1958.

———. *Church and Ministry III*, edited by Eric W. Gritsch. Vol. 41. Luther's Works. Philadelphia: Fortress, 1966.

———. *Lectures on Galatians (1535): Chapters 1–4*, edited by Jaroslav Pelikan and Walter A. Hansen. Vol. 26. Luther's Works. St. Louis: Concordia, 1963.

———. *Lectures on Genesis Chapters 1–5*, edited by Jaroslav Pelikan. Vol. 1. Luther's Works. St. Louis: Concordia, 1958.

———. *Lectures on Genesis Chapters 6–14*, edited by Jaroslav Pelikan. Vol. 2. Luther's Works. St. Louis: Concordia, 1960.

———. *Lectures on Genesis: Chapters 26–30*, edited by Jaroslav Pelikan and Walter A. Hansen. Vol. 5. Luther's Works. St. Louis: Concordia, 1968.

———. *Lectures on Isaiah Chapters 40–66*, edited by Hilton C. Oswald. Vol. 17. Luther's Works. St. Louis: Concordia, 1972.

———. *Lectures on Titus, Philemon, and Hebrews*, edited by Walter A. Hansen. Vol. 29. Luther's Works. St. Louis: Concordia, 1968.

———. "On the Last Words of David." In *Ecclesiastes, Lectures on Song of Solomon, Treatise on the Last Words of David*, edited by Jaroslav Pelikan and Hilton C. Oswald. Vol. 15. Luther's Works. St. Louis: Concordia, 1972.

——. *Selected Psalms II*, edited by Jaroslav Pelikan. Vol. 13. Luther's Works. St. Louis: Concordia, 1956.

——. *Selected Psalms III*, edited by Jaroslav Pelikan and Daniel E. Poellot. Vol. 14. Luther's Works. St. Louis: Concordia, 1958.

——. *Table Talk*, edited by Theodore G. Tappert. Vol. 54. Luther's Works. Philadelphia: Fortress, 1968.

——. *What Luther Says*, edited by Ewald M. Plass. St. Louis: Concordia, 2006.

——. *Word and Sacrament I*, edited by E. Theodore Bachmann. Vol. 35. Luther's Works. Philadelphia: Muhlenberg, 1960.

Luy, David J. "A Wondrous Strife: Luther's Baroque Soteriology." In *Savior and Lord: The Work of Jesus Christ*, edited by Paul R. Hinlicky and R. David Nelson. Delhi, NY: American Lutheran Publicity Bureau, forthcoming.

Maag, Karin. *Seminary or University? The Genevan Academy and Reformed Higher Education, 1560–1620*. Aldershot, England: Scolar, 1995.

Manetsch, Scott W. *Calvin's Company of Pastors: Pastoral Care and the Emerging Reformed Church, 1536–1609*. New York: Oxford University Press, 2013.

——. "The Gravity of the Divine Word and the Corinthian Correspondence in the Reformation Era." *Concordia Theological Quarterly* 81 (2017): 55–76.

——. "Reassessing the Reformation: Contemporary Themes and Approaches." *Fides et Historia* 48 (2016): 131-40.

——, ed. *Reformation Commentary on Scripture: 1 Corinthians*. Vol. 9A. Downers Grove, IL: InterVarsity Press, 2017.

Marbach, Johann. *Von Mirackeln vnd Wunderzeichen . . .* (s.l. 1571).

Marsh, Charles. *Strange Glory*. New York: Vintage, 2014.

Marsh, Christopher. "'Departing Well and Christianly': Will-Making and Popular Religion in Early Modern England." In *Religion and the English People, 1500–1640: New Voices and Perspectives*, edited by Eric Josef Carlson. Kirksville, MO: Thomas Jefferson University Press, 1998.

Marsh, William M. *Martin Luther on Reading the Bible as Christian Scripture: The Messiah in Luther's Biblical Hermeneutic and Theology*. Princeton Theological Monographs. Eugene, OR: Pickwick, 2017.

Marshall, Peter, ed. *The Oxford Illustrated History of the Reformation*. Oxford: Oxford University Press, 2015.

Mastricht, Peter von. *Theoretico-Practica Theologica*. 2nd ed. 1698.

Mathesius, Johannes. *Das Tro[e]stliche De Profvndis, Welches Ist Der CXXX. Psalm Davids*. Nuremberg, 1567.

Matheson, Peter, ed. *Argula von Grumbach. A Woman's Voice in the Reformation.* Edinburgh: T&T Clark, 1995.

McClay, Wilfred M. "The Strange Persistence of Guilt." *The Hedgehog Review* 19, no. 1 (Spring 2017). Accessed April 18, 2017. www.iasc-culture.org/THR /THR_article_2017_Spring_McClay.php.

McGrath, Alister E. *Iustitia Dei: The History of the Doctrine of Justification.* 3rd ed. Cambridge: Cambridge University Press, 2005.

———. *Passion for the Gospel: Hugh Latimer (1485–1555) Then and Now.* London: Latimer Trust, 2005.

———. *Reformation Thought: An Introduction.* Oxford: Blackwell, 1999.

McKim, Donald, ed. *Dictionary of Major Biblical Interpreters.* Downers Grove, IL: IVP Academic, 2007.

McNeill, John T. Review of *Hugh Latimer, Apostle to the English*, by Allan G. Chester. *Church History* 24, no. 1 (1955): 77–78.

McNutt, Jennifer Powell, and David Lauber, eds. *The People's Book: The Reformation and the Bible.* Downers Grove, IL: IVP Academic, 2017.

Melanchthon, Philipp. *Loci Communes.* Translated by J. A. O. Preus. St. Louis: Concordia, 1992.

Metaxas, Eric. *Bonhoeffer: Pastor, Prophet, Martyr, Spy.* Nashville: Thomas Nelson, 2011.

Meuser, Fred W. "Luther as Preacher of the Word of God." In *The Cambridge Companion to Martin Luther*, edited by Donald K. McKim. Cambridge: Cambridge University Press, 2003.

Moeller, B. "Scripture, Tradition and Sacrament in the Middle Ages and in Luther." In *Holy Book and Holy Tradition*, edited by F. F. Bruce and E. G. Rupp, 120-22. Manchester, England: Manchester University Press, 1968.

Monter, William. *Judging the French Reformation: Heresy Trials by Sixteenth-Century Parlements.* Cambridge, MA: Harvard University Press, 1999.

Montgomery, John Warwick. *In Defense of Luther.* Milwaukee: Northwestern, 1970.

Moo, Douglas J. *The Epistle to the Romans.* Grand Rapids: Eerdmans, 1996.

Mueller, J. T. "Luther and the Bible." In *Inspiration and Interpretation*, edited by John F. Walvoord. Grand Rapids: Eerdmans, 1957.

Müller, Gerhard. "Allgemeines Priestertum aller Getauften und kirchliches Amt in der Reformationszeit." *Kerygma und Dogma* 52, no. 1 (2006): 98-104.

———. "Luther's Transformation of Medieval Thought: Discontinuity and Continuity." In *The Oxford Handbook of Martin Luther's Theology*, edited by

Robert Kolb, Irene Dengel, and L'Ubomir Batka, 105-14. Oxford: Oxford University Press, 2014.

Muller, Richard A. *After Calvin: Studies in the Development of a Theological Tradition.* Oxford: Oxford University Press, 2003.

———. *Calvin and the Reformed Tradition: On the Work of Christ and the Order of Salvation.* Grand Rapids: Baker Academic, 2012.

———. "John Calvin and Late Calvinism: The Identity of the Reformed Tradition." In *The Cambridge Companion to Reformation Theology,* edited by David Bagchi and David Steinmetz, 130-49. Cambridge: Cambridge University Press, 2004.

Muller, Richard, and John Thompson, eds. *Biblical Interpretation in the Era of the Reformation.* Grand Rapids: Eerdmans, 1996.

Mumme, Jonathan. *Die Präsenz Christi im Amt: am Beispiel ausgewählter Predigten Martin Luthers, 1535–1546.* Refo500 Academic Studies 21. Göttingen: Vandenhoeck & Ruprecht, 2015.

Murray, Iain. "Lloyd-Jones: Messenger of Grace." *Banner of Truth* 536 (2008): 32.

Needham, Nick. "Justification in the Early Church Fathers." In *Justification in Perspective: Historical Developments and Contemporary Challenges,* edited by Bruce McCormack. Grand Rapids: Baker Academic, 2006.

Niebuhr, H. Richard. *The Kingdom of God in America.* New York: Harper and Row, 1959.

Noll, Mark. "Noun or Adjective? The Ravings of a Fanatical Nominalist." *Fides et Historia* 47, no. 1 (2015): 73-83.

Norden, John. *A Pensive Mans Practice. Or the Pensive Mans Complaint and Comfort.* London, 1623.

Null, Ashley. *Thomas Cranmer's Doctrine of Repentance: Renewing the Power to Love God.* Oxford: Oxford University Press, 2007.

Oberman, Heiko A. *Luther: Man Between God and the Devil.* New Haven, CT: Yale University Press, 1989.

Ocker, Christopher. *Biblical Poetics Before Humanism and Reformation.* Cambridge: Cambridge University Press, 2002.

Old, Hughes Oliphant. *The Reading and Preaching of the Scriptures in the Worship of the Christian Church.* 7 vols. Grand Rapids: Eerdmans, 2007.

Olin, John C., ed. *John Calvin and Jacopo Sadoleto: A Reformation Debate.* Grand Rapids: Baker Academic, 1976.

Olson, Jeannine Olson. "Jean Crespin, Humanist Printer Among the Reformation Martyrologists." In *The Harvest of Humanism in Central Europe,* edited by Manfred Fleischer, 317-40. St. Louis: Concordia, 1992.

Origen. *Commentary on the Epistle to the Romans, Books 1–5.* Translated by Thomas P. Scheck. Washington, DC: Catholic University of America Press, 2001.

Ozment, Steven. *The Age of Reform: An Intellectual and Religious History of Late Medieval and Reformation Europe.* New Haven, CT: Yale University Press, 1980.

———. *The Reformation in the Cities: The Appeal of Protestantism to Sixteenth-Century Germany and Switzerland.* New Haven, CT: Yale University Press, 1975.

Pak, G. Sujin. *The Judaizing Calvin: Sixteenth-Century Debates over the Messianic Psalms.* New York: Oxford University Press, 2010.

Parker, T. H. L. *Calvin's Preaching.* Louisville: Westminster John Knox, 1992.

Parker, Thomas D. "The Interpretation of Scripture: A Comparison of Calvin and Luther on Galatians." *Interpretation* 17 (1963): 61-75.

Pasquarello, Michael, III. *God's Ploughman. Hugh Latimer: "A Preaching Life" (1485–1555).* Studies in Christian History and Thought. Eugene, OR: Wipf & Stock, 2014.

———. *Sacred Rhetoric: Preaching as Theological and Pastoral Practice of the Church.* Grand Rapids: Eerdmans, 2005.

Patterson, Mary Hampson. *Domesticating the Reformation: Protestant Best Sellers, Private Devotion, and the Revolution of English Piety.* Madison, NJ: Fairleigh Dickinson University Presses, 2007.

Pauck, Wilhelm. "The Ministry in the Time of the Continental Reformation." In *The Ministry in Historical Perspectives,* edited by H. Richard Niebuhr and Daniel D. Williams. New York: Harper and Brothers, 1956.

Paulson, Steven D. *Lutheran Theology.* London: T&T Clark, 2011.

Payne, J. B. *Erasmus: His Theology of the Sacraments.* Richmond: Bratcher, 1970.

Pelikan, Jaroslov. *Luther the Expositor.* St. Louis: Concordia, 1959.

———. *The Reformation of the Bible. The Bible of the Reformation.* New Haven, CT: Yale University Press, 1996.

Pereira, Jairzinho Lopes. *Augustine of Hippo and Martin Luther on Original Sin and the Justification of the Sinner.* Göttingen: Vandenhoek & Ruprecht, 2013.

Peterson, Cheryl M. "Martin Luther on the Church and Its Ministry." In *Oxford Research Encyclopedia of Religion,* n.d.

Pettegree, Andrew. *Brand Luther.* New York: Penguin, 2015.

Pfeffinger, Johann. *Trostbu[e]chlin Aus Gottes Wort.* Leipzig, 1552.

Polanus, Amandus. *De Partibus Gratuitae Iustificationis Nostrae Coram Deo: Theses Theologica*. Basel, 1598.

———. *Syntagma Theologiae Christianae*. Basel, 1609.

Preus, James Samuel. "Luther on Christ and the Old Testament." *Concordia Theological Monthly* 43 (1972): 488-97.

Putnam, Rhyne R. *In Defense of Doctrine: Evangelicalism, Theology, and Scripture*. Minneapolis: Fortress, 2015.

Reilly, Robert R. *Making Gay Okay: How Rationalizing Homosexual Behavior Is Changing Everything*. San Francisco, CA: Ignatius Press, 2014.

Reimer, Jonathan. "The Life and Writings of Thomas Becon, 1512–1567." PhD diss., Cambridge University, 2016.

Rieske-Braun, Uwe. *Duellum mirabile: Studien zum Kampfmotiv in Martin Luthers Theologie*. Forschungen zur Kirchen- und Dogmengeschichte 73. Göttingen: Vandenhoeck & Ruprecht, 1999.

Rittgers, Ronald K. "The Age of Reform as an Age of Consolation." *Church History: Studies in Christianity and Culture* 86, no. 3 (2017): 607-42.

———. *The Reformation of the Keys: Confession, Conscience, and Authority in Sixteenth-Century Germany*. Cambridge, MA: Harvard University Press, 2004.

———. *The Reformation of Suffering: Pastoral Theology and Lay Piety in Late Medieval and Early Modern Germany*. New York: Oxford University Press, 2012.

———. "The Word-Prophet Martin Luther." *The Sixteenth-Century Journal: The Journal of Early Modern Studies* 48, no. 3 (2017): 951-76.

Roberts, Alexander, James Donaldson, and A. Cleveland Cox, eds. "The Epistle to Diognetus." In *Apostolic Fathers, Justin Martyr, Irenaeus*. Vol. 1. Ante-Nicene Fathers. Edinburgh: T&T Clark, 1989.

Rogers, Mark. "A Dangerous Idea? Martin Luther, E. Y. Mullins and the Priesthood of All Believers." *The Westminster Theological Journal* 72 (2010): 119-34.

Rupp, G. *Luther's Progress to the Diet of Worms*. New York: Harper, 1964.

Ryle, J. C. *Five English Reformers*. London: The Banner of Truth Trust, 1960.

Ryrie, Alec. *Being Protestant in Reformation Britain*. Oxford: Oxford University Press, 2013.

Sasse, Herman. "Luther and the Word of God." In *Accents in Luther's Theology: Essays in Commemoration of the 450th Anniversary of the Reformation*, edited by Heino O. Kadal. St. Louis: Concordia, 1967.

Schaff, Philip, ed. *The Creeds of Christendom*. Rev. ed. Grand Rapids: Baker, 1985.

Scheck, Thomas P. "Introduction to Origen." In *Commentary on the Epistle to the Romans, Books 1–5*. Translated by Scheck. Washington, DC: Catholic University of America Press, 2001.

Schmid, Heinrich. *The Doctrinal Theology of the Evangelical Lutheran Church*. Minneapolis: Augsburg, 1899.

Schwager, Raymund. *Der wunderbare Tausch: zur Geschichte und Deutung der Erlösungslehre*. München: Kösel, 1986.

Scribner, Robert W. "The Incombustible Luther: The Image of the Reformer in Early Modern Germany." *Past and Present* 110 (1986): 38-68.

———. *Religion and Culture in Germany (1400–1800)*. Edited by Lyndal Roper. Leiden: Brill, 2001.

Sehling, Emil. *Die Evangelischen Kirchenordnungen Des XVI Jahrhunderts*. 19 vols. Leipzig: O. R. Riesland, J. C. B. Mohr (Paul Siebeck), 1902.

Shelton, Raymond Barry. "Martin Luther's Concept of Biblical Interpretation in Historical Perspective." PhD diss., Fuller Theological Seminary, 1974.

Siggins, I. D. K. *Martin Luther's Doctrine of Christ*. Publications in Religion. New Haven, CT: Yale University Press, 1970.

Silcock, Jeffrey G. "Luther on the Holy Spirit and His Use of God's Word." In *The Oxford Handbook of Martin Luther's Theology*, edited by Robert Kolb, Irene Dingel, and Ľubomír Batka, 294-309. Oxford: Oxford University Press, 2014.

Soergel, Philip M. "Miracle, Magic, and Disenchantment in Early Modern Germany." In *Envisioning Magic: A Princeton Seminar and Symposium*, edited by Peter Schäfer and Hans G. Kippenberg, 215-34. Leiden: Brill, 1997.

———. *Wondrous in His Saints: Counter-Reformation Propaganda in Bavaria*. Berkeley: University of California Press, 1993.

Spangenberg, Johannes. *A Booklet of Comfort for the Sick, & On the Christian Knight by Johann Spangenberg (1548)*. Edited by Robert Kolb. Translated by Robert Kolb. Milwaukee: Marquette University Press, 2007.

Spitz, L. W., Sr. "Luther's Sola Scriptura." *Concordia Theological Monthly* 31 (1960): 740-45.

———. "The Universal Priesthood of Believers with Luther's Comments." *Concordia Theological Monthly* 23 (1952): 1-15.

Stanglin, Keith D. *Arminius on the Assurance of Salvation: The Context, Roots, and Shape of the Leiden Debate, 1603–1609*. Leiden, Brill: 2007.

Stanglin, Keith D., and Thomas H. McCall. *Jacob Arminius: Theologian of Grace*. New York: Oxford University Press, 2012.

Staupitz, Johann von. "The Eternal Predestination of God." In *Forerunners of the Reformation: The Shape of Late Medieval Thought*, edited by Heiko A. Oberman, 151-64. Philadelphia: Fortress, 1966.

Steiger, Johann Anselm. "Die Gesichts- und Theologie-Vergessenheit der heutigen Seelsorgelehre. Anlaß für einen Rückblick in den Schatz reformatorischer und orthodoxer Seelsorgeliteratur." *Kerygma und Dogma* 39 (1993): 64-87.

———. *Medizinische Theologie. Christus Medicus und Theologia Medicinalis bei Martin Luther und im Luthertum der Barockzeit*. Leiden: Brill, 2005.

Steinmetz, David. *Luther in Context*. 2nd ed. Grand Rapids: Baker Academic, 2002.

———. *Taking the Long View: Christian Theology in Historical Perspective*. New York: Oxford University Press, 2011.

Stephens, W. P. *The Theology of Huldrych Zwingli*. Oxford: Clarendon, 1986.

Stott, John. *The Cross of Christ*. 1988. Reprint, Downers Grove, IL: InterVarsity Press, 2006.

Strauss, Gerald. *Luther's House of Learning: Indoctrination of the Young in the German Reformation*. Baltimore: Johns Hopkins University Press, 1978.

Surburg, Raymond F. "The Presuppositions of the Historical-Grammatical Method as Employed by Historic Lutheranism." *Springfielder* 38, no. 4 (1975): 278-88.

———. "The Significance of Luther's Hermeneutics for the Protestant Reformation." *Concordia Theological Monthly* 24 (1953): 241-61.

Tanneberg, Hieronymus. *Trostbu[e]chlein*. Leipzig, 1999.

Tanner, Norman P. *Decrees of the Ecumenical Councils*. 2 vols. Washington, DC: Georgetown University Press, 1990.

Taylor, Charles. *Sources of the Self: The Making of the Modern Identity*. Cambridge: Cambridge University Press, 2012.

Taylor, Larissa, ed. *Preachers and People in the Reformations and Early Modern Period*. Leiden: Brill, 2001.

Thayer, Anne T. "Judge and Doctor: Images of the Confessor in Printed Model Sermon Collections, 1450–1520." In *Penitence in the Age of Reformations*, edited by Katharine Jackson Lualdi and Anne T. Thayer, 10-29. Aldershot, England: Ashgate, 2000.

Thiselton, Anthony. "The New Hermeneutic." In *New Testament Interpretation: Essays on Principles and Methods*, edited by I. Howard Marshall, 308-33. Grand Rapids: Eerdmans, 1977.

———. *Two Horizons*. Grand Rapids: Eerdmans, 1980.

Thomas, Keith. *Religion and the Decline of Magic: Studies in Popular Beliefs in Sixteenth and Seventeenth Century England*. New York: Oxford University Press, 1971.

Thompson, Mark. *A Sure Ground on Which to Stand: The Relation of Authority and Interpretative Method in Luther's Approach to Scripture*. Eugene, OR: Wipf & Stock, 2007.

Trelcatius, Lucas, Jr. *Disputatio theologica de justificatione hominis coram Deo*, XX. Leiden, 1604.

———. *Opscula theologica omnia, duorum catalogum, prima edita* XIII. Leiden, n.d.

Trento, Jean-Baptiste, and Pierre Eskrich. *Mappe-monde nouvelle papistique: Histoire de la mappe-monde papistique, en laquelle est déclairé tout ce qui est contenu et pourtraict en la grande Table, ou Carte de la Mappe-Monde (Genève, 1566)*, edited by Frank Lestringant and Alessandra Preda. Geneva: Droz, 2009.

Trigg, Jonathan D. *Baptism in the Theology of Martin Luther*. Leiden: Brill, 1994.

Trueman, Carl R. *Luther on the Christian Life: Cross and Freedom*. Wheaton, IL: Crossway, 2015.

———. "Martin Luther." In *Christian Theologies of Salvation: A Comparative Introduction*, edited by Justin S. Holcomb, 191-207. New York: New York University Press, 2017.

Turretin, Francis. *Institutio Theologiae Elencticae, XVII* in *Opera Tomus I*. Edinburgh, 1847.

Vanhoozer, Kevin J. *Biblical Authority After Babel: Retrieving the Solas in the Spirit of Mere Protestant Christianity*. Grand Rapids: Brazos, 2016.

———, ed. *Dictionary for Theological Interpretation of the Bible*. Grand Rapids: Baker, 2005.

———. *First Theology: God, Scripture, Hermeneutics*. Downers Grove, IL: InterVarsity Press, 2002.

———. *Is There Meaning in This Text? The Bible, the Reader, and the Morality of Literary Knowledge*. Grand Rapids: Zondervan, 1998.

Vermigli, Peter Martyr. "Locus on Justification." In Frank A. James III, introduction to *Peter Martyr Vermigli: Predestination and Justification*. The Peter Martyr Library, vol. 8. Translated and edited by Frank A. James III. Kirksville, MO: Sixteenth Century Essays and Studies, 2003.

Voss, Hank. *The Priesthood of All Believers and the Missio Dei: A Canonical, Catholic, and Contextual Perspective*. Princeton Theological Monograph Series 223. Eugene, OR: Pickwick, 2016.

Wabuda, Susan. "'Fruitful Preaching' in the Diocese of Worcester: Bishop Hugh Latimer and His Influence, 1535–1539." In *Religion and the English People 1500–1640: New Voices, New Perspectives*, edited by Eric Josef Carlson. Vol. 45. Sixteenth Century Essays & Studies. Kirksville, MO: Thomas Jefferson University Press, 1998.

Walker, D. P. "The Cessation of Miracles." In *Hermeticism and the Renaissance: Intellectual History and the Occult in Early Modern Europe*, edited by Ingrid Merkel and Allen G. Debus, 111-24. London: Associated University Press, 1988.

Warfield, B. B. "Introductory Essay on Augustine and the Pelagian Controversy." In *Nicene and Post-Nicene Fathers: First Series*. Vol. V, *St. Augustine: Anti-Pelagian Writings*, edited by Philip Schaff., ii-xxi. 1887.

Watson, David. "Jean Crespin and the First English Martyrology of the Reformation." In *John Foxe and the English Reformation*, edited by David Loades, 192-209. Aldershot, England: Scolar, 1997.

———. "Jean Crespin and the Writing of History in the French Reformation." In vol. 2 of *Protestant History and Identity in Sixteenth-Century Europe*, edited by Bruce Gordon, 39-58. Aldershot, England: Scolar, 1996.

Weber, Max. *The Protestant Ethic and the Spirit of Capitalism*. Translated by Talcott Parsons. New York: Charles Scribner's Sons, 1958.

Wengert, Timothy J., ed. *Dictionary of Luther and the Lutheran Tradition*. Grand Rapids: Baker Academic, 2017.

———. *Priesthood, Pastors, Bishops: Public Ministry for the Reformation and Today*. Minneapolis: Fortress, 2008.

Westhead, Nigel. "Calvin and Experimental Knowledge of God." In *Adorning the Doctrine: Papers Read at the 1995 Westminster Conference*. London: The Westminster Conference, 1995.

Wiles, Maurice F. *The Divine Apostle: The Interpretation of St. Paul's Epistles in the Early Church*. Cambridge: Cambridge University Press, 1967.

Wise, Michael, Martin Abegg, Jr., and Edward Cook, trans. *A New Translation of the Dead Sea Scrolls*. New York: HarperOne, 2005.

Wollebius, Johannes. *An Abridgement of Christian Divinity*. Translated by Alexander Ross. London, 1660.

———. *Christianae Theologiae Compendium*. Basel, 1634.

Wood, A. Skevington. "Luther as an Interpreter of Scripture." *Christianity Today* 3 (November 24, 1958): 7-9.

———. *The Principles of Biblical Interpretation as Enunciated by Irenaeus, Origen, Augustine, Luther, and Calvin*. Grand Rapids: Zondervan, 1967.

Wood, Charles. *The Formation of Christian Understanding*. Philadelphia: Westminster Press, 1982.

Woodbridge, John D. *Biblical Authority: Infallibility and Inerrancy in the Christian Tradition*. Grand Rapids: Zondervan, 2015.

Wright, David F. "Augustine and Justification by Faith." In *Justification in Perspective: Historical Developments and Contemporary Challenges*, edited by Bruce L. McCormack, 50-60. Grand Rapids: Baker Academic, 2006.

———. "Martin Bucer." In *Dictionary of Major Biblical Interpreters*, edited by Donald K. McKim. Downers Grove, IL: InterVarsity Press, 2009.

Yeago, David. "A Christian, Holy People: Martin Luther on Salvation and the Church." In *Spirituality and Social Embodiment*, edited by L. Gregory Jones and James J. Buckley, 101-20. Oxford: Wiley-Blackwell, 1997.

———. "Gnosticism, Antinomianism, and Reformation Theology: Reflections on the Costs of a Construal." *Pro Ecclesia* (1993): 37-49.

———. "Martin Luther on Renewal and Sanctification: *Simul Iustus et* Revisited." *Sapere teologico e unita' della defe: studi in onore del Prof. Jared Wicks* (2004): 655-74.

Zambelli, Paola, ed. *"Astrologi hallucinati": Stars and the End of the World in Luther's Time*. Berlin: De Gruyter, 1986.

List of Contributors

Kevin DeYoung
Senior Pastor and Assistant Professor of Theology
Christ Covenant Church (Matthews, North Carolina)
Reformed Theological Seminary—Charlotte

David S. Dockery
President
Trinity International University

Timothy George
Founding Dean and Professor of Theology
Beeson Divinity School

Michael A. G. Haykin
Professor of Church History
Southern Baptist Theological Seminary

Michael S. Horton
Professor of Systematic Theology and Apologetics
Westminster Seminary California

David J. Luy
Associate Professor of Biblical and Systematic Theology
Trinity Evangelical Divinity School

Scott M. Manetsch
Professor of Church History and the History of Christian Thought
Trinity Evangelical Divinity School

Thomas H. McCall
Professor of Biblical and Systematic Theology
Trinity Evangelical Divinity School

Ronald K. Rittgers
Erich Markel Professor of History and Theology
Valparaiso University

AUTHOR INDEX

Subject Index

Scripture Index

Finding the Textbook You Need

The IVP Academic Textbook Selector
is an online tool for instantly finding the IVP books
suitable for over 250 courses across 24 disciplines.

ivpacademic.com